Flowers for Lisa

Abelardo Morell

Flowers for Lisa

A DELIRIUM OF PHOTOGRAPHIC INVENTION

Abelardo Morell

CONVERSATION WITH LAWRENCE WESCHLER
AFTERWORD BY LISA MCELANEY

ABRAMS, NEW YORK

Tell all the truth but tell it slant.
EMILY DICKENSON

Contents

Foreword

Lisa McElaney and I have been together since we were twenty and twenty-eight, respectively. My relationship with her is at the core of my life as a man and as an artist. Our love for each other—in all kinds of weather—grounds my resolve to be hopeful and vital, even when that feels like a challenge. She is always my first audience, and I count on her eyes to see things that I may not. A couple of years ago, for her birthday, I made Lisa a picture of flowers—it felt more enduring than actual flowers. In creating that image, I had no idea that a series would follow. However, something in the making of that first photograph gave me a newfound spark to experiment in ways I had not done before.

I chose the subject of flowers because they are lovely things—often exchanged between lovers—and a part of the long tradition of still life in art. Precisely because flowers are such a conventional subject, I felt a strong desire to describe them in new ways. I love how Jan Brueghel the Elder, Édouard Manet, Georgia O'Keeffe, Giorgio Morandi, Irving Penn, Joan Mitchell, and David Hockney reworked the look of common flowers to show unexpected versions of them. So while the subject of my work may be flowers, the photographs are also pictures about perspective, love, jealousy, hate, geometry, sex, life, the passage of time, and death. In choosing to limit myself to one subject, I was able to open doors to a world where I felt inventive, improvisational, and fresh.

Technically, these images involve a number of approaches, such as making multiple exposures to create floral explosions; combining my own painting with living bouquets; and using ink to produce dense *cliché verre* (glass plate) pictures. I believe that new possibilities in art are always around the corner, and these works have been giving me plenty of opportunities to prove that to myself again and again. At the same time, they serve an emotional impulse to show my dedication to the woman with whom I share my life.

AM
Newton, Massachusetts, October 2017

Note: The photographs in the Plates section are sequenced in the chronological order in which they were made, reflecting the evolution of ideas and processes that I explore in *Flowers for Lisa*. For further information about the images, please refer to Notes on the Photographs on pages 128–143.

Exuberance

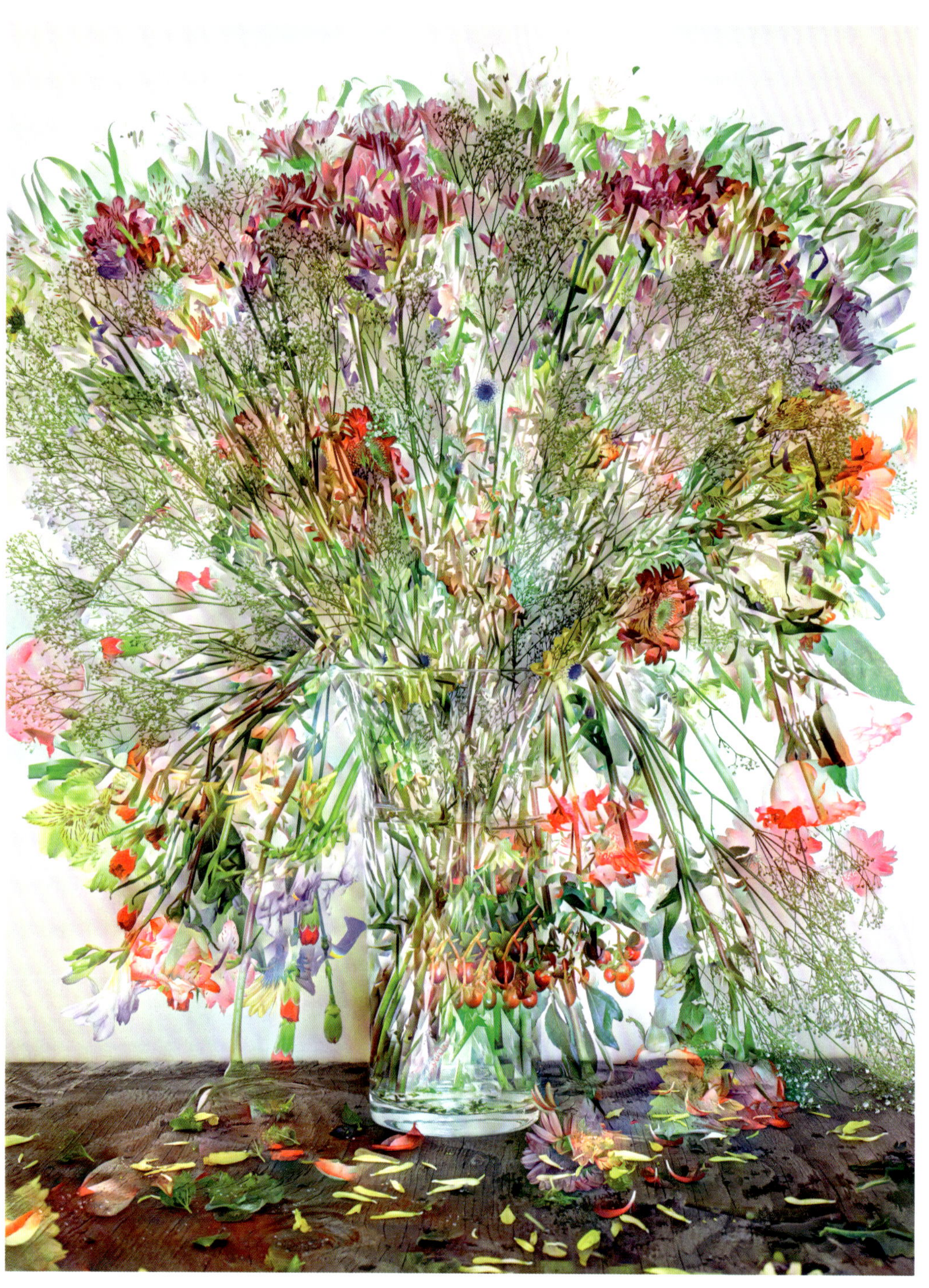

Figure 1. Abelardo Morell, *Flowers for Lisa #1*, 2014

Abelardo Morell and I meet in the ground-floor studio of a two-story unit he and his wife moved into a few years ago, in an apartment compound for artists—the onetime Claflin Elementary School in Newton, Massachusetts. He'd launched the current series of images back in his old, longtime home in nearby Brookline, but he tells me how it had really taken off only once he'd settled into these much more spacious haunts. . . .

LAWRENCE WESCHLER: I want to get to the first picture in this remarkable new series of yours, your *Flowers for Lisa* series, this one here (Figure 1), in just a moment, but allow me perhaps to surprise you here at the outset by telling you that some of my own first associations upon seeing it were with this earlier picture of yours, your *Light Bulb* from 1991 (Fig. 2). Bear with me. Perhaps you could first tell me the story of that lightbulb picture.

ABELARDO MORELL: I'm intrigued, if a bit dubious, but, okay. So in 1991, I had been teaching for a while, and one of my desires was to be clear about the fundamentals of photography. So I decided to make pictures that offered an explanation of how photography works, and this lightbulb picture was a way—

LW: A photograph interrogating itself, in a way?

AM: A way of showing the process, but one that would look nice as well. By way of a certain kind of simplicity—a plain cardboard box that had once contained wine bottles, as it happens, some duct tape, a lens—nevertheless arriving at a level of mystery and awe.

LW: So outside the box you have a bare lightbulb, turned on, and there on the other side of the photo, through the lens, you have an image of that same bulb, projected upside down on the far side of the box.

AM: Yep.

LW: One of the things that, to me, is absolutely astonishing about the resultant photo, though, is that the most real-seeming thing in the picture is the projected image of the bulb!

AM: Indeed. That's in part on account of the length of the exposure required—I had to do a lot of experimenting, trial and error, both in taking the photograph and then in developing the negative. The exposure ended up being something like five minutes, so that the actual bulb virtually whites itself out, whereas the projection takes on palpable substance, that sense of reality as you describe it, albeit upside down. You can even see the filament of the bulb burning there inside the projection, which you couldn't see looking at the actual bulb.

LW: And just as David Hockney likes to point out, the process of projection, of pushing the image through the pinhole, as it were, and spreading it out on the other side,

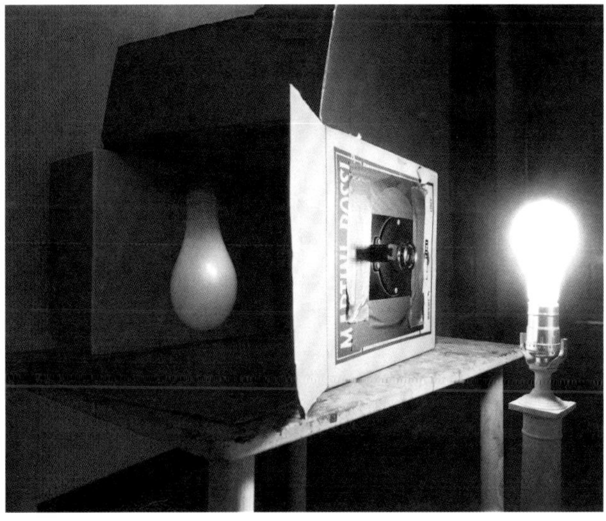

Figure 2. Abelardo Morell, *Light Bulb*, 1991

harmonizes relations and values within the projected image—almost makes it look like a painting. Were you amazed when you first saw the results?

AM: Absolutely, and I was also delighted, because postmodernism was at its highest then, in the early nineties, with all its nonsensical claims that everything had been done already, there was no room for anything original, and I could say, "Oh yeah?"

LW: "Did you ever see *this*?"

AM: So it was a way of rebelling against that kind of mindset. But it also really kind of made me think, "Oh, wow . . . ," and started me out on the series of optical experiments, projecting the outside world, upside down, into interiors of darkened rooms, literal cameras obscura.

LW: Photos like this one here (Fig. 3).

AM: And it's true that those all grew out of the germ of that lightbulb image.

LW: Indeed, but do you hear what you are saying, especially in the context of this latest series, *Flowers for Lisa?* Because the lightbulb photo portrays precisely, especially in the projected image, a sort of bulb. Like a tulip bulb.

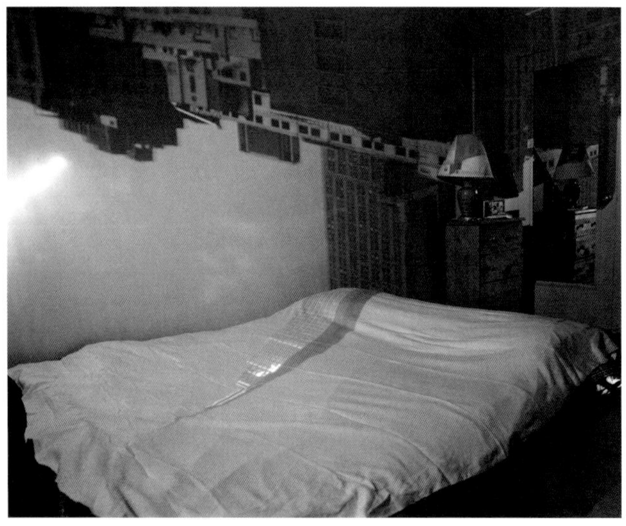

Figure 3. Abelardo Morell, *Camera Obscura Image of the Empire State Building in Bedroom*, 1994

AM: Hmm. Wow, I hadn't thought of that.

LW: And that sort of association has a history.

AM: How do you mean?

LW: Well, back in the sixteenth and seventeenth centuries, when, again as Hockney has pointed out, painters began deploying lenses and cameras obscura of all sorts, a whole series of diagrams of the process were being published, and it's funny, because over and over the thing being projected onto the far wall in these diagrams turns out to be a tree (Figs. 4–7).

What's more, in certain such renderings, the process of pinhole projection is consciously being likened to that of vision itself, the way, say, the image of a tree out there in the world goes through the pinhole pupil of the human eye before getting projected, upside down, onto the retina at the back of the eye. And look for a second at that diagram of vision (Fig. 5), or better yet at this version here (Fig. 8), where the diagram has been rotated by ninety degrees, and you begin to see that vision itself, seen in this way, replicates what happens with a tree (Fig. 9)! The branches . . . the trunk penetrating the pinhole earth . . . the roots. Indeed, centuries later, you get Lee Friedlander capturing this remarkable image (Fig. 10), where the curvature of the hill in the background suggests, if you squint your gaze just right, the curvature of an eyeball.

AM: And the shadows reading like the veins inside the eyeball.

LW: Yes, but also like the rays of light piercing the pupil of the eyeball and getting projected beyond.

AM: That's fascinating, but—

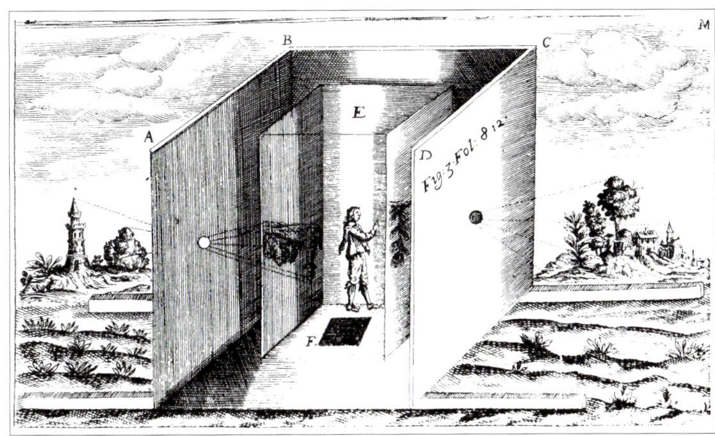

Figure 4. Illustration of a portable camera obscura, from Athanasius Kircher's *Ars Magna Lucis et Umbrae*, 1646

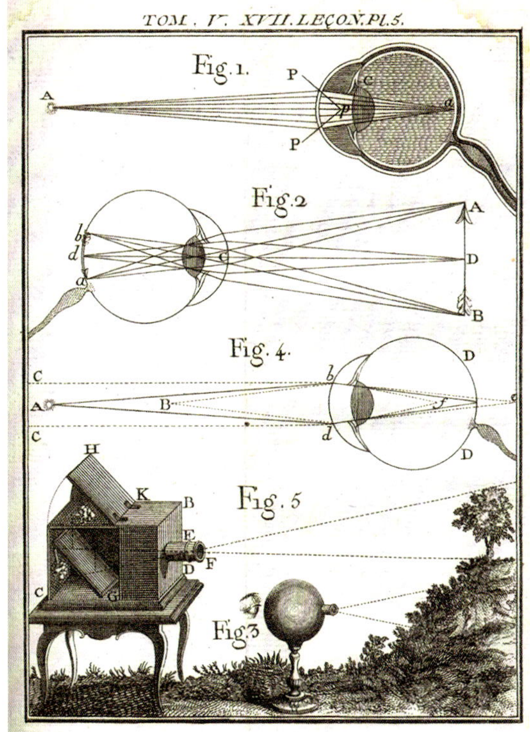

Figure 5. Illustration of a camera obscura compared to the mechanism of the eye, from Jean Antoine Nollet's *Leçons de physique expérimentale*, vol. 5, 1764

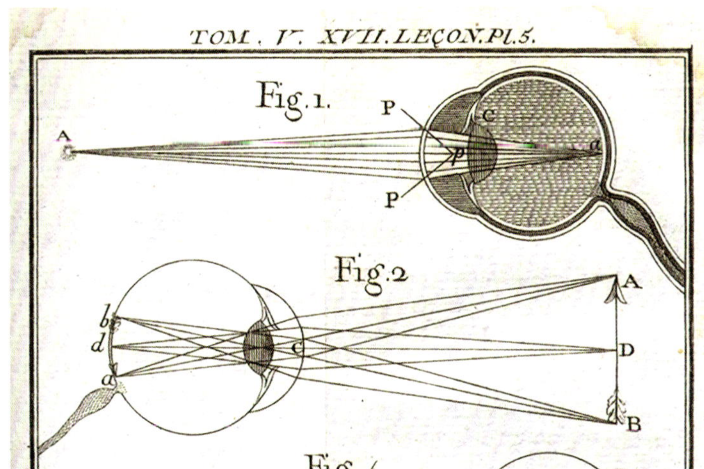

Figure 6. *Optics: The Principle of the Camera Obscura*, 1752

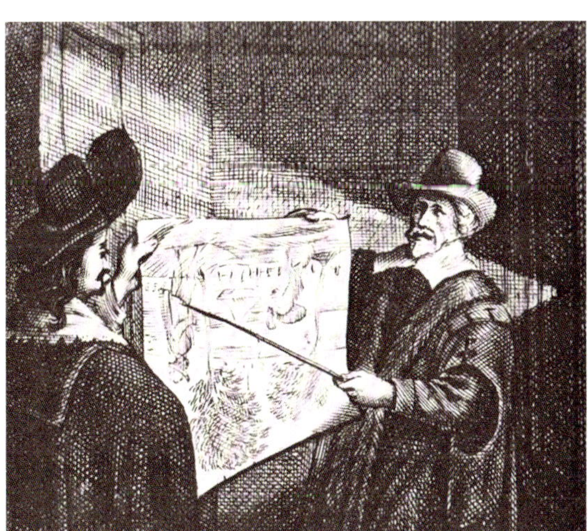

Figure 7. Illustration of the mechanism of the eye, from Johan van Beverwijck's *Schat der ongesontheyt*, 1664

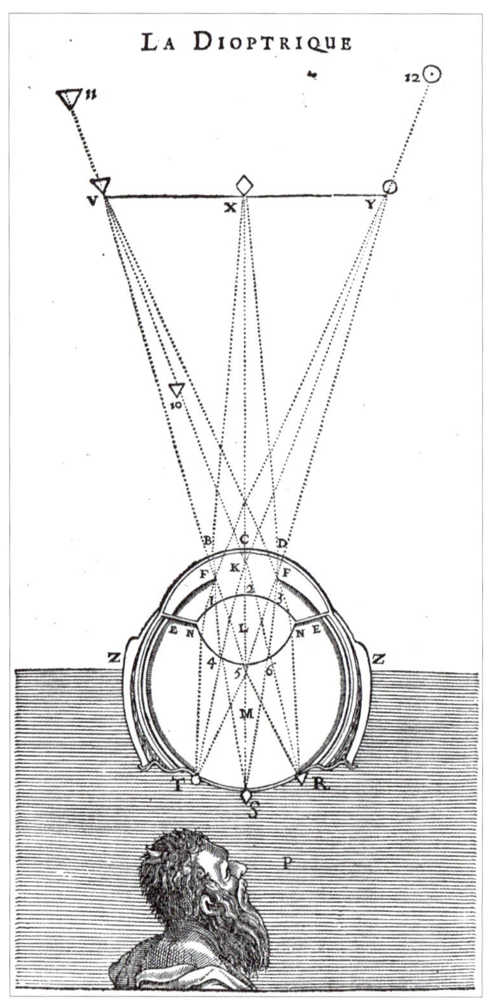

Figure 8. Diagram of ocular refraction, from
René Descartes's *Discourse on the Method*, 1637

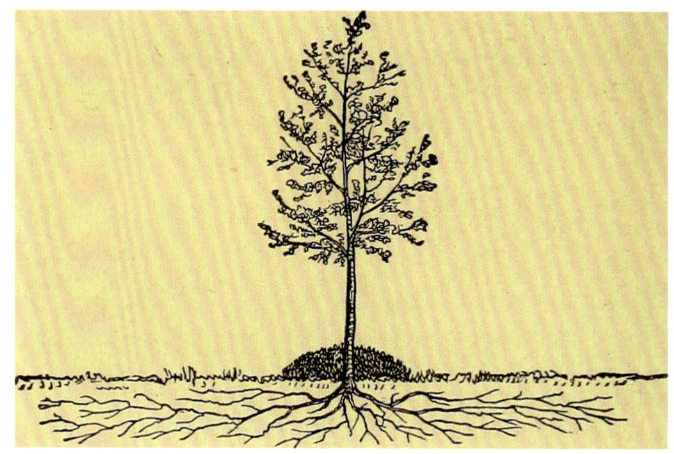

Figure 9. Tree and root illustration, from John Jacob Thomas's
The American Fruit Culturist, 1903

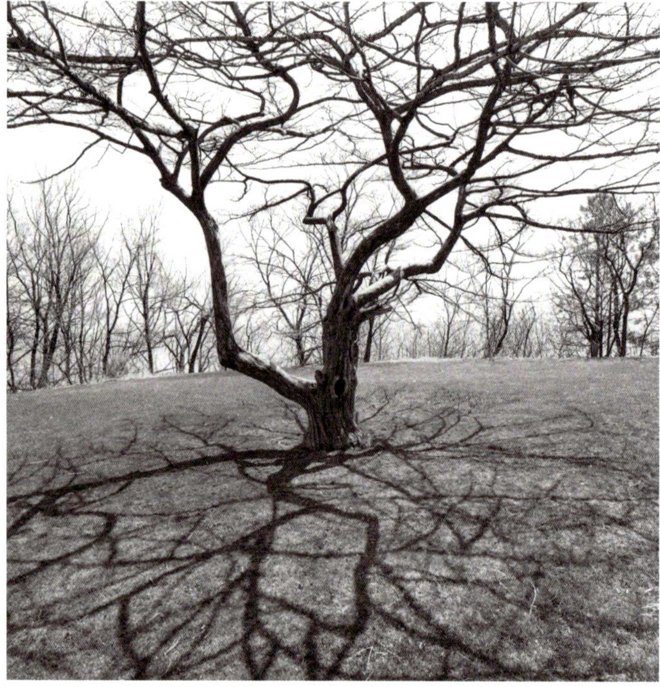

Figure 10. Lee Friedlander, *Central Park, New York City*, 1992

LW: But what does it have to do with the subject at hand? Well, look again at that first image in your *Flowers* series. Remind you of anything?

AM: Hah! I never thought of that, and it certainly wasn't my conscious intention. If anything, my associations had been with good old American fireworks, but I see what you mean.

LW: I'm certainly not the first to note the way that the pupil of the eye, or the eye more generally, is often deployed as a metaphor for the artist him- or herself: The world out there gets refracted through the sensibility incarnated in the artist-eye—Isherwood's "I am a camera . . ."—and then projected, in a form transmuted by the unique personality of the artist, onto the page or canvas. Impression becoming expression.

Which in turn reminds me of one of my favorite books, albeit a very odd and recondite one, the English philologist R. B. Onians's mid-twentieth-century *The Origins of European Thought about the Body, the Mind, the Soul, the World, Time, and Fate*—

AM: Great title!

LW: Yeah, but what Onians does, with near-maniacal erudition, is to probe the linguistic roots of some of the key concepts in early pre-Socratic, pre-Hippocratic—and, for that matter, early Sanskrit usage, thereby generating a sense of how those people thought of, say, the body. And in this context, he was able to show that they believed that the seat of thought, and more especially of vision, was in the lungs, of all places, not the brain. That for them, vision, like breathing, was a question of in-and-out: Breathe in, breathe out; the world enters one's pupils, to be sure, but one's gaze just as clearly bores out through the pupils and into the world: back and forth. Hence the overlap of words like *inspiration* and *respiration*.

AM: Which is exactly how a photographer moves through the world.

LW: Indeed, but your comment just now about fireworks makes me realize how that splay of light through the pupil or, for that matter, flower stems converging into a vase, applies to you even more profoundly.

AM: How so?

LW: Precisely because you are not a "good old American," or, rather, the status of your Americanness is decidedly more complex, more nuanced. You were born in Cuba, after all, yes?

AM: Yes, in 1948.

LW: How old were you when your family moved to the United States?

AM: Thirteen.

LW: Thirteen, whereupon your life turned inside out, as it were . . .

AM: Yeah. Literally . . . [*laughs*]

LW: . . . through the pinhole of immigration, of exile and displacement.

AM: Yes, that's a good point. In fact, there's something I have to show you.

When my parents, my sister, and I first came to New York, it was 1962. We were hardly fancy Cubans: My father was a mechanic in the navy, and afterward, as refugees, we were really lower class, living in a basement apartment on West 69th Street. And West 69th in those days was not like it is today: It was fairly bleak. I bought, with money from a pharmacy delivery job, a Brownie camera with a flash, sort of square like Diane Arbus's, who of course I had not yet heard of. My English was not so good at the beginning, and so I mediated some of my interactions with the world through that camera. But here (Fig. 11) is a photo I took of our apartment.

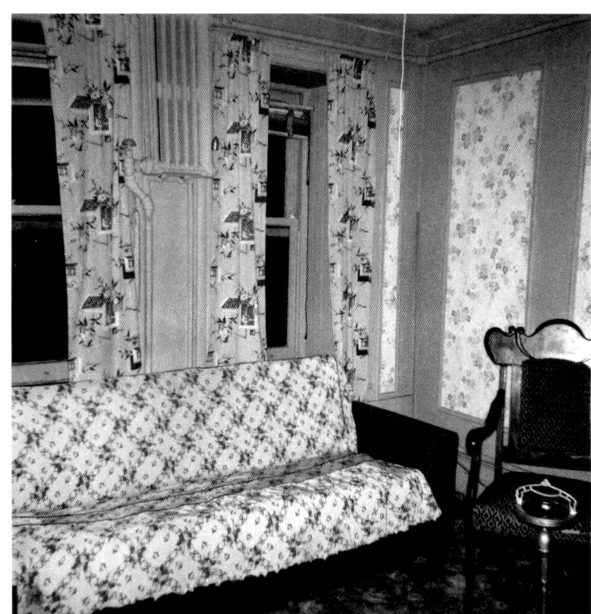

Figure 11. Abelardo Morell, *Our Living Room*, 1963

LW: That's uncanny, because it really does look like the kind of thing Arbus was doing some years later, for example, that one of *A Jewish giant at home with his parents in the Bronx*. Same sort of vantage, same cramped kind of room.

AM: As I say, newly arrived, at thirteen, I'd never heard of her. The only light we were getting in that apartment was through those small windows that looked up, because it was a basement apartment. So those windows were kind of important. It was sort of a peeping system, with all the bustle of New York up there rushing by.

LW: Another peephole.

AM: Well, I've always been grateful for that, because we were literally starting at the bottom, which gave one's life even more of a sense of the aspirational.

LW: You were a seed, transplanted into the loam of New York, and your life would rise up from that. Reminds me of that diagram we were looking at a few moments ago, of the bearded guy looking up from underground at the splay of vision through the eyeball. A theme that in your life clearly goes way back, and in turn comes forward through your subsequent pinhole images; for example, the one of that upside-down projection of the Empire State Building across the bed, which, come to think of it, also sort of rhymes with the photo of your basement apartment.

***

LW: Well, let's fast-forward in time a little. Can you describe the kind of work you were doing immediately before *Flowers for Lisa*?

AM: Well, that would have been a series of different tent projects. About ten years ago, I got a commission from the Alturas Foundation to do some camera obscura–type work in Texas, in Big Bend National Park, and I told them, "The thing is, there are no rooms in the desert." But then I thought maybe I could make a room, a portable thing, such as a tent.

LW: A camping tent . . .

AM: Well, a camping tent, but completely dark inside, pitch-black, and outfitted with a periscope on top, which could look out—a little bit like some NASA rover—at the surrounding landscape (Fig. 12), projecting the image of that landscape onto the bare ground below, within the tent, whatever that ground might happen to be: pebbles, grass, pavement, or the like.

LW: A sort of open-faced sandwich, with the ground as the bread and the periscope-projected image evenly spread out across it.

AM: Okay, yeah, and I could then photograph that projection from within the tent. And over the years I proceeded to create several different series using that technique: the Golden Gate Bridge as projected onto pavement; Monet's gardens at Giverny as projected onto the gravelly pathways; more recently, Constable-like vistas spread across the very grass that Constable, whose work I love, would have trod (Fig. 13). It was my way to reinvent the nature of landscape pictures—something I'd never thought I was any good at before.

LW: Gotta love those trees! Interesting, too, in that periscopes have a history of their own in American photog-

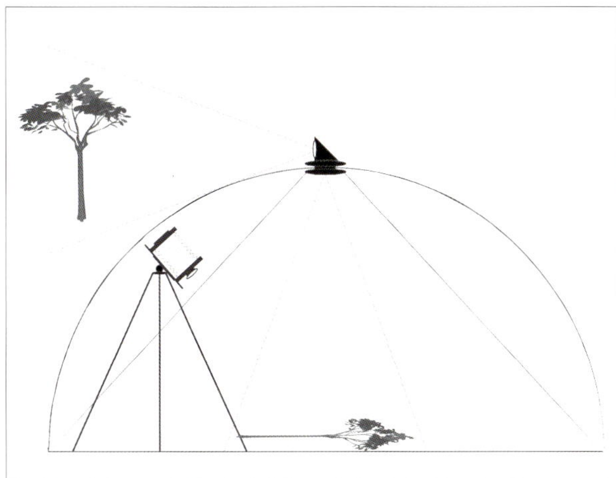

Figure 12. Diagram of camera obscura tent

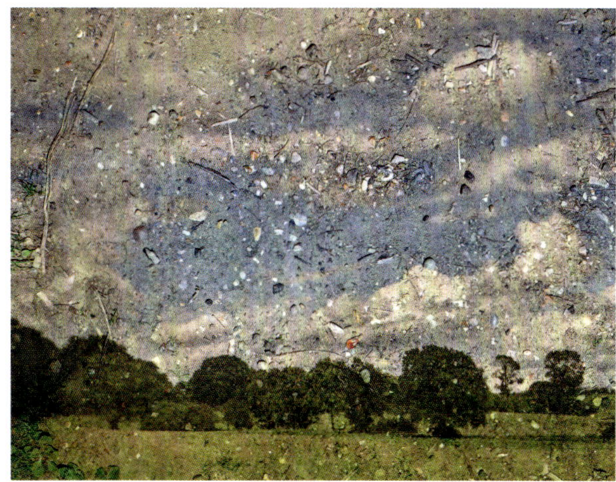

Figure 13. Abelardo Morell, *Tent-Camera Image: Rapidly Moving Clouds over Field, Flatford, England #1*, 2017

raphy: Both Helen Levitt and Ben Shahn in their street work deployed primitive periscopes, although lateral ones, mounted in front of the forward-facing lenses of their boxy cameras, so that looking down into the viewfinder, they could seem to be aiming straight ahead when in fact they were focusing on something or someone at a right angle to what they seemed to be aiming at. Hence some of the incredibly unselfconscious vantages of common people that they were able to capture.

AM: Which I love.

LW: But that in turn reminds me of a great passage from Nathaniel Hawthorne, of all people, from his journal, where he writes:

> I have before now experienced, that the best way
> to get a vivid impression and feeling of landscape,
> is to sit down before it and read, or become other-
> wise absorbed in thought; for then, when your
> eyes happen to be attracted to the landscape,
> you seem to catch Nature at unawares, and see
> her before she has time to change her aspect.
> The effect lasts but for a single instant, and
> passes away almost as soon as you are conscious
> of it; but it is real, for that moment. It is as if you
> could overhear and understand what the trees
> are whispering to one another; as if you caught
> a glimpse of a face unveiled, which veils itself

from every wilful glance. The mystery is revealed, and after a breath or two, becomes just as much a mystery as before.

AM: Wonderful. Marvelous.

LW: The world at a slant. Which in turn also reminds me of a terrific late poem of Seamus Heaney's, the last poem in his book *Spirit Level* ("spirit levels" being those little bubble things that carpenters and curators use to make sure something is perfectly level), entitled "Postscript":

> And some time make the time to drive out west
> Into County Clare, along the Flaggy Shore,
> In September or October, when the wind
> And the light are working off each other
> So that the ocean on one side is wild
> With foam and glitter, and inland among stones
> The surface of a slate-grey lake is lit
> By the earthed lightning of a flock of swans,
> Their feathers roughed and ruffling, white on white,
> Their fully grown headstrong-looking heads
> Tucked or cresting or busy underwater.
> Useless to think you'll park and capture it
> More thoroughly. You are neither here nor there,
> A hurry through which known and strange things pass
> As big soft buffetings come at the car sideways
> And catch the heart off guard and blow it open.

With your periscope tents, though, you did in fact contrive a way to "park and capture" nature more thoroughly, "Nature at unawares," and to catch our hearts off guard and blow them open.

AM: Hmmm. That last poem is gorgeous, and especially uncanny for me, because back in 1978 my wife and I traveled to Scotland and then to Ireland, and we found a cottage in County Clare (Fig. 14), and for three months we lived inside the very center of that poem! And we loved it, though it was rough.

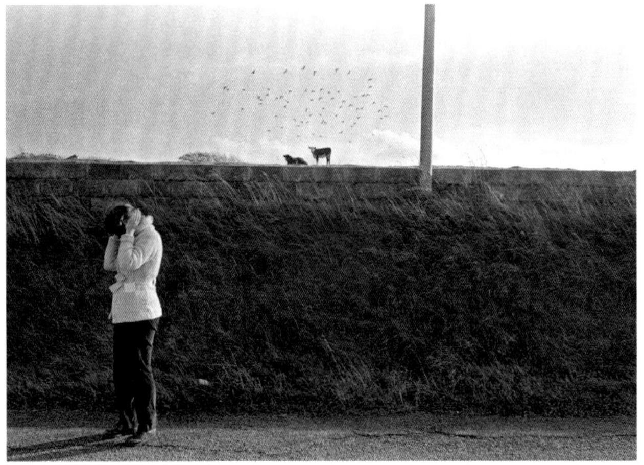

Figure 14. Abelardo Morell, *Lisa in County Clare*, 1978

LW: "Roughed and ruffling."

AM: Extraordinary.

***

LW: Okay, though, enough with these preliminaries. Let's turn to *Flowers for Lisa*. When did you start making these images?

AM: Let's see, that would have been in 2014, in February sometime, because that was her birthday. I'd been in the habit of giving her big bouquets on her birthdays, but that year I decided to try something a little different.

LW: So I guess I should begin by asking, who is this "her," this Lisa person?

AM: Well, that would be my wife, Lisa, and we've been together since—really, since 1976. So it's a long marriage. And I think she saved my life. I was a bit of a mess and her love just kind of transformed me.

LW: How so? You met where, in what context?

AM: Well, fresh out of high school in New York, I'd gotten a scholarship to go to Bowdoin College in Maine, which was Nathaniel Hawthorne's college, too, incidentally.

LW: And about as far from Cuba as you could find.

AM: Yes, and there I discovered music. I mean, I reported to college with Lawrence Welk albums. I mean really, I liked Muzak, and not in an ironic way, either, I thought, "This is good!" [*laughs*] But within a year, I had a radio show on the campus station and I was playing John Coltrane and Stockhausen, and John Cage was my bible. It was a radical, radical change for me at Bowdoin, which is reverberating still. And I discovered photography, and thought, "Oh, shit. This is—I can talk, I can say something." And that was very immediate.

LW: Would you say that with this visual medium, you found your voice?

AM: Yeah, yeah. I could put things together in a kind of a sentence that made visual sense, which I still couldn't have done in words at the time. My English has gotten better in the years since. But in other ways, I was not nearly prepared to do the work. I mean, I was planning to be an engineer, but I failed a lot of classes—I failed physics and I failed math. So in 1971, I dropped out, a year short of getting my degree.

LW: A lot of people were doing that in those days.

AM: Perhaps. I suppose so. But I came back to New York, lived with my parents, and worked in a hospital. Still I kept making photographs. And by 1975, I had the idea that maybe I should go to graduate school in photography. But I needed to finish Bowdoin first, so I went back for my final year. And there was Lisa, who was in her true senior year, and that's when we met. And we've been together since.

LW: What was she doing?

AM: She was a history person, interested in music, politics, and history, and very different. And soon after we met, she got an MFA from Columbia in filmmaking. And went on to make films about women's and children's health, after which she did research about behavior change in response to her media interventions.

LW: And you say she saved your life? How?

AM: Well, she gave me a sense of what a life together with someone else could be. With her, it felt like—another visual thing—it felt like I could see for miles. And that was really reassuring, you know? We could fight here and there, but there was a long road together.

LW: I imagine when you first started, you weren't a famous photographer—

AM: Not at all.

LW: And it wasn't at all clear that you were going to be one, and so that must have required a lot of support from her . . .

AM: Support, and belief, absolutely. But we traveled together, County Clare and so forth, and that sense of steady love, especially in the context of the whole immigrant thing, was fundamental. Because exile is inherently unstable.

LW: She was not an exile?

AM: No, she's an American, of Irish background: Lisa McElaney. But I really envied people who were just Americans, you know? Seemed to have no baggage.

LW: On the train up here just now, I was looking at a survey of your early work, and it strikes me that one picture in particular of yours marked a clear breakthrough, and it's

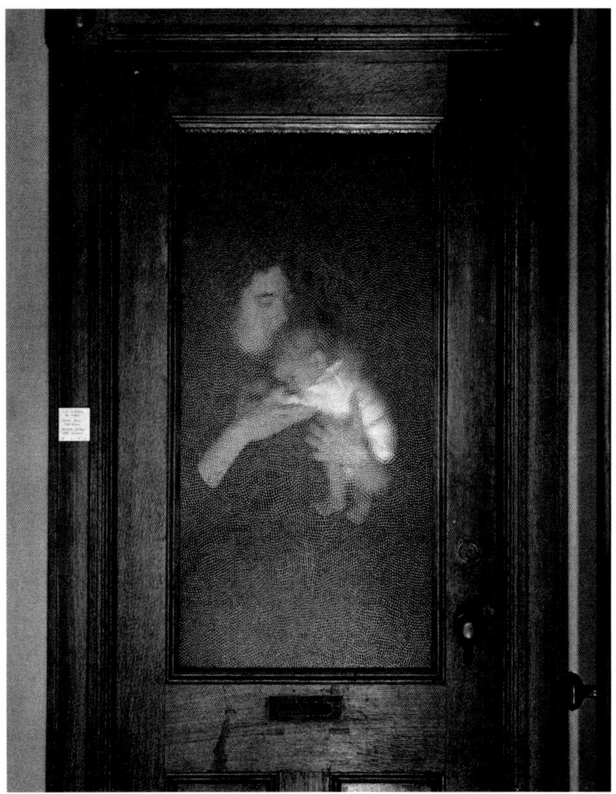

Figure 15. Abelardo Morell, *Lisa and Brady behind Glass*, 1986

a picture of her from 1986, seen through a frosted door, holding your first baby together, Brady (Fig. 15).

AM: Oh, absolutely. Huge breakthrough.

LW: I mean, it's interesting, if you think about it, in terms of what you're going to do later on. On the one hand, it anticipates all the ways you were going to be playing with lenses and so forth, but also there's such intimacy.

AM: Right!

LW: You'd been off to photograph the world, and turning back, you'd seen that, and suddenly you recognized your subject, or at least one of them—the intimacy of family life.

AM: And it redirected me. It felt like someone saying as E. E. Cummings did, "Where are you going?" Just like that: "Listen: there's a hell of a good universe," and not even next door.

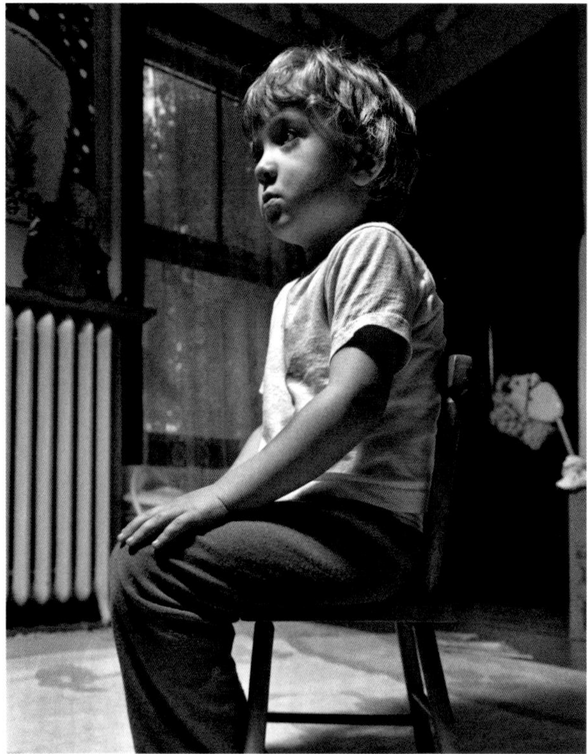

Figure 16. Abelardo Morell, *Brady Sitting*, 1989

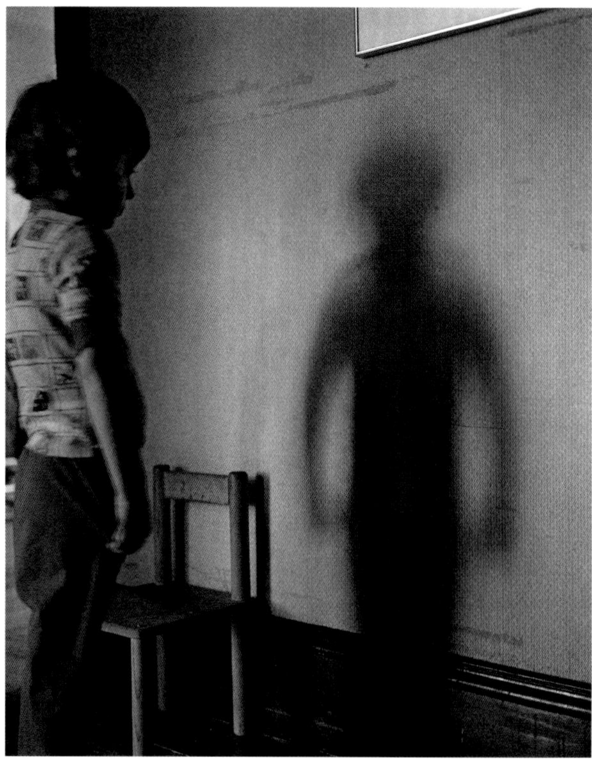

Figure 17. Abelardo Morell, *Brady Looking at His Shadow,* 1991

LW: "Let's go!"

AM: "Let's go." I didn't know that Cummings poem ["pity this busy monster, manunkind"] then, but it was like that. Guess what? Right here is your salvation. In the meantime I'd gone to grad school at Yale University, where a lot of cool people went, and the idea of photographing babies was probably a no-no or something. So I had to work my way through some of those insecurities.

LW: And all that's tied in your mind with Lisa?

AM: Oh, very much. The idea that we could have children together, and that in some ways I could thrive with her love. And that my love for her could make me a better man.

LW: Ironically, as I think about your career, when you had children, you really hadn't found your vocation yet, so that was a tremendous leap of faith. But it was in the having of the children, and that particular child, as a subject and so forth that you really began to discover yourself as an artist (Figs. 16 and 17).

AM: You know, it took me years to really finally get it all together. My earlier street pictures were a little bit of, "Oh, those Americans, or those people that are doing things over there." Whereas with the baby, and the pictures that came after, it's no longer "They're there" but, rather, "We're here." I found a way to blend my perceptions with love and intimacy.

LW: It's interesting that you say that, because as it happens, the Nathaniel Hawthorne passage I referenced a few minutes ago, with its notion of "catching Nature at unawares," very much applies to some of your studies of your kids, Brady, for instance, and the weird thing is that the Hawthorne passage is from a section of his journal that's been excerpted in book form under the title *Twenty Days with Julian and Little Bunny by Papa*, which happens to concern three weeks that Hawthorne spent by himself in the company of his five-year-old son, Julian, while his wife and two daughters went to West Newton. Catching intimacy at unawares.

***

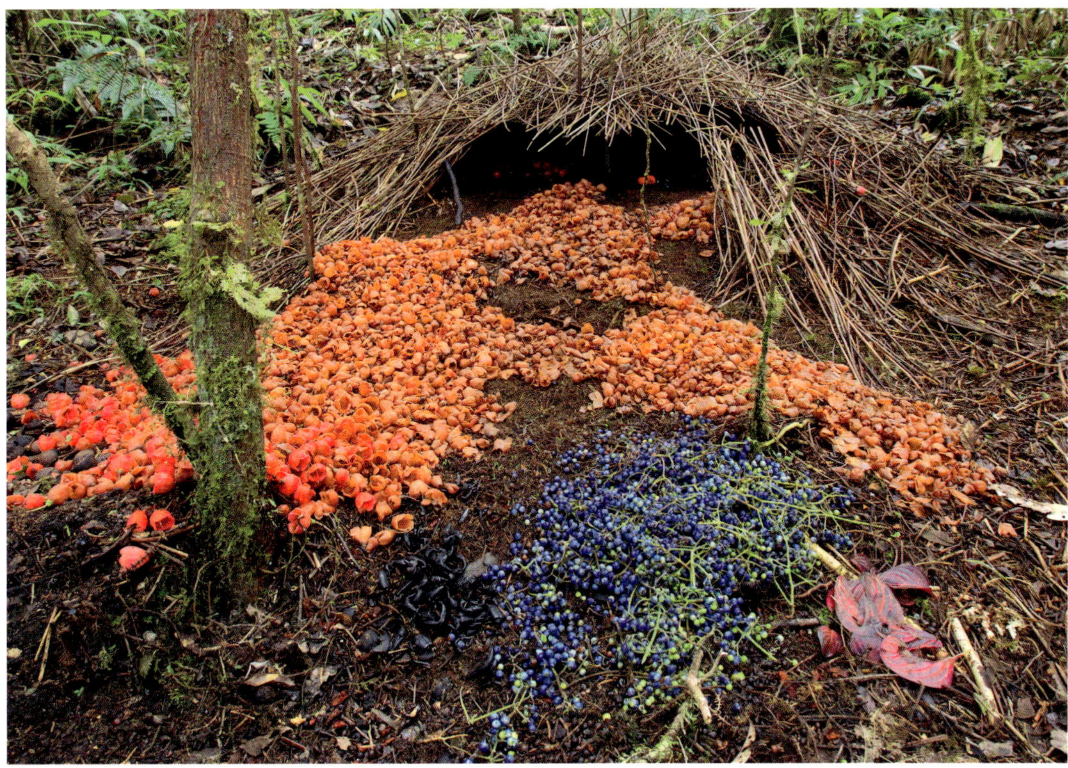

Figure 18. A bowerbird's nest

LW: But okay, one last time. *Flowers for Lisa*: Let's talk about those images themselves, and for starters, once again, that first one.

AM: As I mentioned, I had long had a tradition of giving Lisa a big bouquet of flowers for her birthday, but this time, in February 2014, I thought to myself, "Maybe I can make a picture instead: For one thing, it will last longer." But I didn't want to do my regular thing. I wanted, almost in some weird way, that it be like a display of plumage. Like a peacock. A little bit of a show-off, as if to catch her attention and gain her attraction. Sort of "Oh yeah? Look what I brought you this time. Watch *this*." And I wanted to start with a bang.

LW: Do you know about those male bowerbirds in Australia and New Guinea who as part of their mating rituals build gloriously colorful nests out of anything at hand?

AM: Oh? I don't know those . . .

LW: Well (Fig. 18) . . . Pretty great, no?

AM: That's real?

LW: Yes. You might have some competition. But keep going.

AM: Incredible. Well, I, too, wanted to make something special. And I started thinking about multiple exposures, but blended digitally somehow, testing a few ideas using Photoshop.

LW: Had you been using Photoshop much up to this point?

AM: Yes, but just in the normal ways of a conventional photographic, digital practice. You shoot a picture, and then you need to import it and work on it in Photoshop. Not like I was adding things to the image.

LW: So here you were deploying Photoshop in a new way?

AM: Yes. But in a way that I had not seen before, to my knowledge—even my assistant had no idea; he said: "What the hell is this?"

LW: Well, frankly, I have no idea, either, so describe what is going on here.

AM: So there's a vase, a table, and a pale background, and all that is immovable. That has to stay in one place. And the lighting, fairly straight on, also has to stay the same throughout. But then the first photograph consisted of, say, three or four strands of flowers leaning out of the vase. And then I would remove that bunch and insert another small bouquet, and photograph that one. In fact, in this instance, I photographed twenty separate small bouquets, all in the same vase.

LW: It might be noted at this point that in so doing you were behaving exactly like a seventeenth-century Dutch flower painter. Nowadays, when we come upon one of those bounteous canvases in the midst of our gallery walk, we're likely to imagine—in part because of the relatively recent hegemony of the photographic model—that the painter first put together an amazing bouquet and then simply painted the scene. But of course it couldn't have been like that: The flowers in question were all fast rotting. No, he or she—and many of them were she—would have painted them one flower at a time, slowly, with great consideration, building the floral array over many weeks, one bud and stem at a time.

AM: Huh. Well, in my case, once I'd photographed all twenty of my separate bunches, I then fed all twenty of the photographs into the Photoshop program. Now, when Photoshop is asked to blend such a collection of images together, it can get confused, for example, over which line is meant to flow into which.

LW: So the program itself is doing the rest of the work? This is not you doing it? You're saying, "Here are twenty pictures, Photoshop. . . ."

AM: Yeah, ". . . You figure it out." Though I'm giving this computer system what I want considered—there's a random quality to this, which I like—in the way that John Cage sometimes chose musical notes by rolling dice or consulting the I Ching.

LW: And Photoshop grinds away on the problem, doggedly applying all its algorithms, for, what? Two days or so? . . .

AM: Well, half an hour.

LW: And when it spews out the result, you say . . .

AM: "Good God." [*laughs*] Because you could see how the program was literally trying to integrate and harmonize what was in fact quite chaotic.

LW: Which is not that dissimilar to what the eye and the brain are doing when they look out at the world. Which takes us back to Onians in a way: in and out.

AM: Back and forth, right. Though I, too, would respond to what the program was doing, notice a gap in one place, too much in another, remove some photos from the array, add a few new vantages, run the program again. I love this dance with technology.

LW: Though also not unlike the practice of an abstract expressionist painter.

AM: In a way. But as with the abstract expressionists, the element of surprise was super important to me. Because in some ways, these flower pictures deal not with chaos, exactly, but just with the exuberance of things. Maybe it's something that I've wanted to do for a long time, maybe it's age, but a lot of these flower pictures contain my desire to—

LW: Your late style . . .

AM: Well, it is a little bit like de Kooning, I really wanted expression, and exuberance, and not just neat lines. And this is part of that desire.

LW: Though, as with the abstract expressionists, clarity, too, is of the essence, and that's what seems so striking about this first resultant effort. Because one is striving after a clear view of chaos, of bursting plenitude, not a blurry, out-of-focus one. And for all its exuberance, this image is preternaturally *in focus*.

AM: I'm glad you think so, that's what I was going for.

LW: What did Lisa think?

AM: Loved it. She was crazy for it. And there's of course a great satisfaction in having a client of sorts like that, you know?

LW: A patron . . . A matron . . .

AM: Way more than that.

LW: A muse.

AM: So I thought I was on good ground. And soon after that, I came to feel that if there's one picture like that in me, there must be others. That's an important element for me—maybe it's the modernist in me—this drive, once I get started, to explore themes across myriad variations. Wallace Stevens had "Thirteen Ways of Looking at a Blackbird," and I was curious to see how many "Ways of Looking at Flowers" I could come up with.

LW: Which brings us to your second iteration (page 32) . . .

AM: Which was quite like the first, but I wanted to try a different palette. I started experimenting with more things drooping down, bigger petals. And whereas the first one feels more like early summer to me, this second felt a little bit more like the beginning of fall. And as you can see, different things happen depending on the kinds of flowers you use, and the different backgrounds—raw plywood in this case. But after this I started thinking, "Okay, maybe there are other ideas, other techniques."

LW: You were making most of these just right here in your studio.

AM: Right here on this table.

LW: Funny how from one series to the next you went, in effect, from the great outdoors, Big Bend National Park and the like, to the delimitations of this table—or maybe, rather, the way you managed to turn this table into your own private national park.

AM: Indeed. And believe me, we've had it all, there's been dirt, things growing, bugs, all sorts of wildlife. There was one point, though, where it began to look like a funeral home in here, it got bad. You know, they began to smell, and things like that.

LW: After those first two, you began experimenting with different approaches, and the third and fourth variations indeed seem radically different.

AM: Well, for starters, I decided to give the multiple exposures a rest. And I've always liked the idea of impressions, especially in photography, and these are a little bit like light impressing itself onto film. The technique here is influenced by *cliché verre*, a nineteenth-century French method whereby one would draw or layer flat objects across glass, or some other such surface, and then press the resulting image onto light-sensitive paper in a darkroom. Except here I first layered a board, maybe even that very board from number 2, with a dark putty into which I then physically pressed wildflower stalks in the first instance (#3, page 33)—with, in the second (#4, page 35), a slightly lighter putty and a bit more color and volume in terms of what I pressed into it—and then photographed the result.

LW: So these are just straight photos of the result?

AM: With slightly raking light, simply from those windows. But just one straight shot. If you looked at the object, maybe it wasn't that impressive, but the photograph transformed it in a really interesting way.

I've always been super interested in printmaking, I love printmakers to death. I'm jealous of how they can do markings that look beautiful—even mistakes look great! And this is my attempt to emulate their practice. The result feels primordial, too, like cave paintings or, alternatively, a forest floor.

LW: And also darker, say, or more melancholy than the first two.

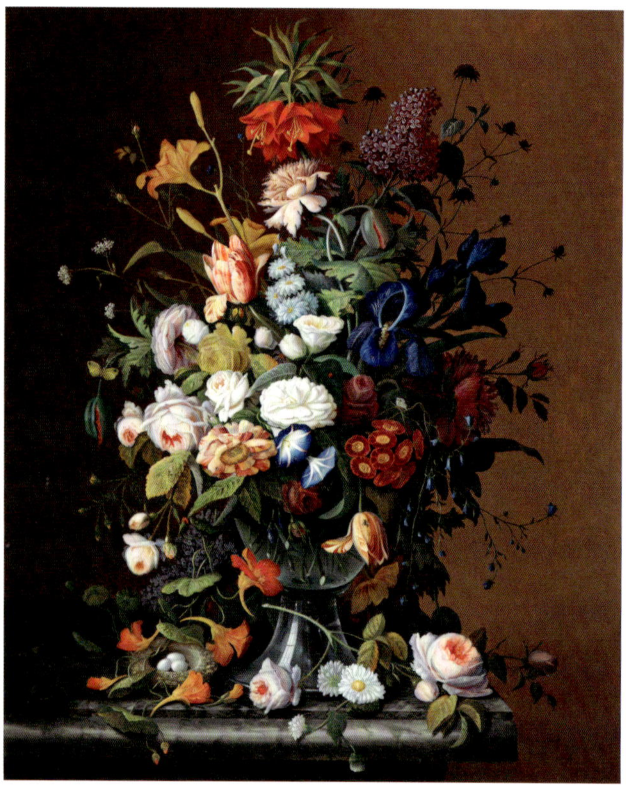

Figure 19. Severin Roesen, *Flower Still Life with Bird's Nest*, 1853

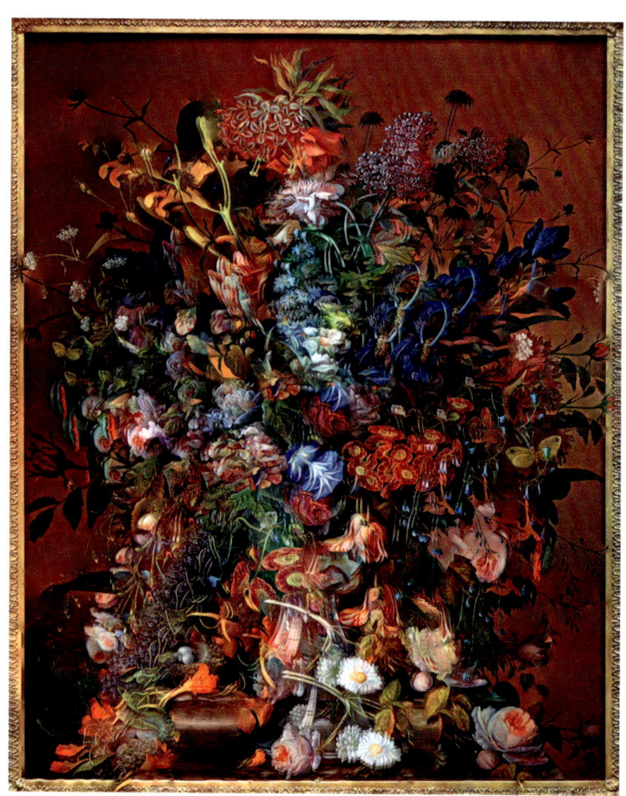

Figure 20. Abelardo Morell, *Flowers for Lisa #5*, 2014

AM: Well, yes, one wants to vary the register. I was especially interested in varying not just the imagery but the techniques as well. I was also interested in the particular challenge that this subject brought. In some circles, flowers can seem too pretty and trite.

LW: Which brings us to this next one (Fig. 20), which really looks like a Dutch seventeenth-century still life.

AM: Not surprisingly, because it is. Or anyway is based on one, or, rather, on a painting that is based on one. In this case, I decided to take my camera on a field trip to the Philadelphia Museum of Art, where I happened upon a mid-nineteenth-century American painting by Severin Roesen (Fig. 19), which was clearly riffing off those Dutch models, and I took eight or nine shots of it, from different distances and different angles, close-ups, details, and the like, and then, coming back, fed them to Photoshop and said, "Do what you will!"

LW: Great name for the process: "What You Will." Almost sounds Shakespearean, given the time period of the original. Reminds me of a recent book by the great Shakespearean and cultural critic Harry Berger, Jr., about such Dutch floral still lifes generally, which begins by noting the way that we often rush past the rooms that contain scores of such paintings during our museum walks, whereas Berger advises us to stop and take a closer look, because, as he shows, the seemingly placid surfaces belie fairly conspicuous fields of violence, mayhem, damage, blight, resistance, mortality, and so forth: all those insects and frogs and snails and caterpillars laying siege to beauty, time itself eating away at the leaves and petals, just all kinds of drama. He calls the book *Caterpillage*.

AM: Talk about a great title. But I agree, those paintings are endlessly absorbing. And I especially love some of the things digital technology came up with in resolving this image. I mean look at some of those shadows, the height-

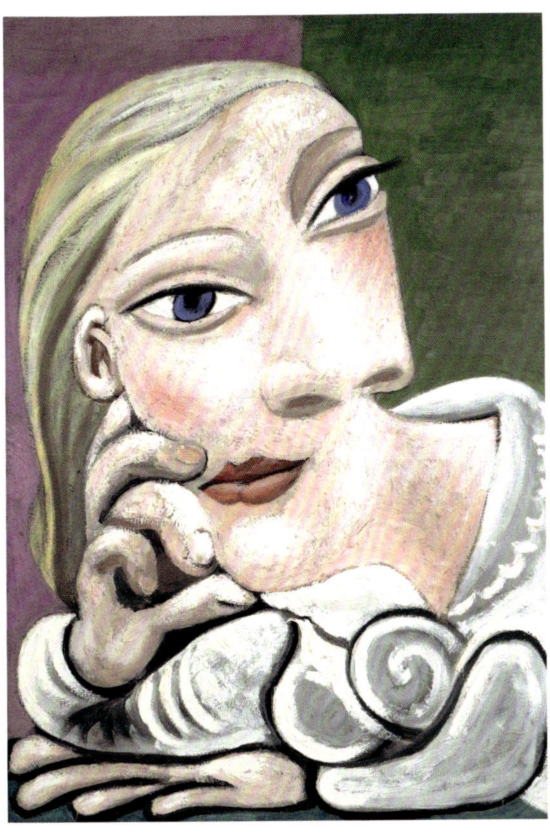

Figure 21. Pablo Picasso, *Marie-Thérèse accoudée*, 1939

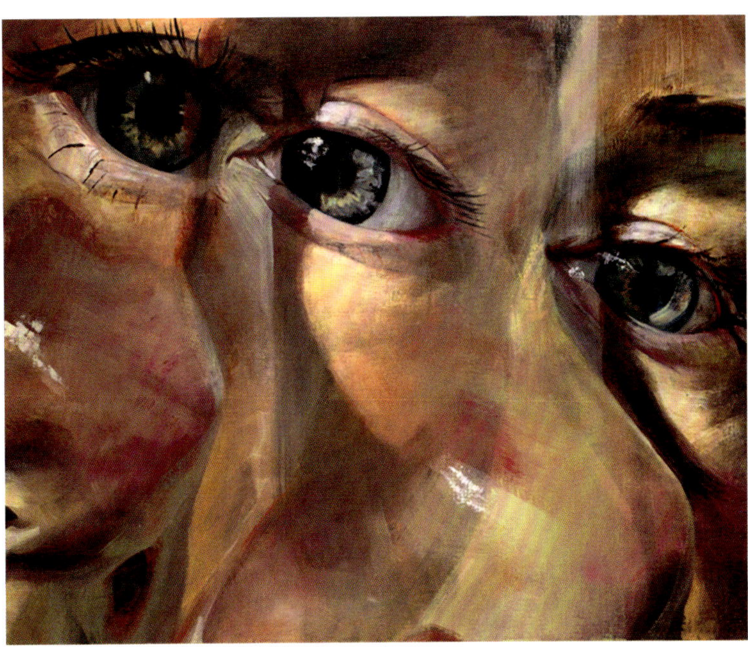

Figure 22. Gerri Davis, *When We Kiss*, 2013

ened tonalities. I wanted the formality of the frame and made a point of including it, but look at the way some of the stalks even seem to hover out *beyond* the frame.

LW: Again, that's Photoshop doing that, it's not you?

AM: Nope, just Photoshop. Though what I'm doing technically is a work in collaboration with it. But it struck me that I could remake all sorts of paintings, not just still lifes. I could just go to museums and say, "Hey, can I do your Picasso?" [*laughs*]

LW: Your mention of Picasso is also interesting in this context. David Hockney talks about the way that when Picasso does one of his pictures of Marie-Thérèse (Fig. 21), say, and she has two eyes on one side of her nose, and her lips are over here, and her nostrils . . . people say, "Oh my God, he's made a monster of her, the image is completely abstract and unrealistic," to which Hockney counters,

"On the contrary, that's completely realistic. That's what happens when you lean in to kiss someone." Things in fact do go all weird. A painter friend of mine, Gerri Davis, in the same vein, literally made a painting called *When We Kiss* (Fig. 22), further thinking all that through . . .

AM: That's wild.

LW: But it seems to me that your Photoshopped riff on that Dutch still life partakes of a similar sort of delirium, a delicious profusion and confusion that I associate precisely with intimacy. Or maybe what it might be like to be a dog, sticking your face deep into all that splendid *stuff*, and smelling, breathing it all in, but with your eyes!

What did you do next? And by the way, how long had it been, say, between number 1 and number 5?

AM: Oh, three or four months—I mean, I was doing them in between other projects, but the deeper I got into the flowers, the more I tended to focus on them to the exclusion of most anything else: playing with all the components of photographic practice within the confines of the theme. And not just the technical, mechanical components.

For example, with number 6 (page 38), I am obviously playing with the idea of receding one-point perspective, which is an inevitable effect with any conventional photography and has always fascinated me: those times when our expectations get violated and we end up going, "Wait? What's that? Where are we?" So in this particular case, across a flat board I have deployed the black and gray putties from earlier in order to create the illusion of such a recession, left to right, across a notional table, seen from above and to the side, and then added to the effect by including flowers atop stems ranged vertically along the table top from biggest to smallest, left to right—the idea being of course that the closer to you, the bigger otherwise identically sized objects will seem—and then I just took a simple photograph of the in fact completely flat panel from directly above.

LW: And number 7 (page 39)?

AM: Well, this is another view of a prepared panel as photographed from directly above, though in this case I am attempting to create the illusion, say, of looking into a forest by ranging variously sized stems, without flowers, as if they were tree trunks receding into the dark distance. The whole thing is pressed into black putty on board, and the forest floor gets suggested by a dusting of little flowers and shredded white petals. In this instance, I had in mind some of the stage sets of William Kentridge and Robert Wilson, for example, who I admire enormously.

LW: It also has the feel of some of Joseph Cornell's boxes, which in turn were consciously suggestive of earlier theatrical and particularly ballet sets. It feels like a winter scene: passing by woods on a snowy night.

AM: Yeah, but it's fascinating, too, how color works, the way its being whiter there at the bottom and less so higher up itself contributes to the image's sense of receding depth.

LW: Well, then you have a triptych, it looks like.

AM: I think of them as funereal scenes, sort of, the kinds of wreaths you might find at a funeral, but just flowers piled up within a frame, seen from above.

LW: And straight, simple photographs again?

AM: Actually, no. Or rather, the first of them (#8, page 40) is, but the other two (#9 and 10, pages 41 and 42) were put through Photoshop, although based on only two or three shots in each case—I was trying to dial back the effect a bit. Still, you can see strange doublings—there, for instance, and there.

LW: And in that last one (Fig. 23), once again you get the flowers tumbling out of the interior bounds of the frame. "Bursting out of all its contours," as Rilke might have put things, "like a star."

AM: Although in that case I myself put the petals there— that's not an effect of Photoshop. I was trying to doff my hat to the great trompe l'oeil painterly tradition of people like William Harnett and John Peto. As I say, in addition to everything else, I am consciously trying to engage the wider history of art with this series, and not just that of photography.

LW: But how does one photograph trompe l'oeil, especially since all of photography is in effect a sort of attempt at tricking the eye?

AM: Precisely: That was one of the things I was trying to play with here.

LW: And then the next one (Fig. 24), it's as if you've taken the funereal theme and gone all the way into death itself, sheer black, like the negative of the prior images. Is that some sort of darkroom trick, or . . . ?

AM: No, in fact I just arranged another collection of flowers in a frame and then spray-painted them black. Although I do love how little blushes of color persist here and there. Straight photograph.

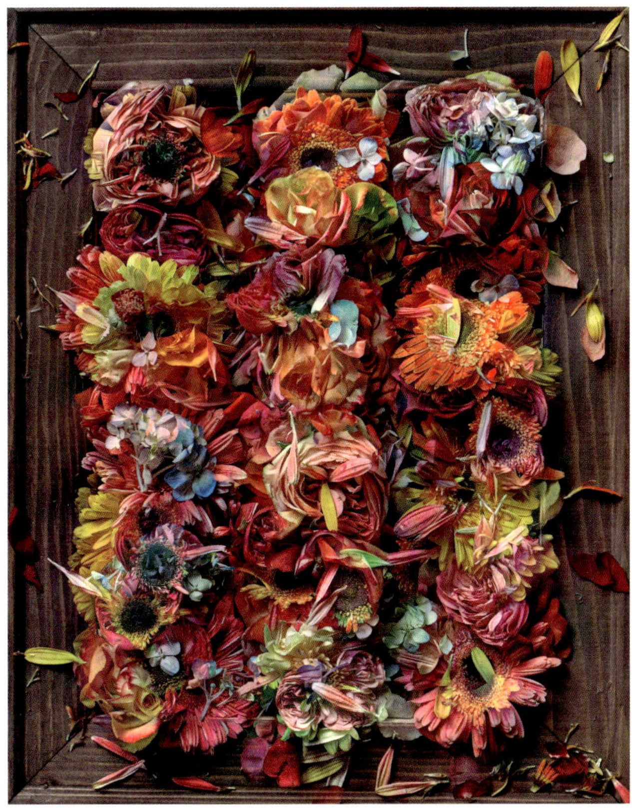

Figure 23. Abelardo Morell, *Flowers for Lisa #10*, 2016

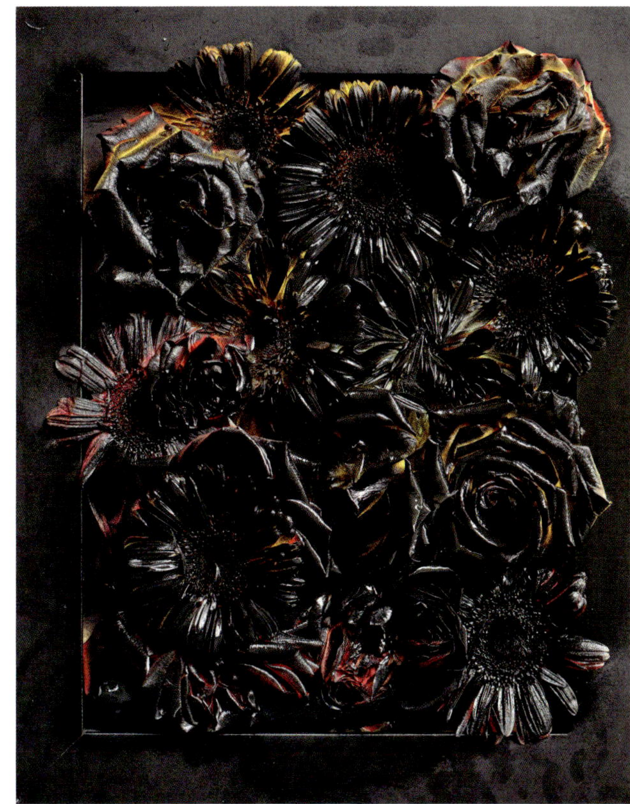

Figure 24. Abelardo Morell, *Flowers for Lisa #11*, 2016

LW: Uncanny lighting, though.

AM: Raking flashlight from the side. Long exposure. I wanted to suggest a sense that notwithstanding its darkness, the thing was still kind of glowing. A feel of varnish.

LW: So on top of everything else, I suppose one could survey this entire series as a master class in lighting technique.

What about the next one (#12, page 45), which, though similarly black, feels somehow even more mysteriously evocative.

AM: Oh, I agree, maybe a little literary in its allusions. I was thinking of the English symbolist painters whom I've always loved, people like Rossetti, their maidens kind of drowning, Ophelia and the like. As I was doing this one, I was thinking that such a maiden might be lurking there behind that curtain of flowers. That's the kind of thing I can get to thinking alone there in my studio.

LW: You're having way too much fun.

AM: I know. Lisa thought so as well, she thought some of these in here were going a bit overboard.

LW: "*What about me!?*" Reminds me of when Hockney was first doing those Polaroid collages back in the early eighties, where because of the relatively narrow depth of field of the Polaroid camera, he had to move all about the room in order to compose the various panels of any eventual grid, and how at one point he was doing a portrait of Stephen Spender seated in a chair, but he'd drifted all the way to the back of the room, twenty feet behind him, to capture a particular corner, and Spender shouted back, "David, are you still photographing *me?*"

At any rate, I can see how in the next one (Fig. 25), you dialed way back, to something more seemingly straightforward.

AM: My homage to Magritte.

LW: But then again, as with Magritte, not as straightforward as all that. Because, wait: Is that a mirror, did you spray-paint the part of the rose facing us gray and leave the other side unsprayed, and, for that matter, is it even three-dimensional, or did you just notch those pieces of plywood together up there at the top . . . ?

AM: [*laughs*] I know, see how one can explore all the variations. No, no mirror, and yes, three dimensions, in fact an open boxlike structure made out of four panels of raw plywood, two vases, two flowers—one sprayed gray, the backdrop beyond the frame stained that deep red.

LW: And the vases themselves looking conspicuously like bulbs—for that matter, like upside-down lightbulbs, which I suppose brings us full circle.

Surveying some of the ensuing images, there are all sorts of jokes and glories and allusions—I note, for example, the vase made out of flowers in number 14 (page 47), the eerie horizon line in the one after that, and is that your Jackson Pollock in number 16 (pages 50–51)? And there's that wonderful play on three-dimensionality in number 18 (pages 54–55), achieved through the simple expedient of four exactingly placed green flower stalks. And then further ahead, riffs on Richter (#25, page 63) and Van Gogh (#23 and #28, pages 61 and 67) and, for that matter, you yourself in number 44 (page 83). Is that, I wonder, a bow to Picasso's bull's head in number 55 (page 97)? There's a witty hourglass in number 37 (page 76), grinding flowers to dust with the passage of time, other images playing off of the Necker cube perceptual illusion (#38, page 77) and its various cousins and, for that matter, a play on that other famous optical allusion of two facing profiles framing, naturally, come to think of it, a vase shape (#40, page 79)—and I notice from the title on that one that the profiles facing each other are none other than yours and Lisa's. Some are clearly Photoshopped, though many not—and wait, number 49 (pages 90–91) even seems to be a throwback to your outdoor tent camera obscura technique. The series in its entirety is like a deck of Rorschach cards—and sure enough, there's even a pair of Rorschach knock-offs (#59 and #60, pages 103 and 104).

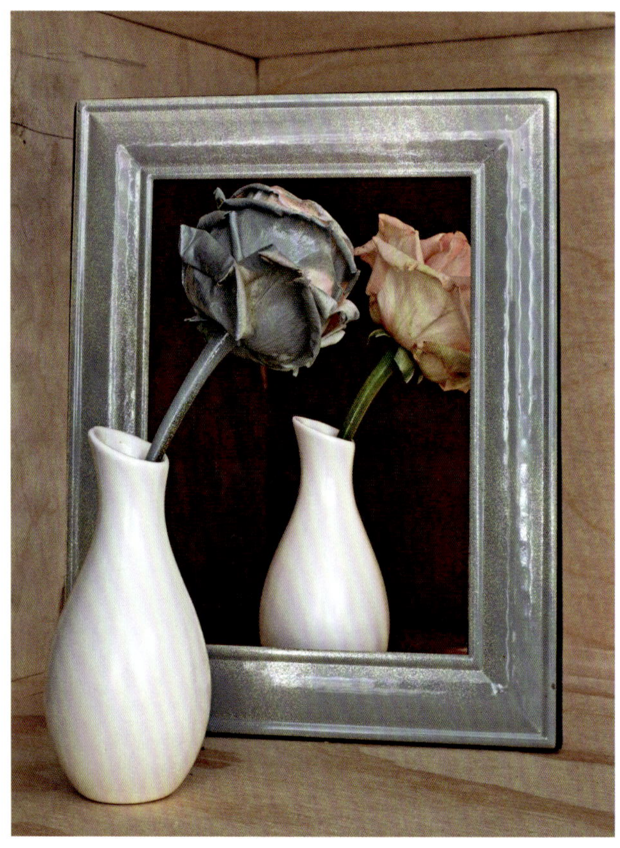

Figure 25. Abelardo Morell, *Flowers for Lisa #13: After René Magritte*, 2016

Well, it's just a whole wide world of associations, teeming away. Maybe the thing to do is to ask you to provide us with a grid at the back of the book where you could annotate thumbnails of each of the images with occasional hints of your process and intention—and, for that matter, we could ask Lisa to offer her thoughts and responses as well.

AM: Sounds good to me.

LW: In closing, though, there's a lot of commentary these days on so-called late style, and I wonder if you think of this series as something like that in your own case.

AM: Well, I hope not *too* late. I hope I still have a lot more to offer. Though I must say that in my own case, I find that aging is giving me a wider sense of freedom and boldness. I have more artistic energy now than when I started. Maybe it's an illusion to make me feel that I'll live forever.

LW: And well you might. But with late works generally, one thinks of summation and transcendence. I suppose I've been free-associating—the sense of a teeming, over-brimming world—to a marvelous late poem by the great Polish master Czeslaw Milosz, "An Honest Description of Myself with a Glass of Whiskey at an Airport, Let Us Say, in Minneapolis" in which he berates himself, old man that he is, for ogling the passing girls, but then goes on to give himself some slack, for, as he says,

> I do what I have always done: compose scenes
>   of this earth under orders from the erotic
>   imagination.
> It's not that I desire these creatures precisely;
>   I desire everything, and they are like a sign
>   of ecstatic union.

going on to celebrate

> the proportions of human bodies, the color
>   of irises, a Paris street in June at dawn, all of
>   it incomprehensible, incomprehensible the
>   multitude of visible things.

And it seems to me something similar is going on here with you: a great upwelling of gratitude, as it were. Of thanks-giving.

AM: Yeah. Thanks to the world.

LW: *Gratitude* and *grace* share the same root.

AM: Well, then, that's what I have. And a feeling of plenty, of exuberance, an overflow of—my peacock turning to Lisa and saying, "I love you, and this is for you."

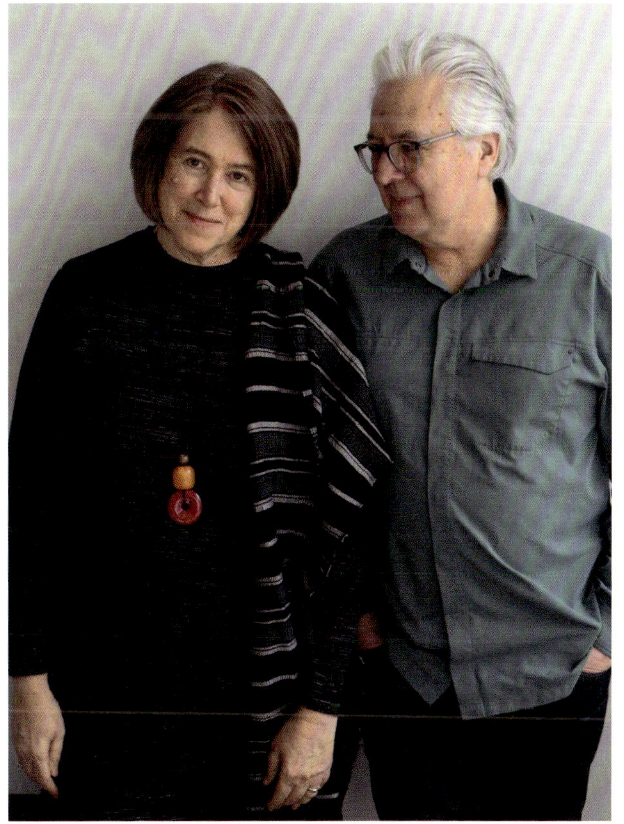

Figure 26. Abelardo Morell and Lisa McElaney, 2018

PLATES

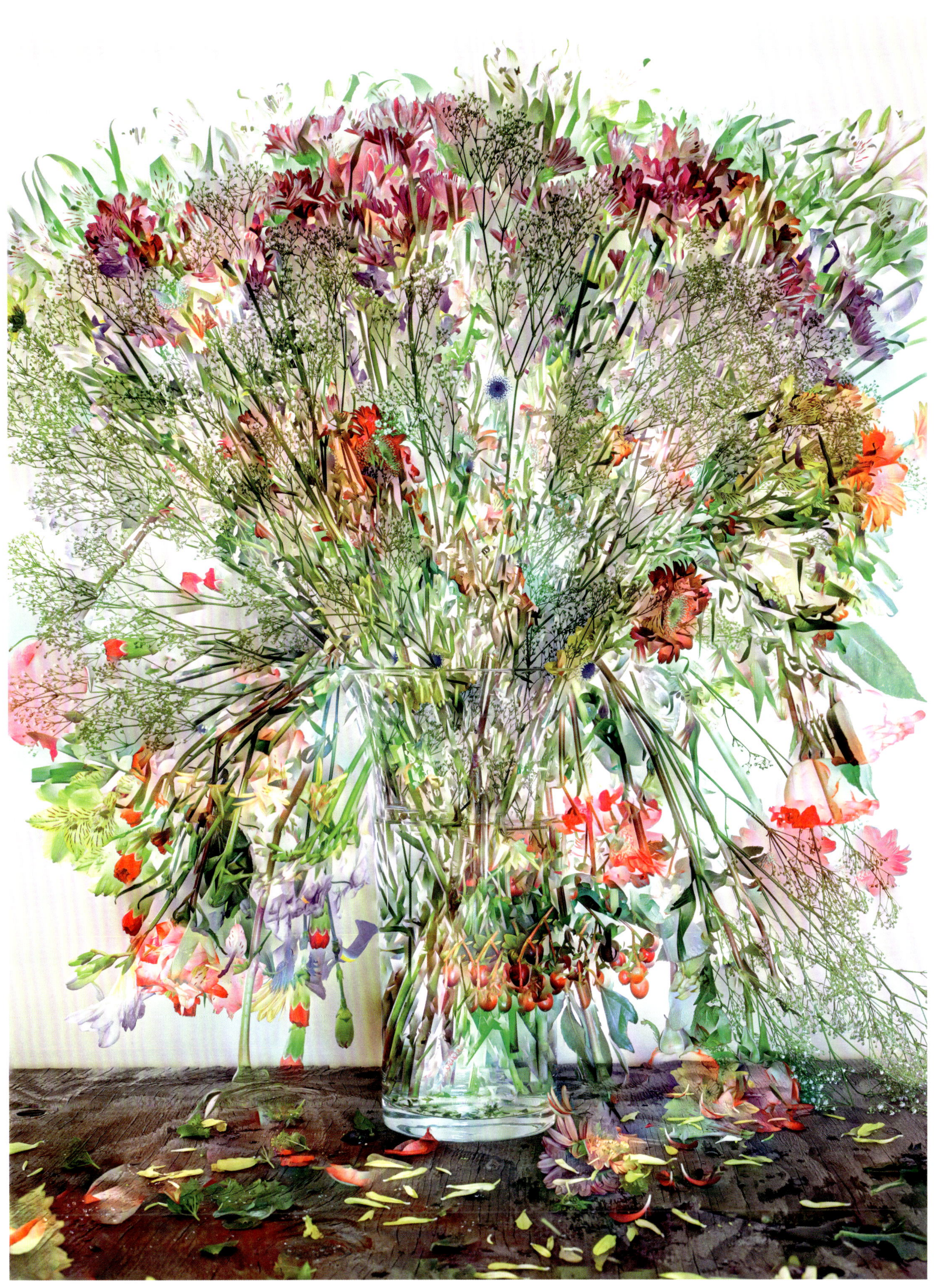

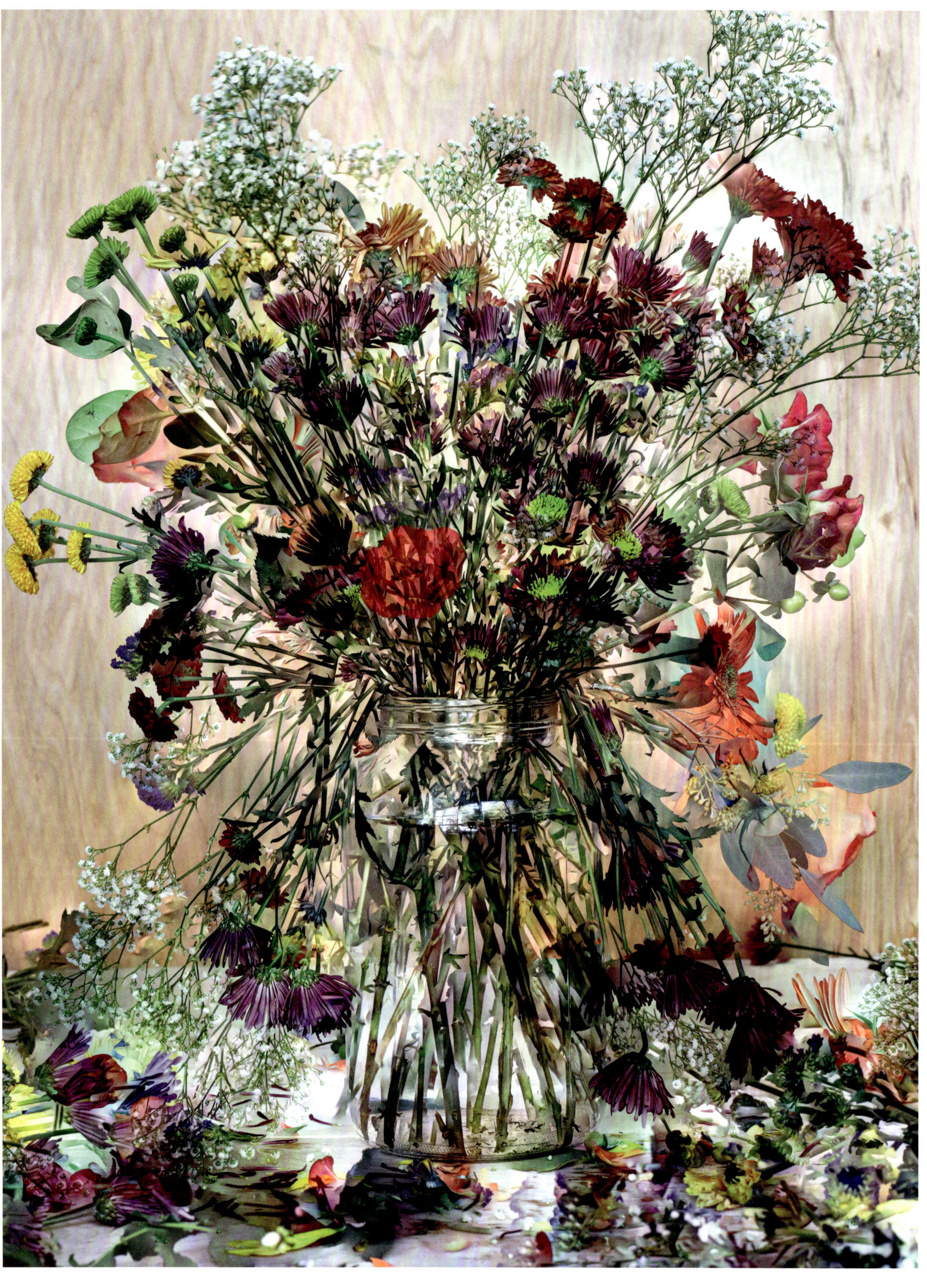

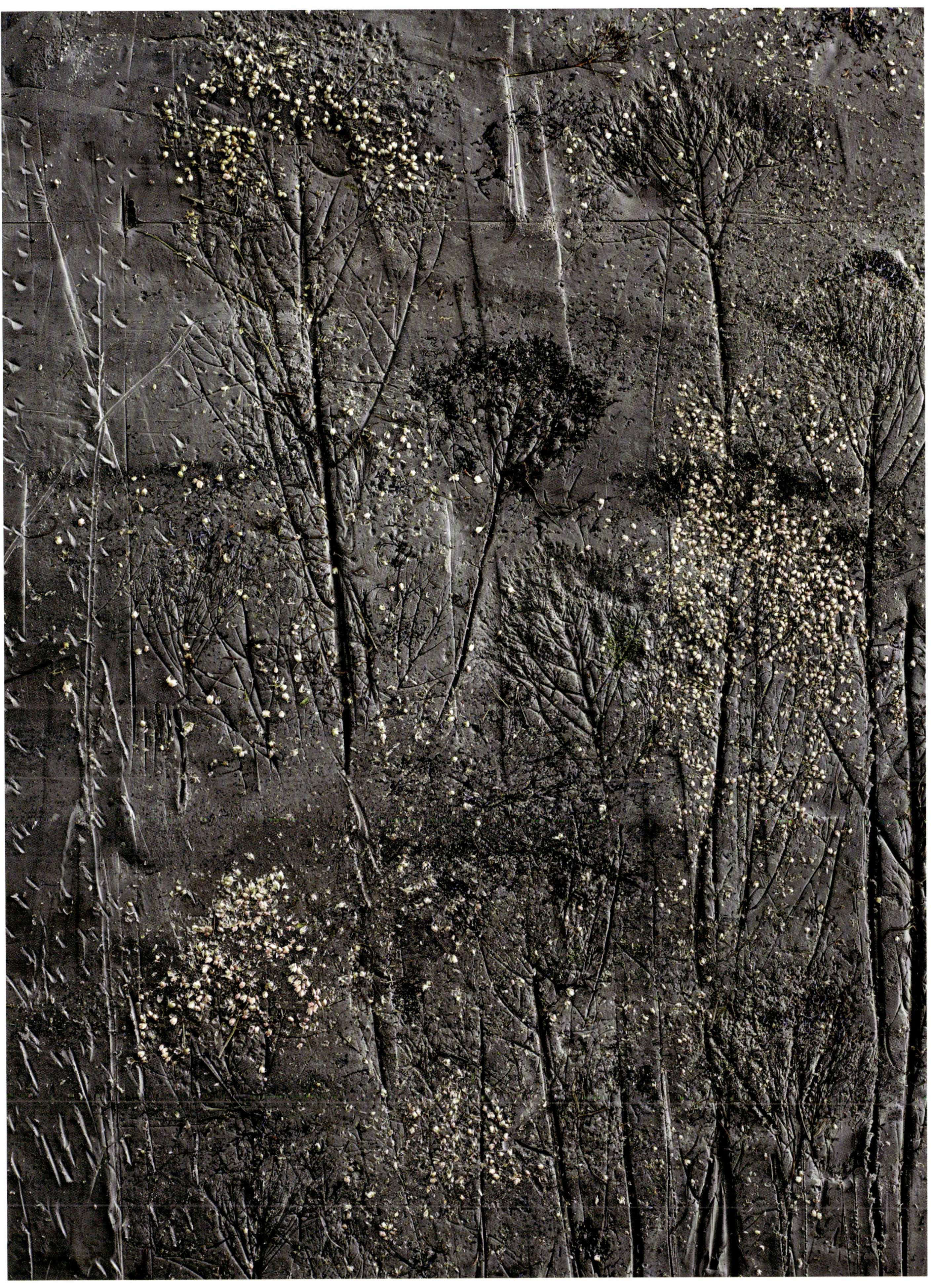

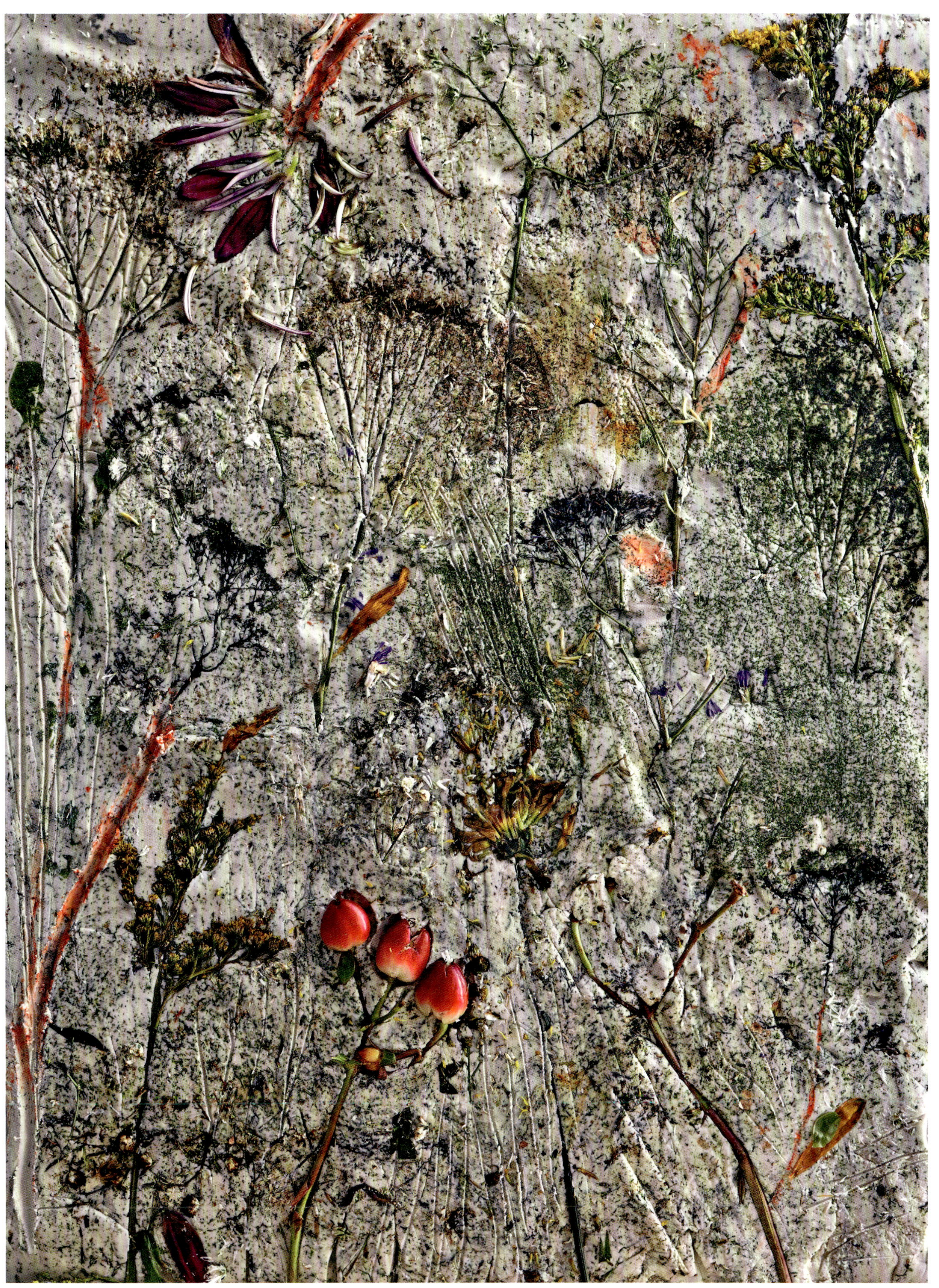

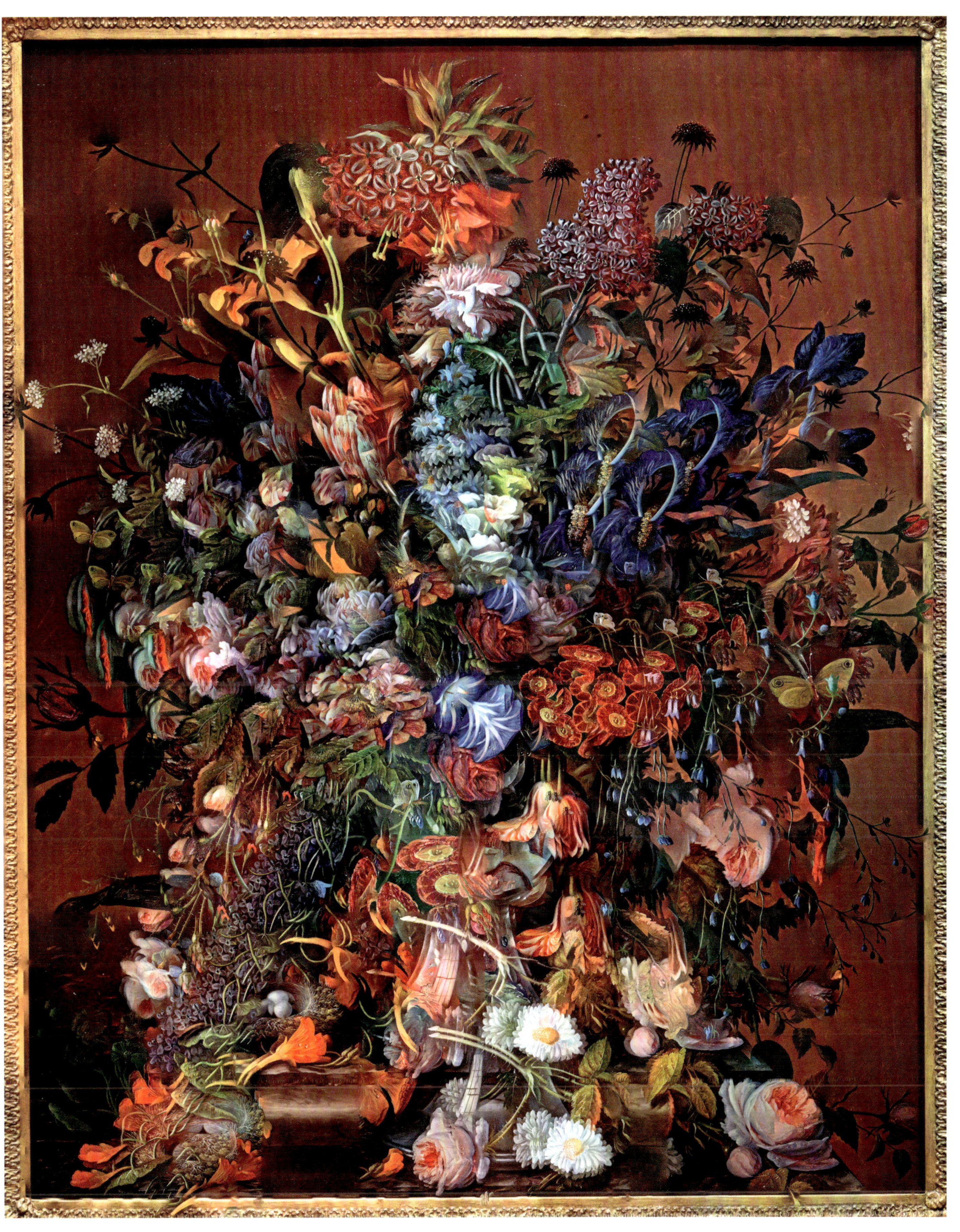

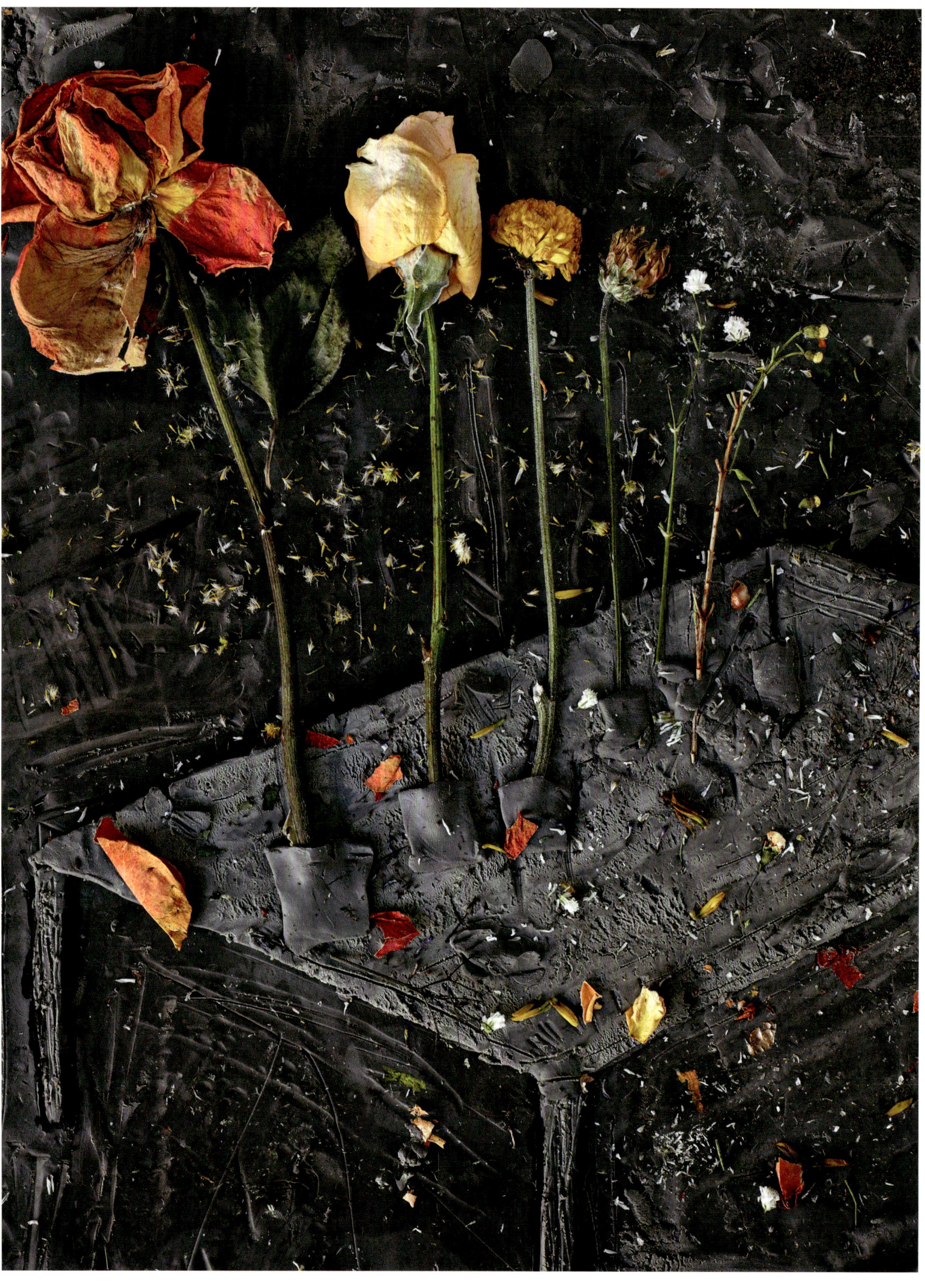

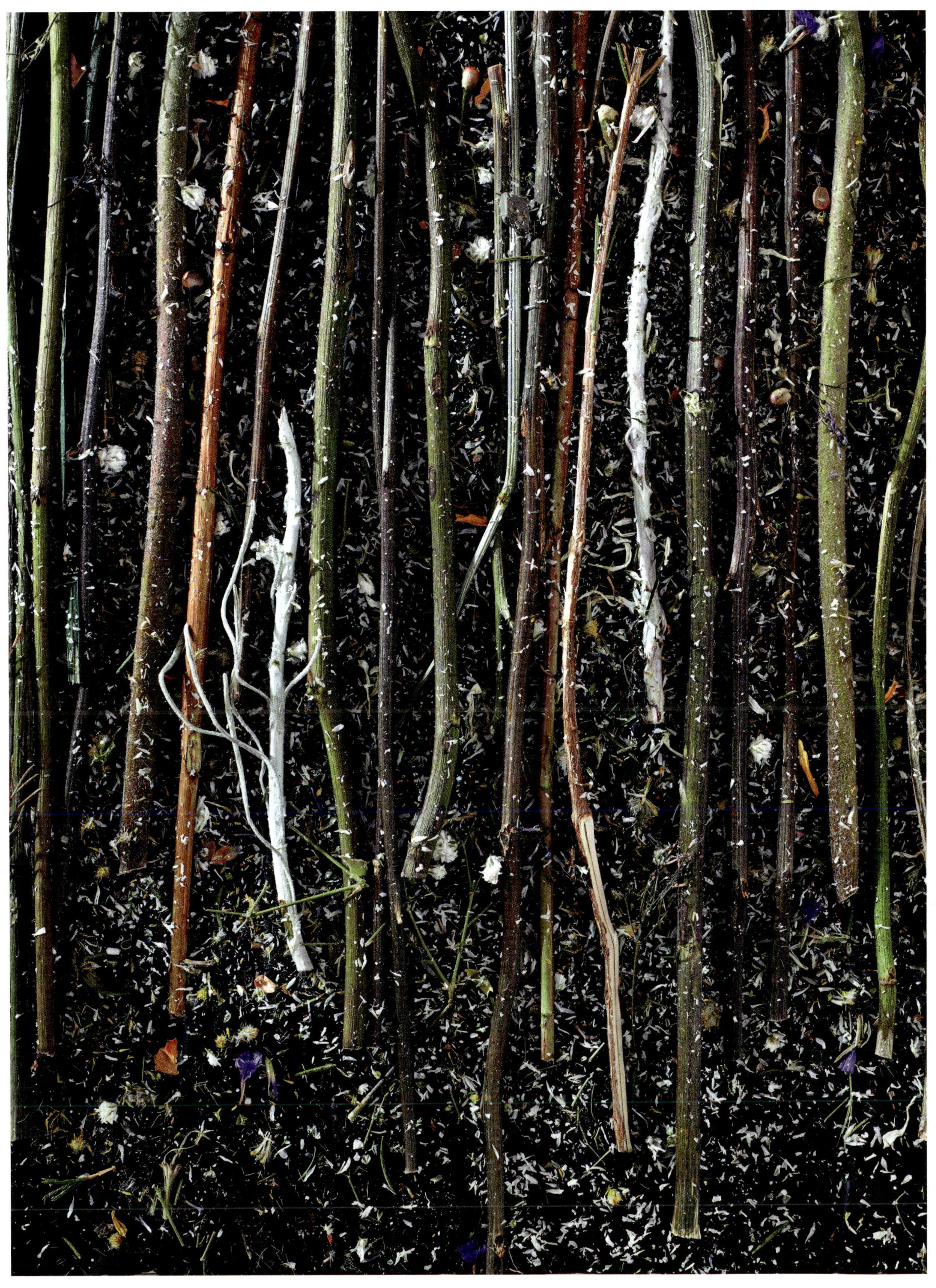

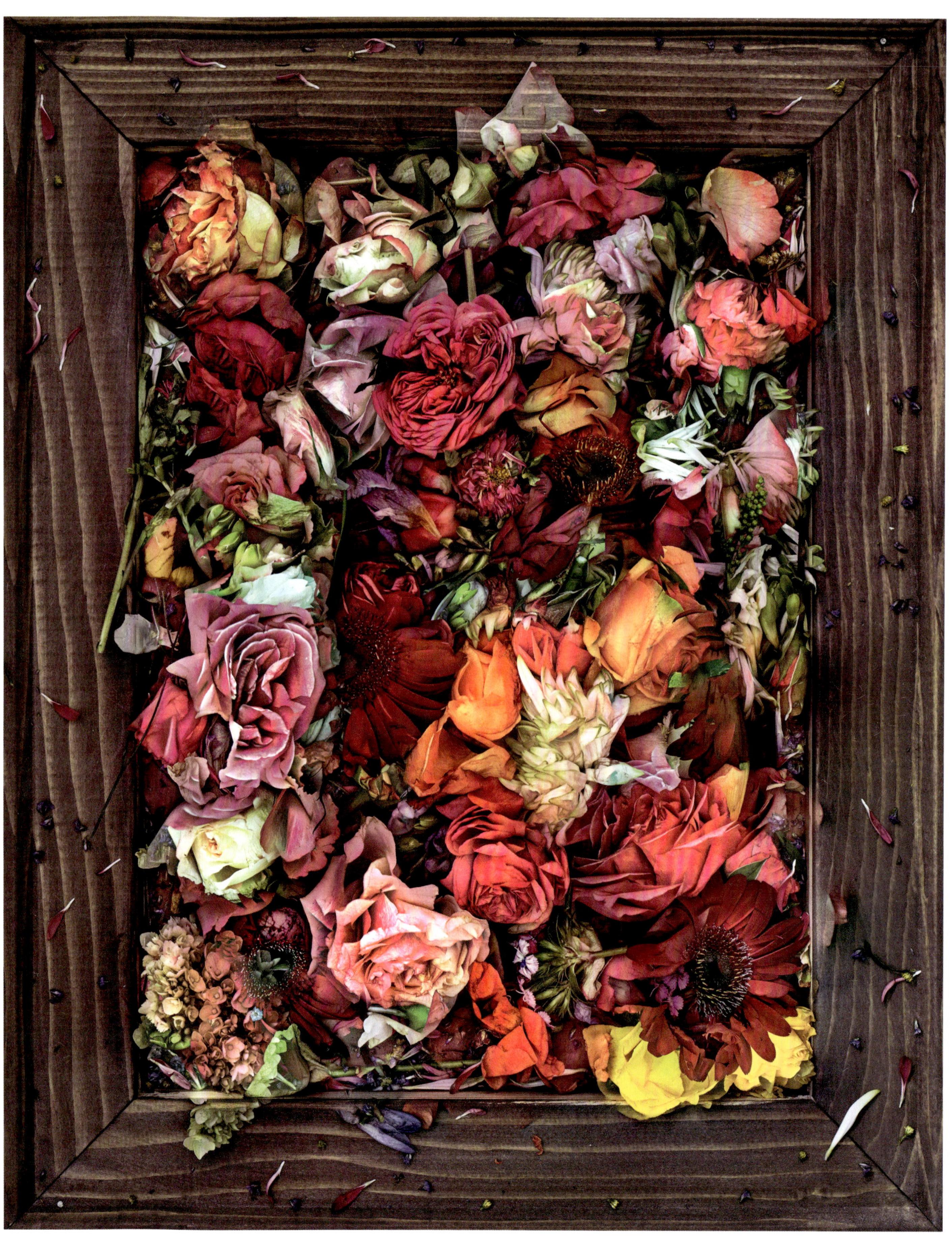

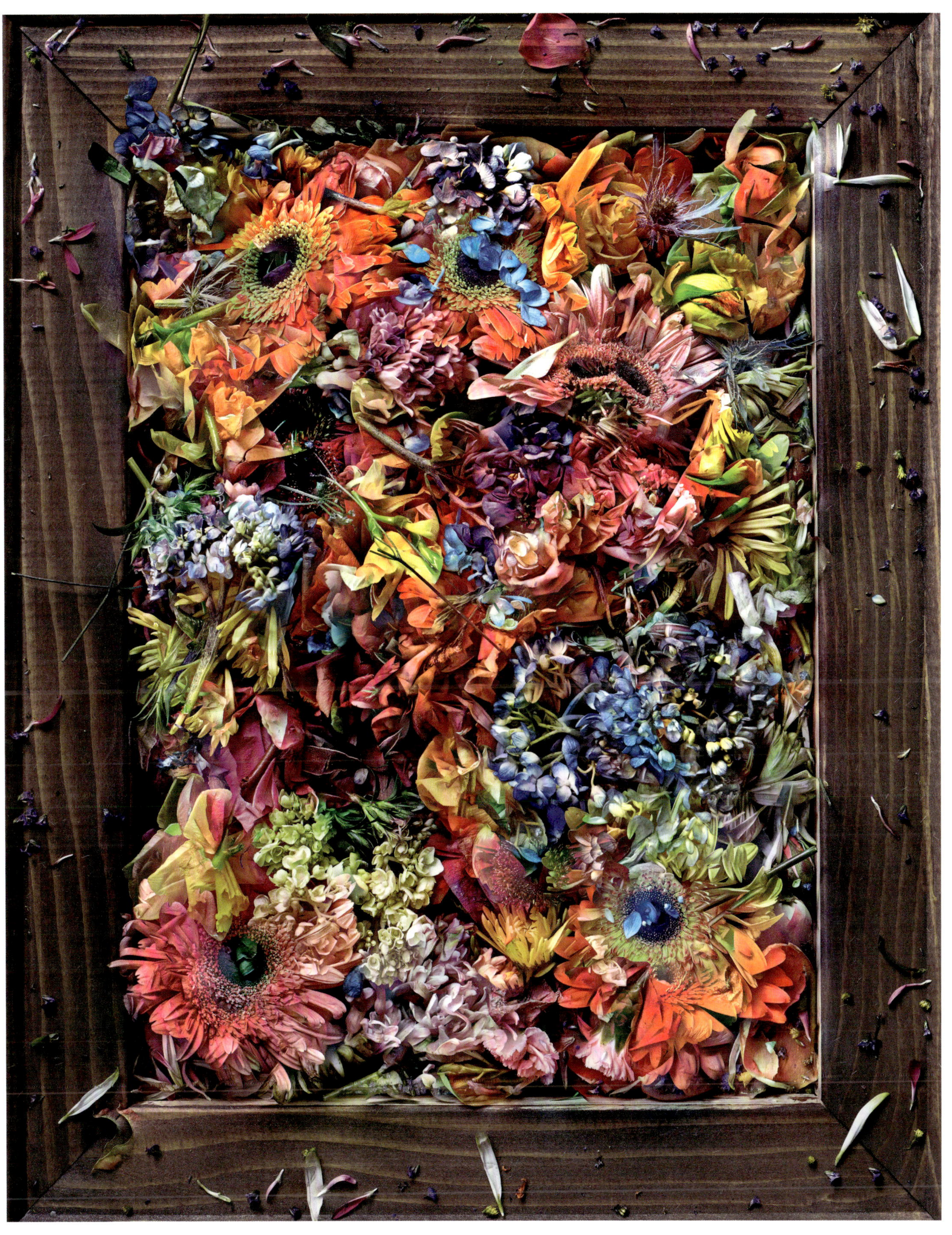

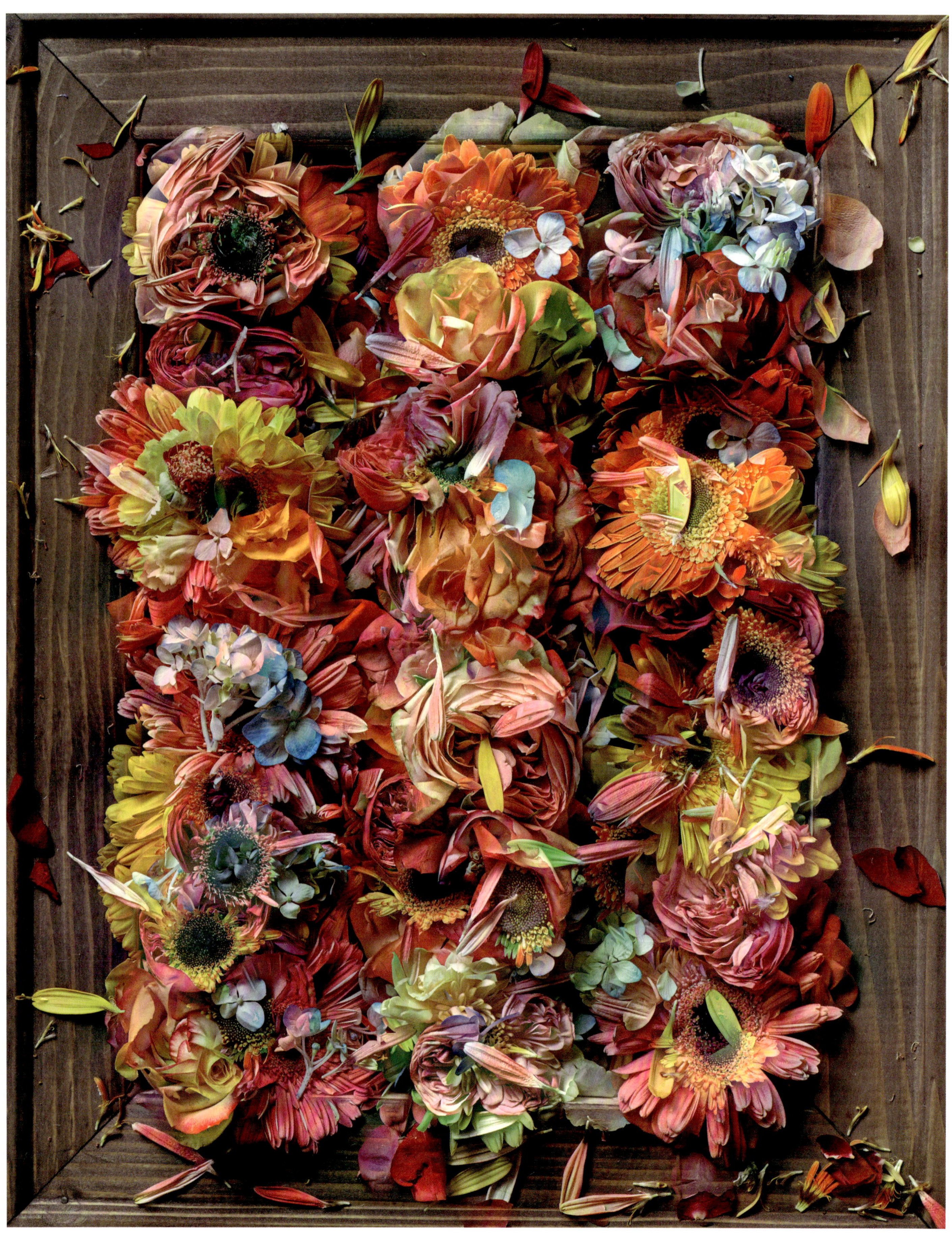

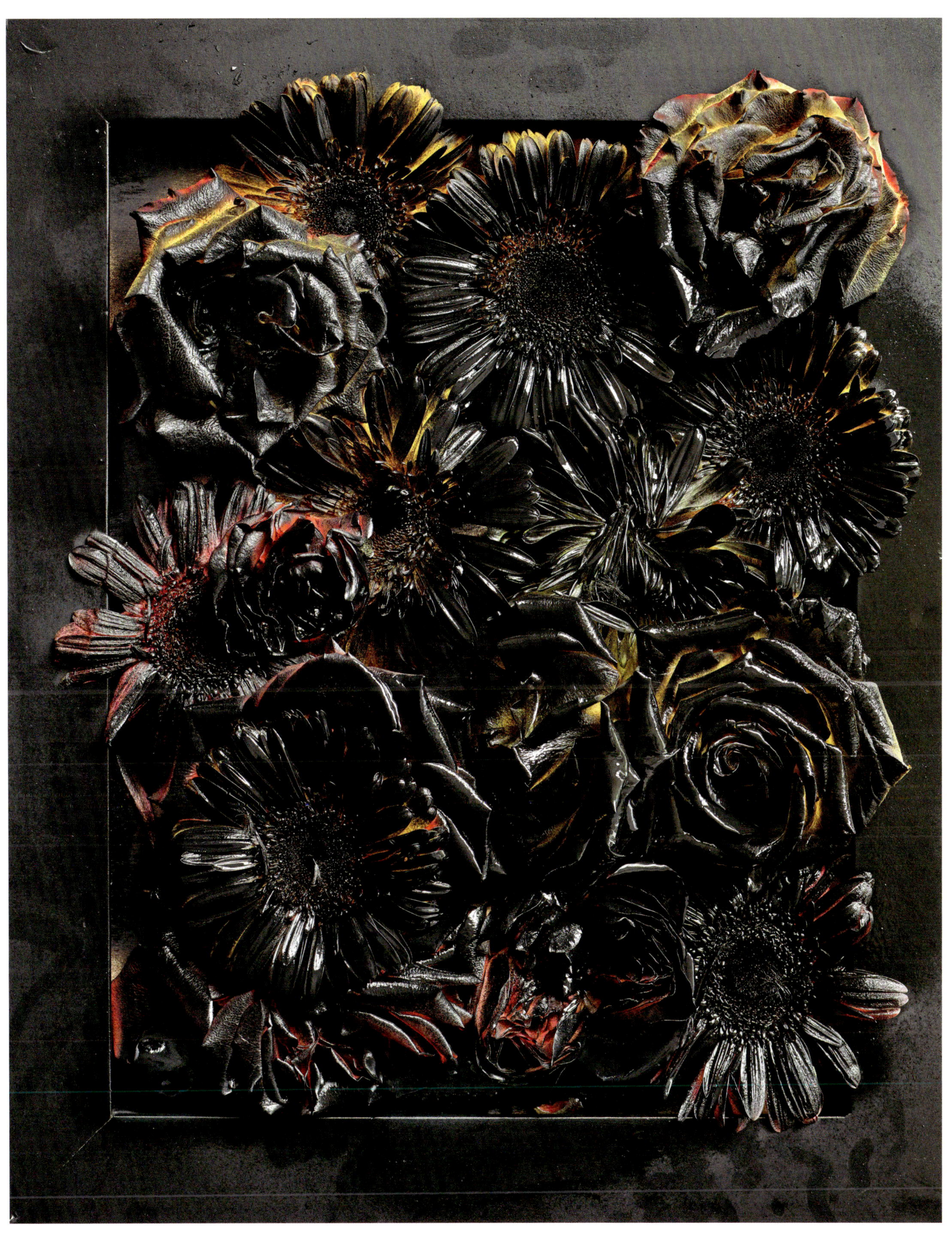

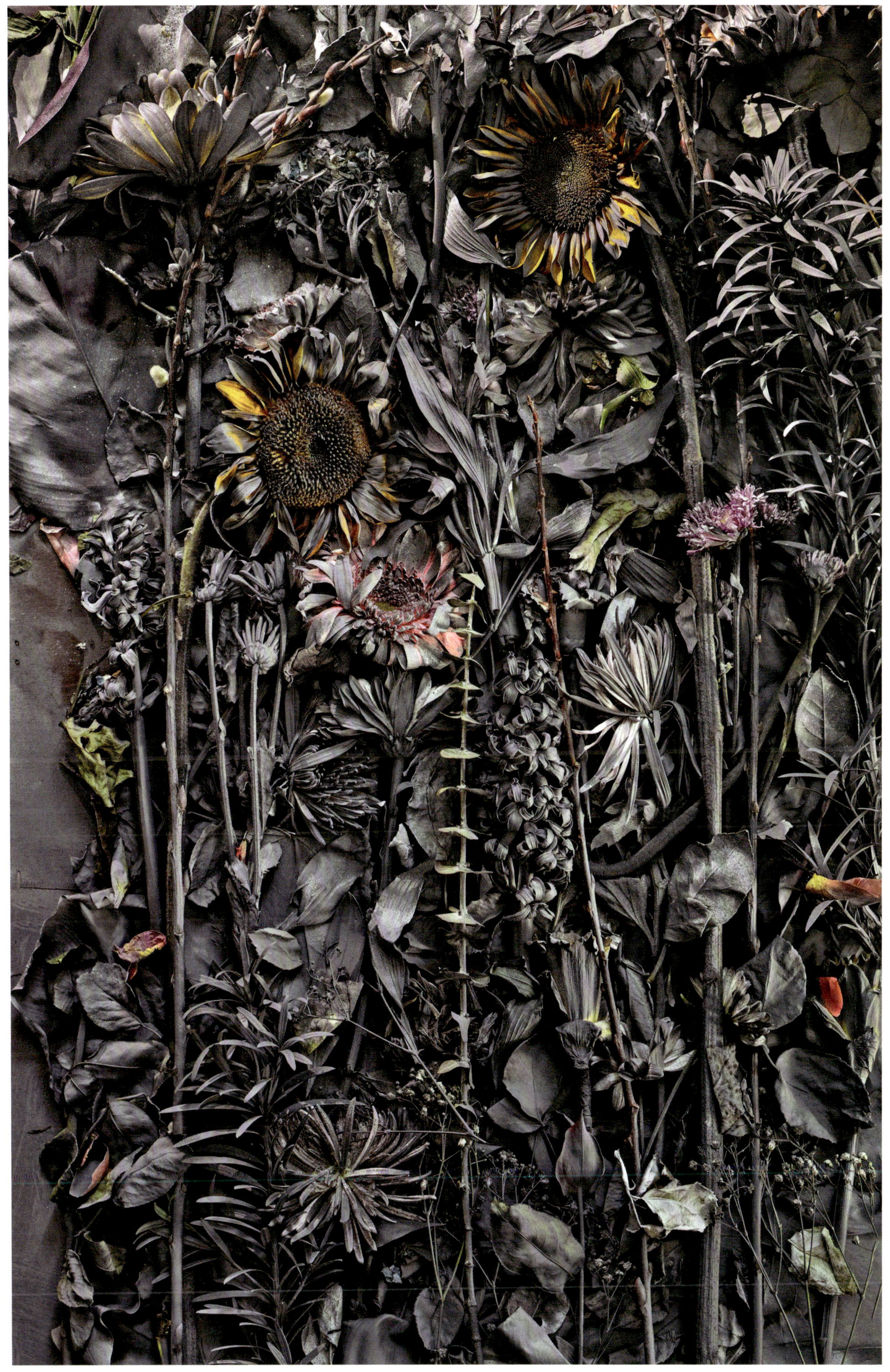

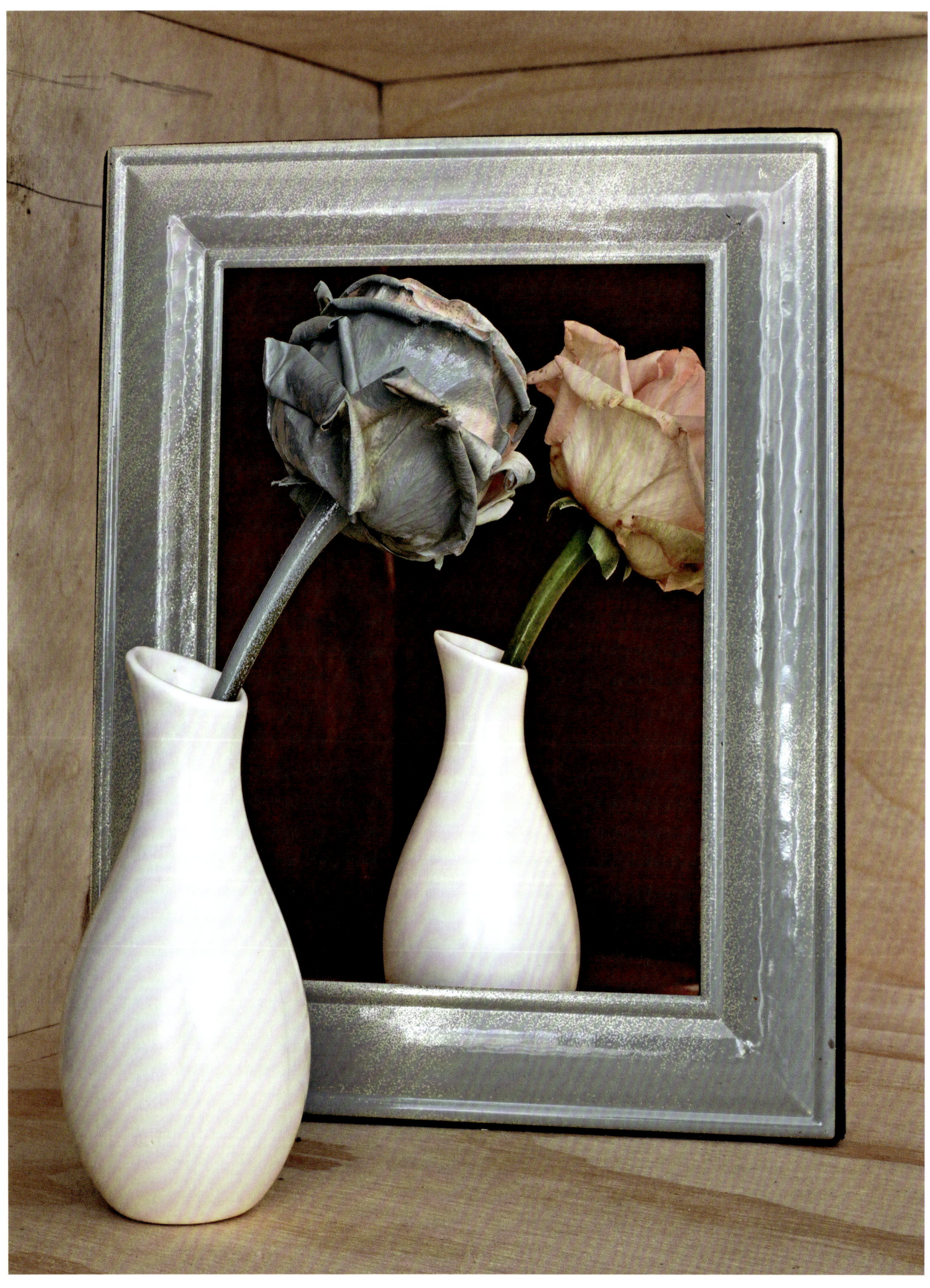

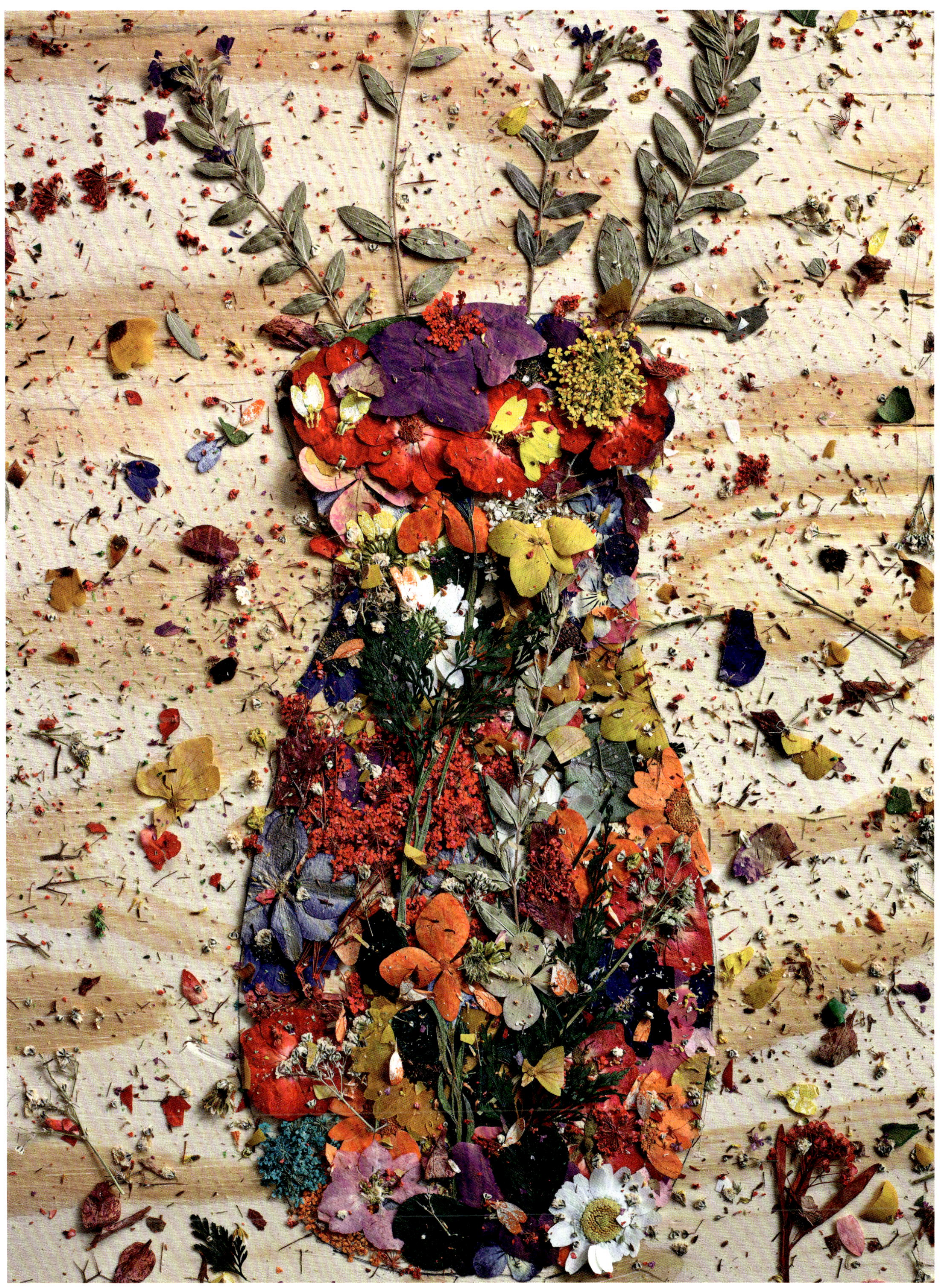

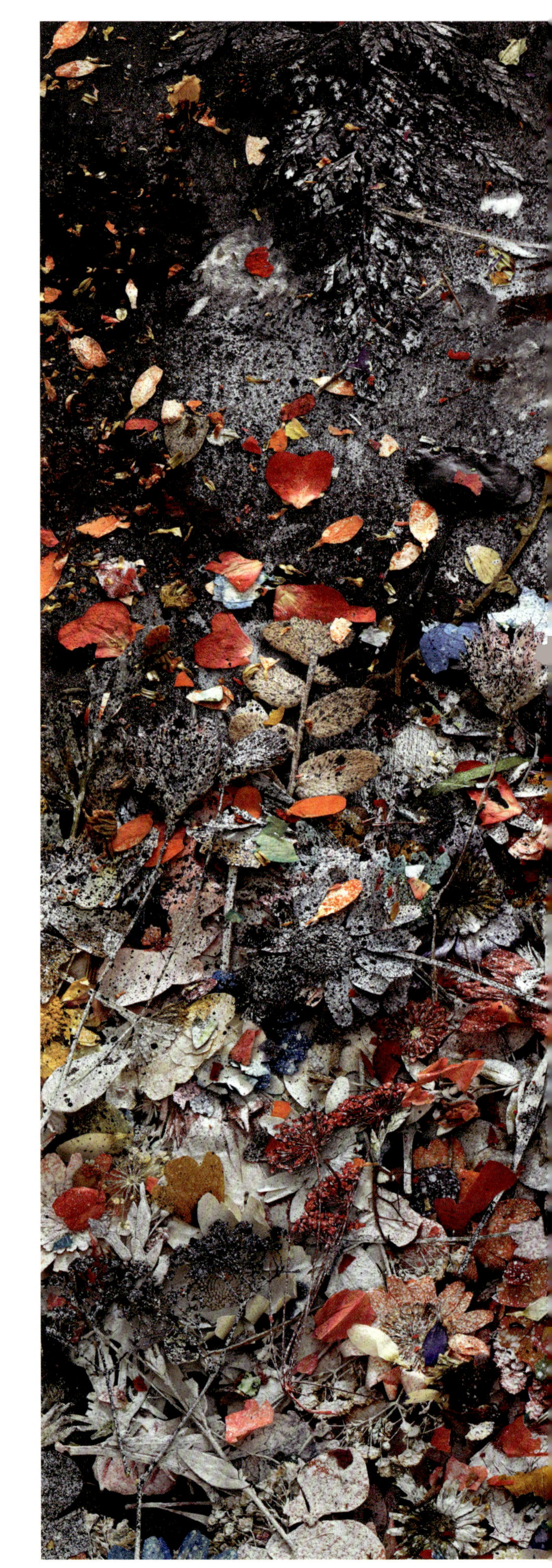

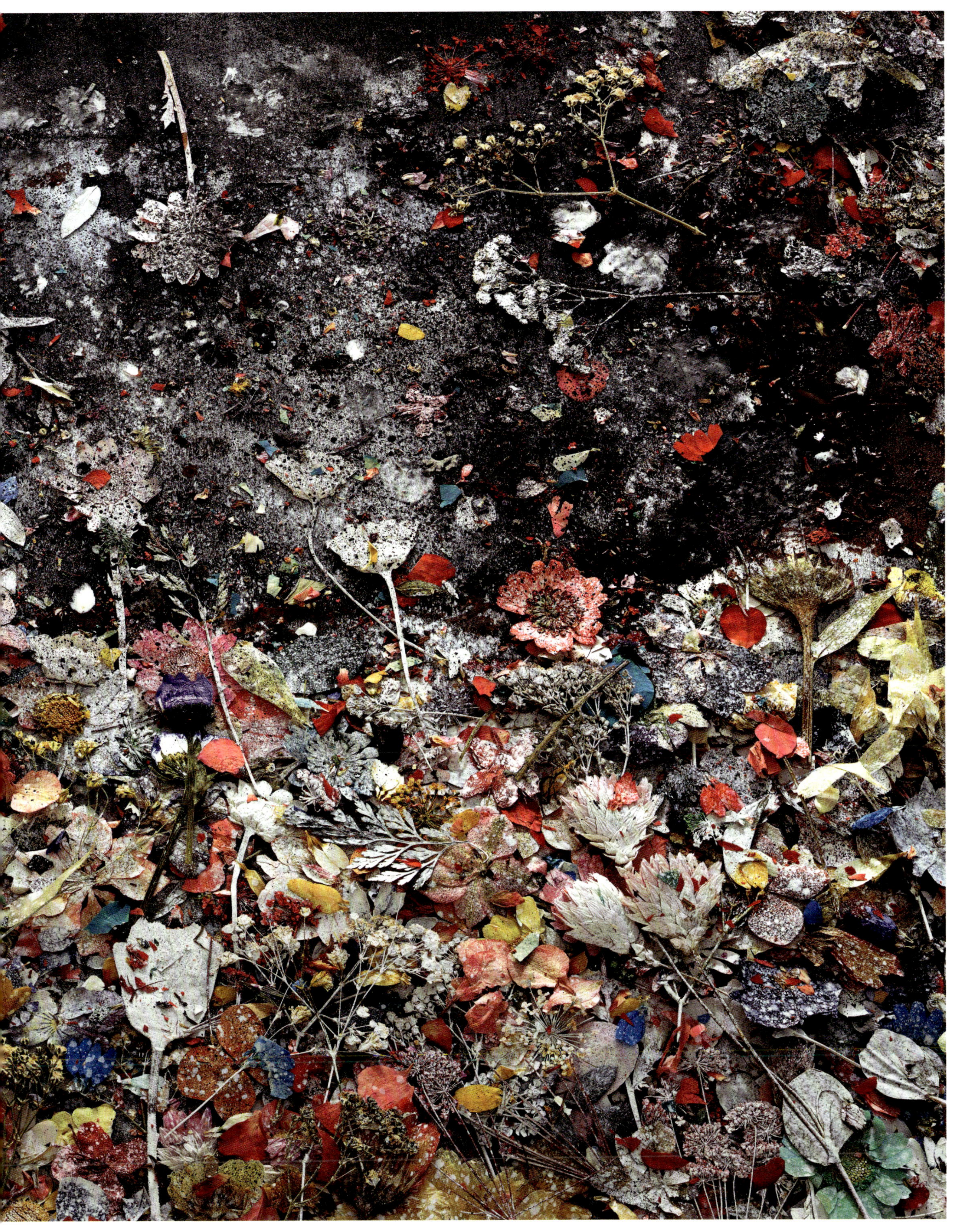

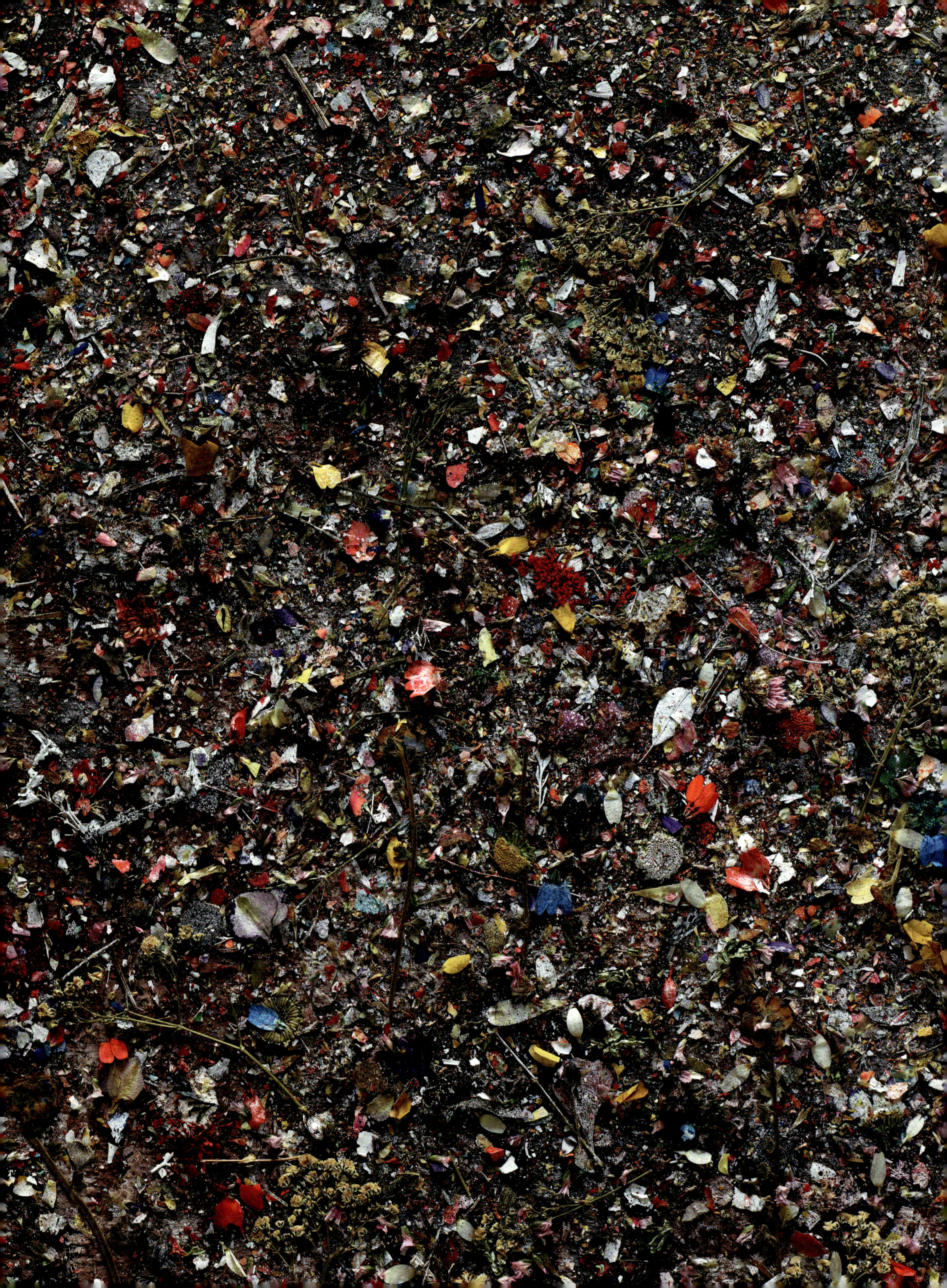

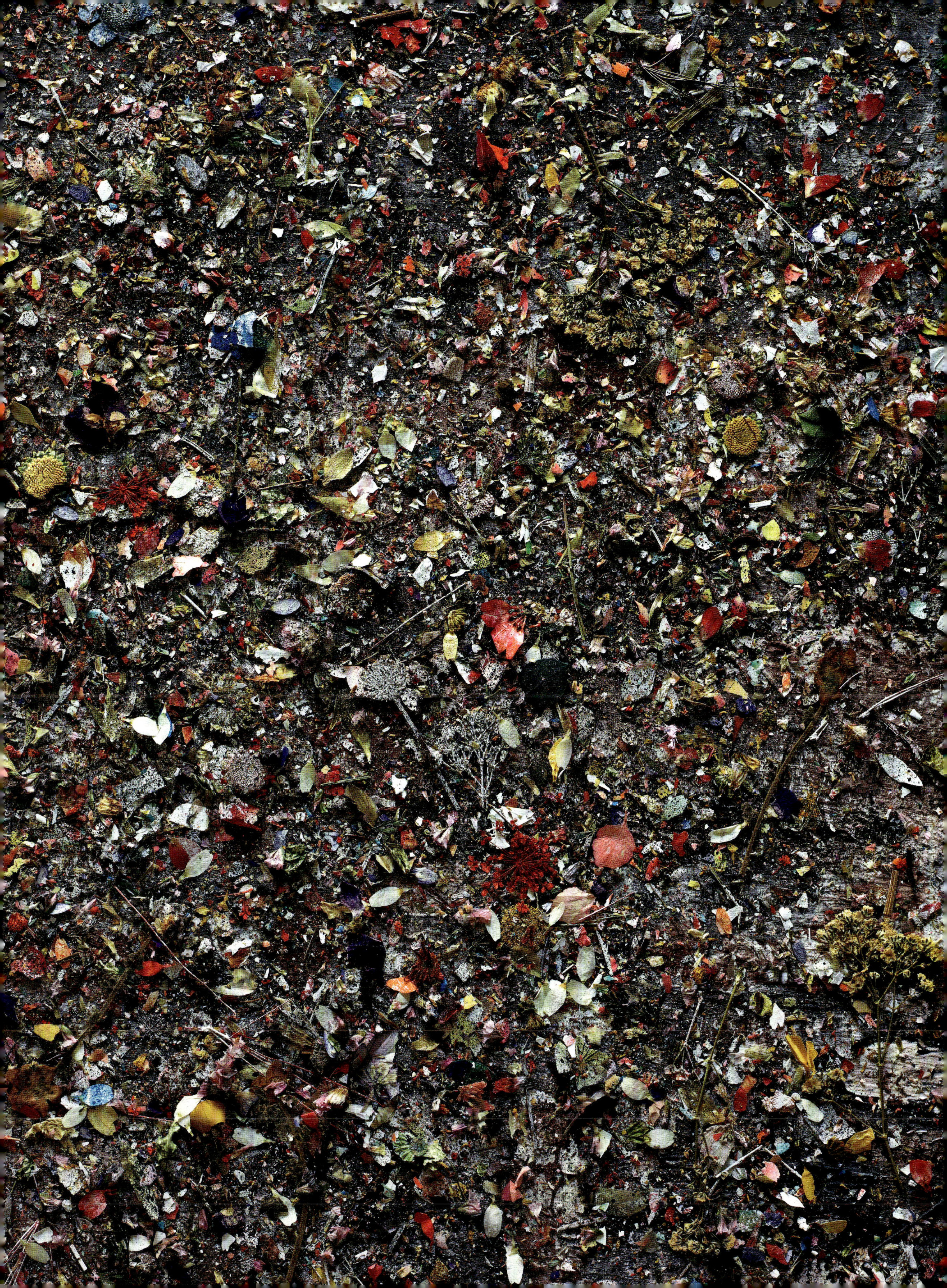

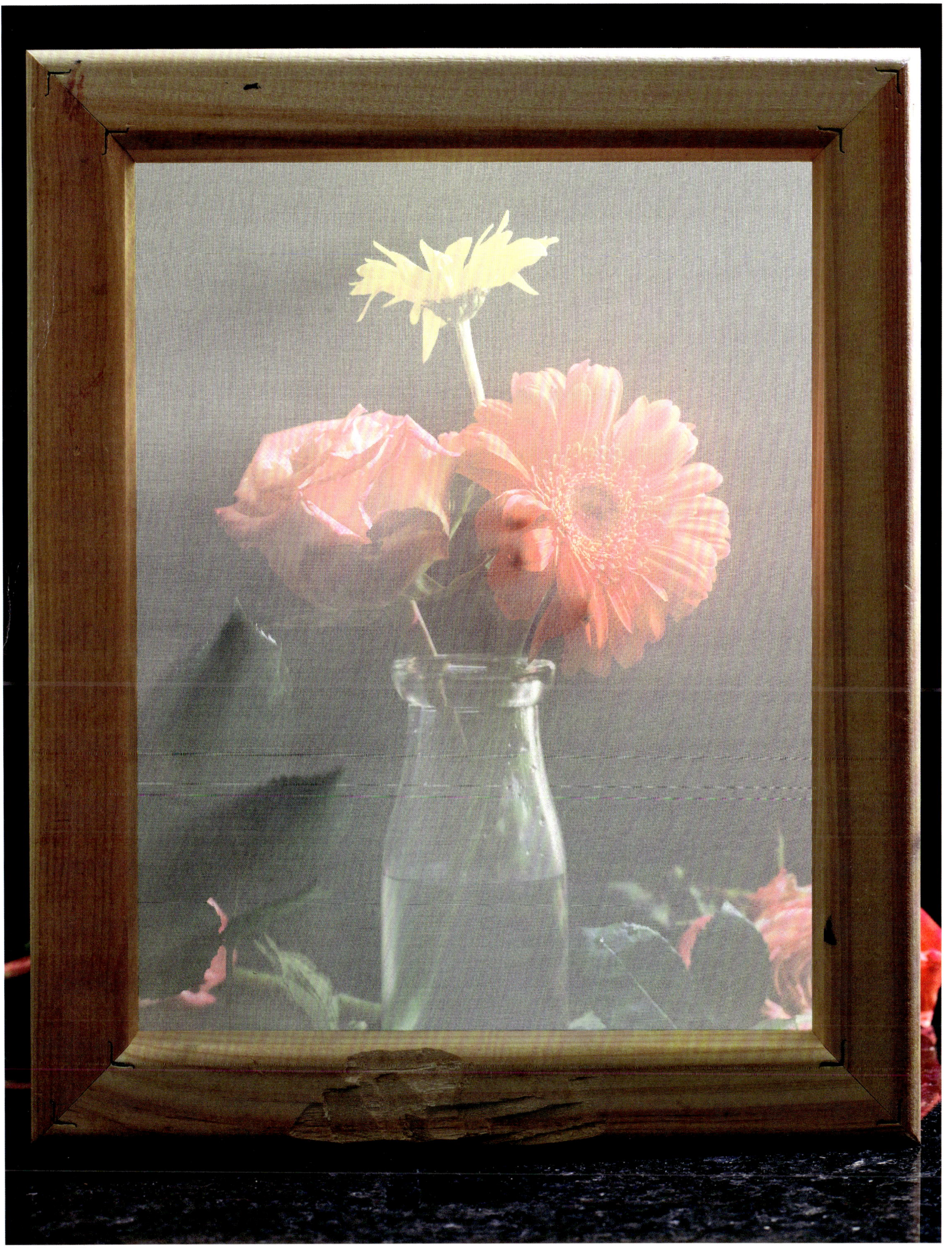

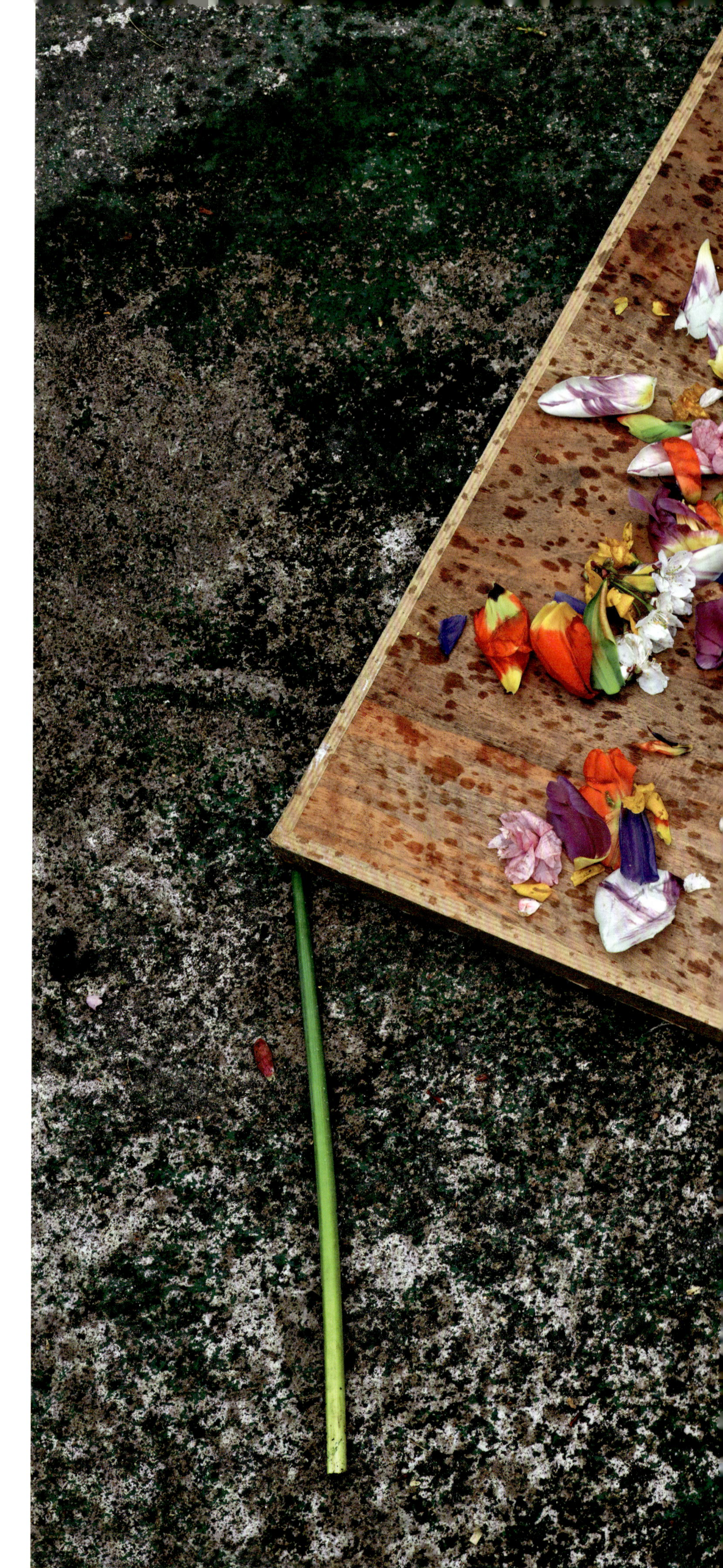

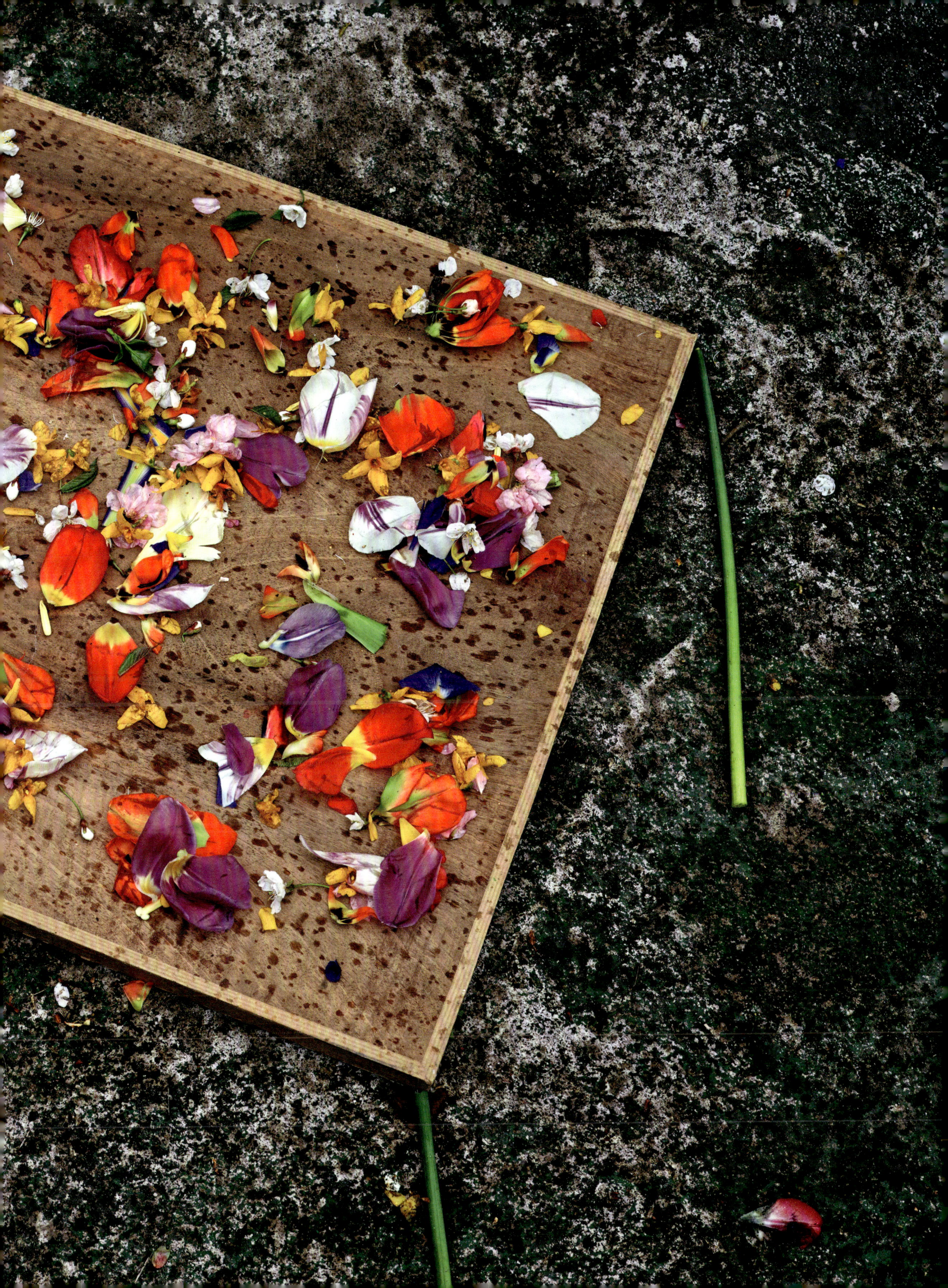

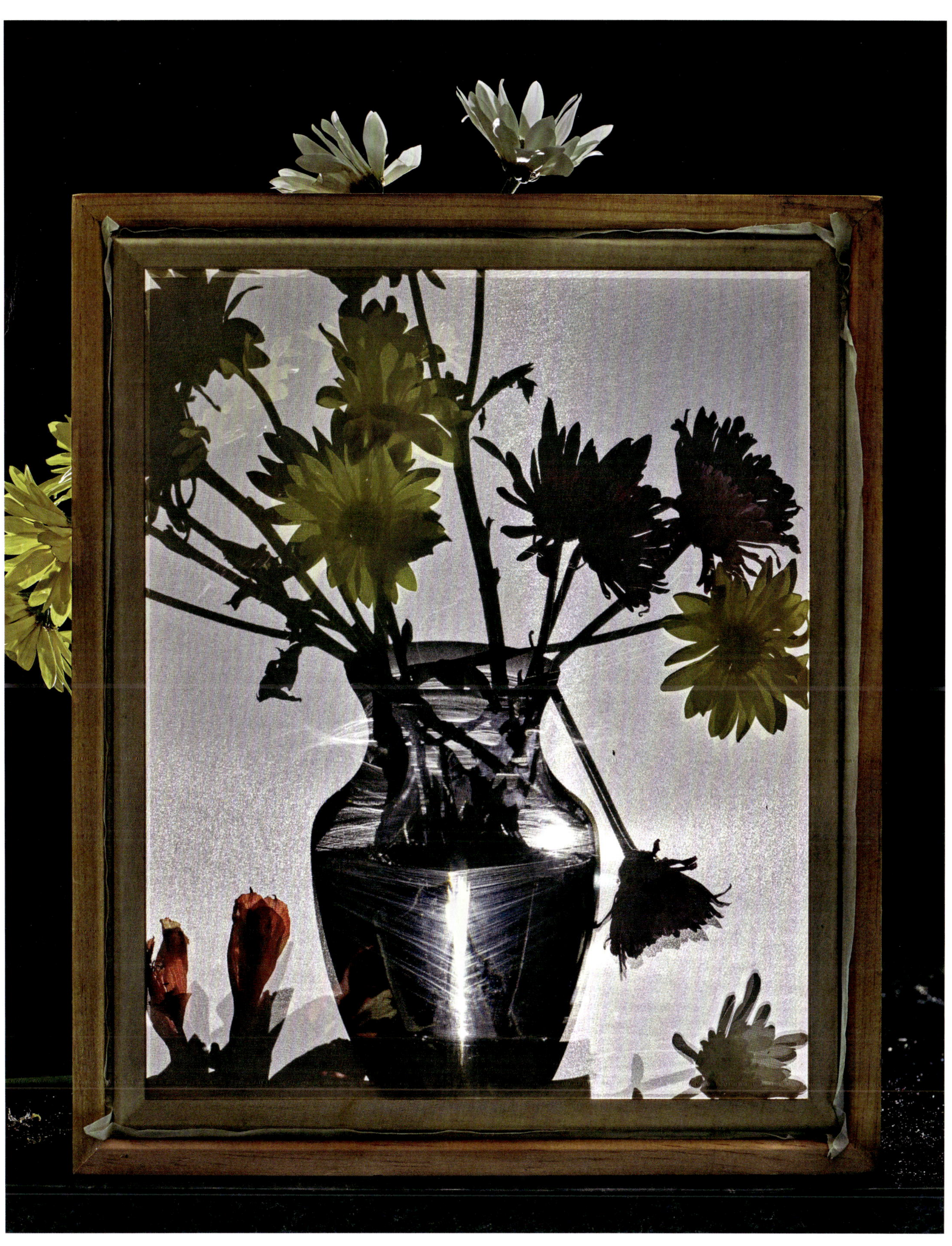

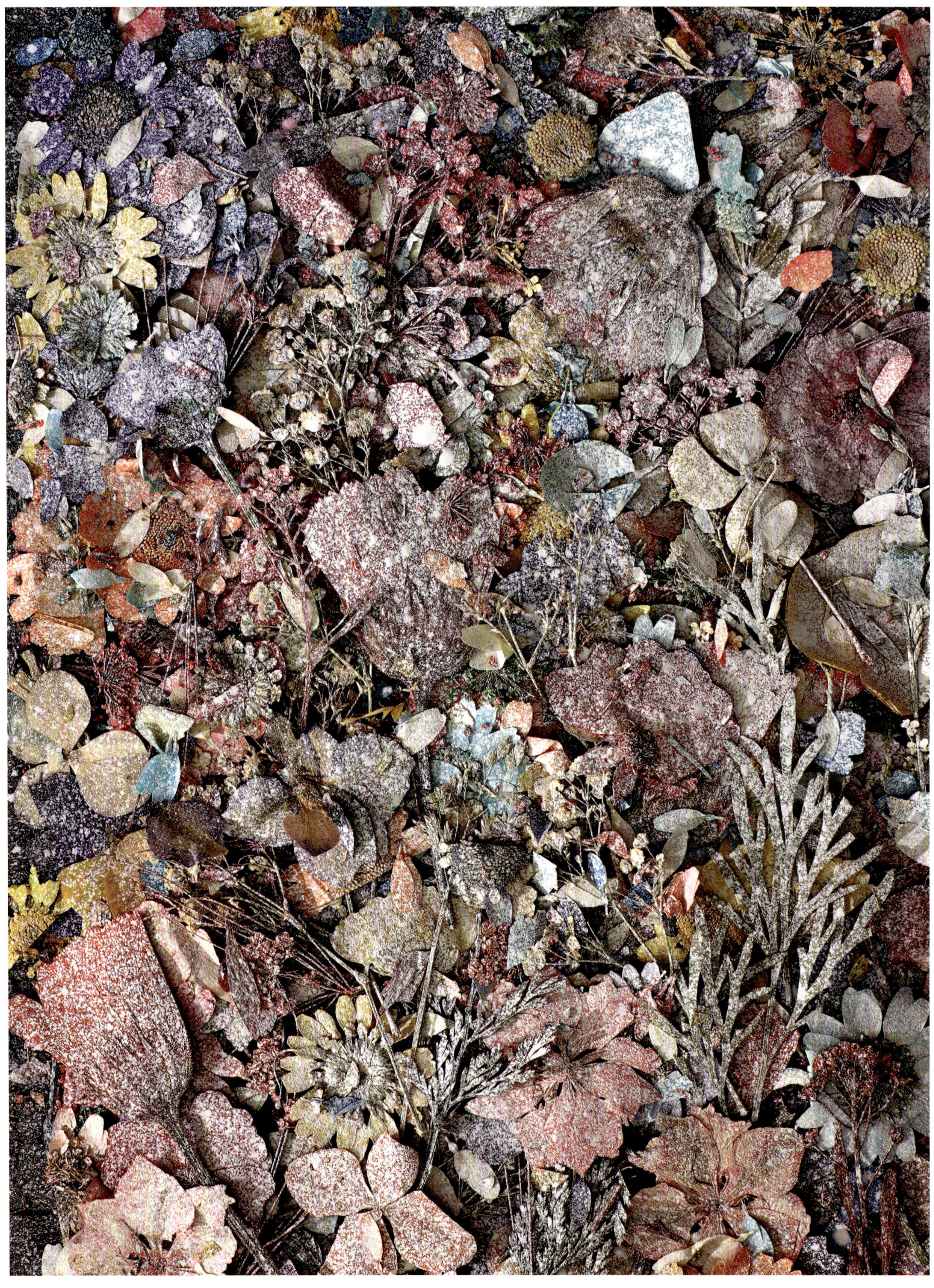

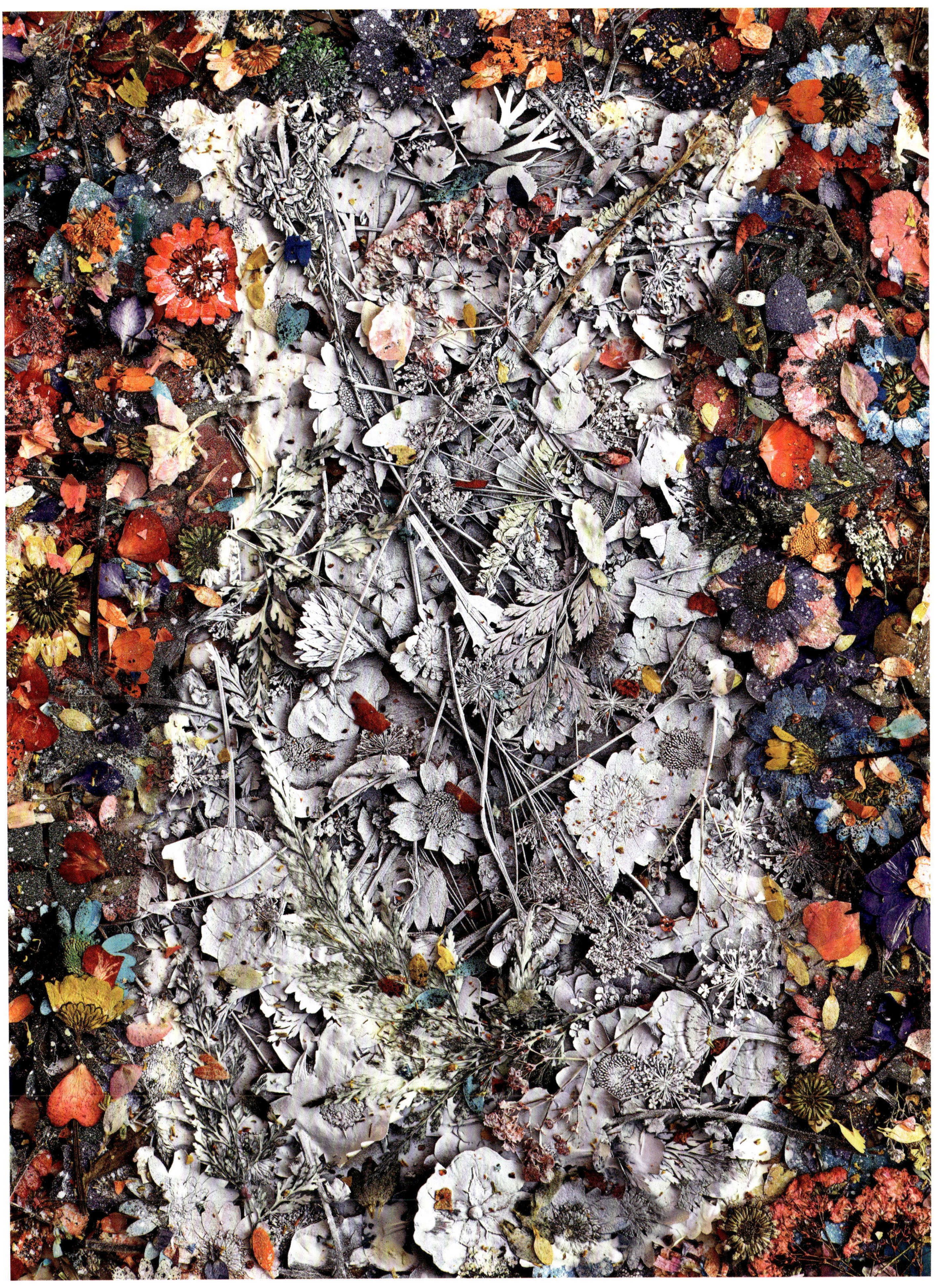

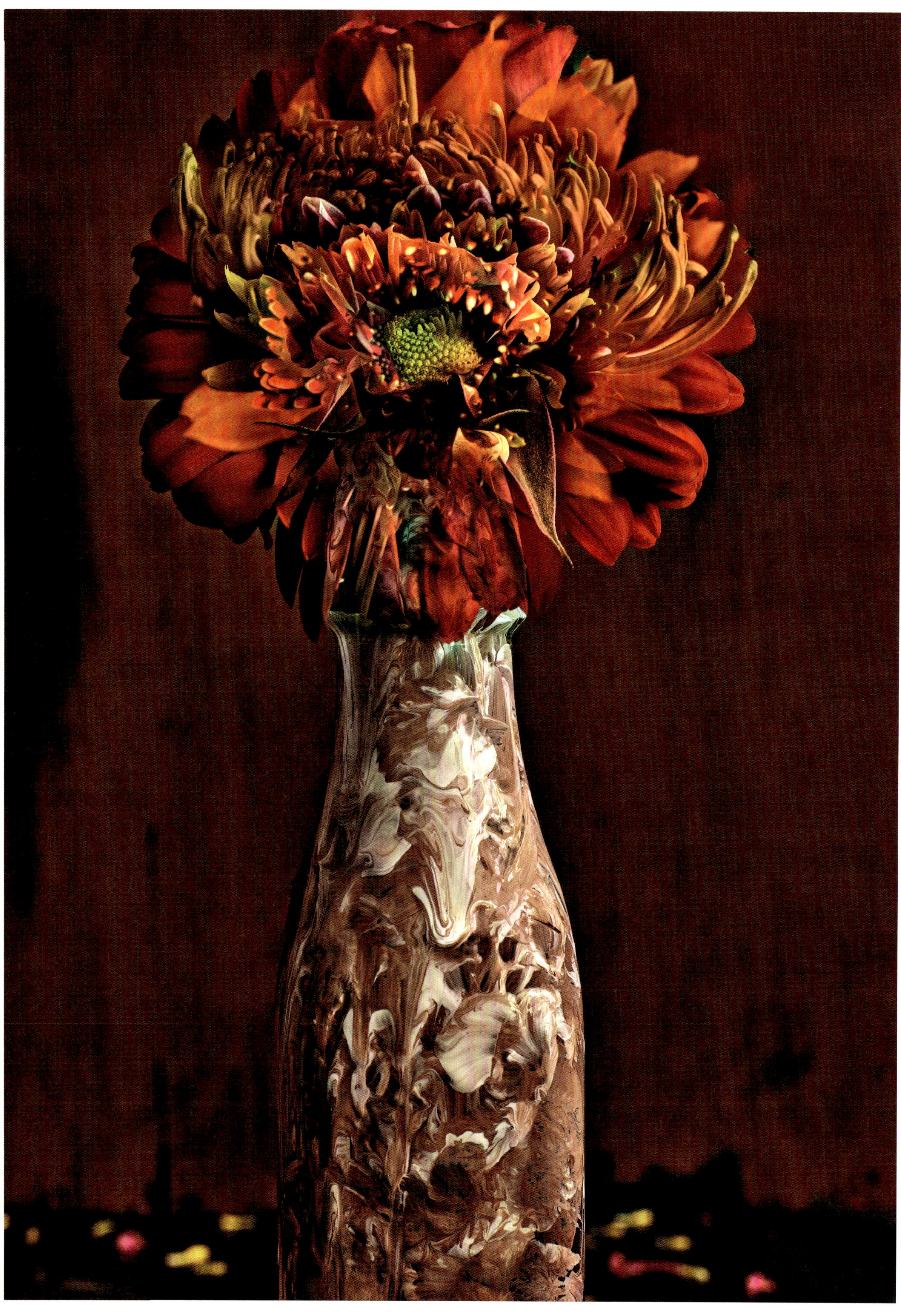

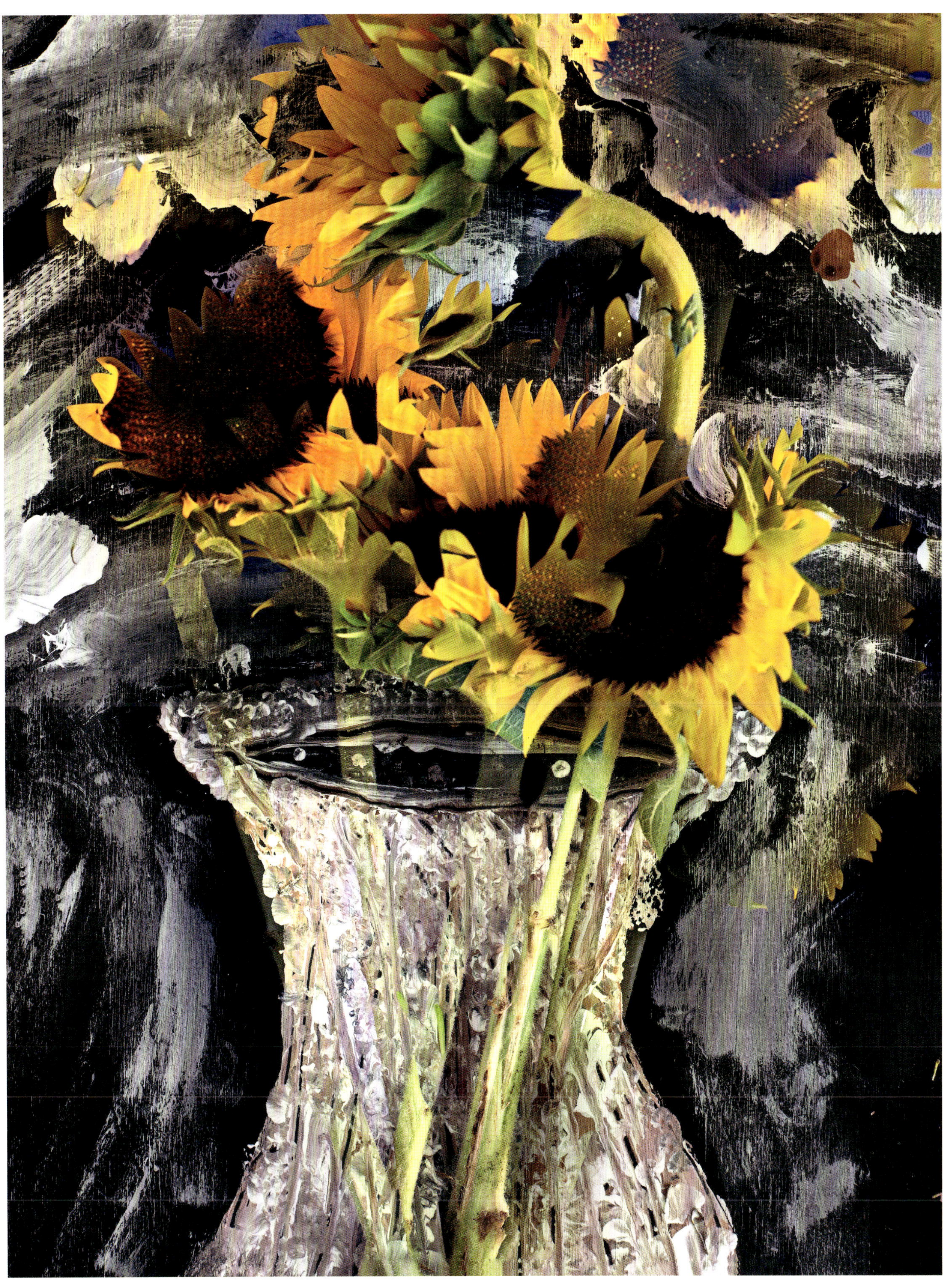

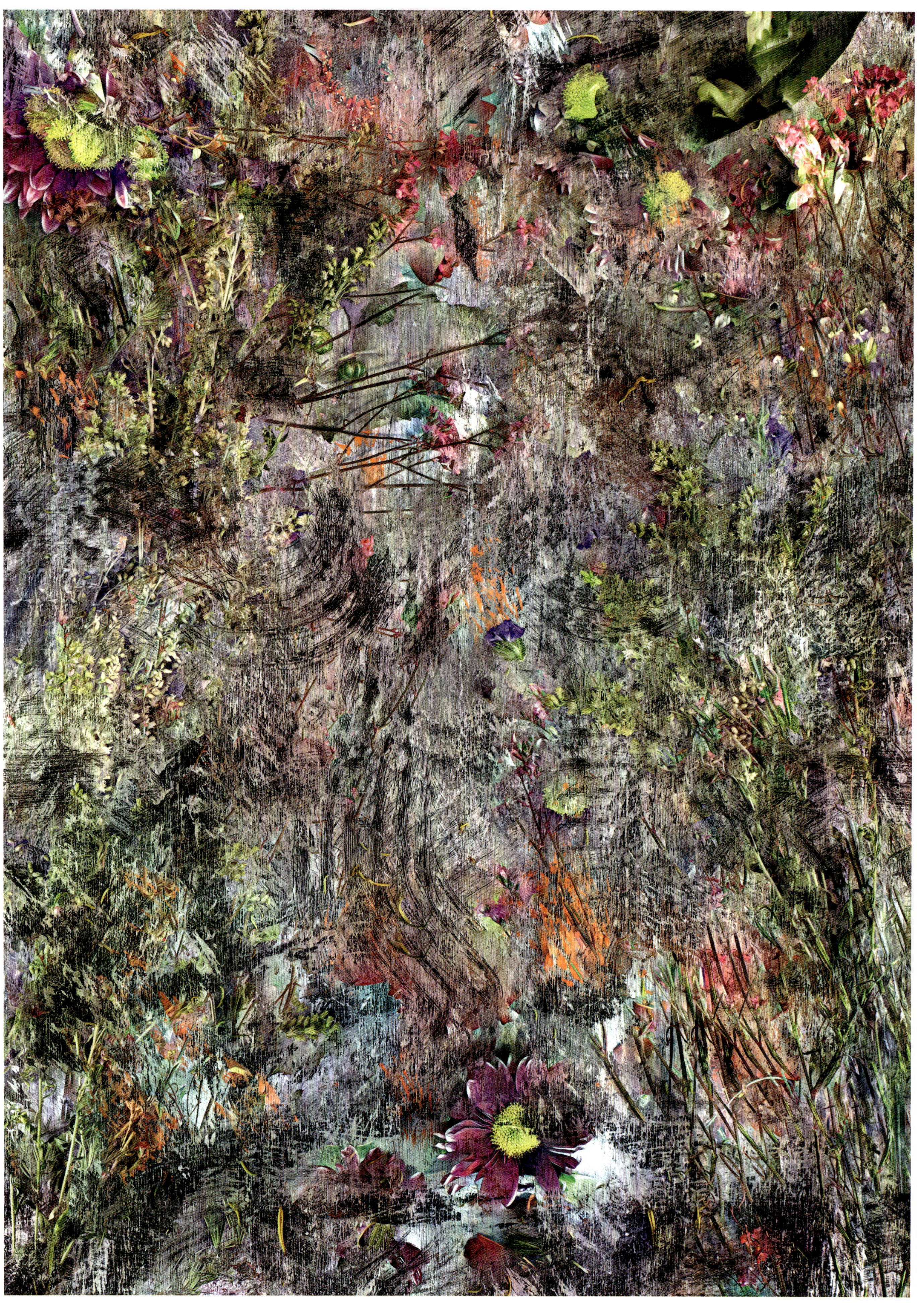

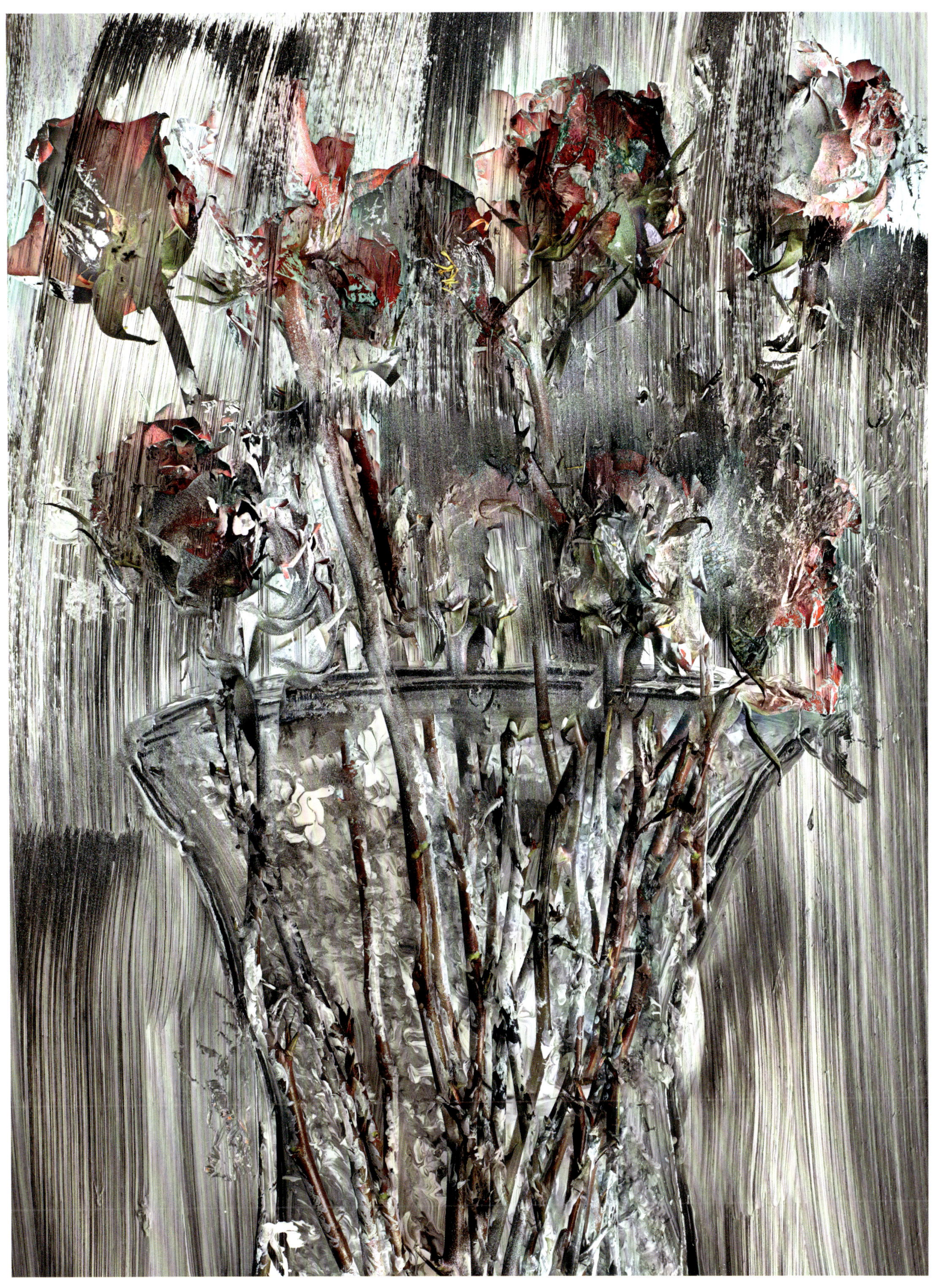

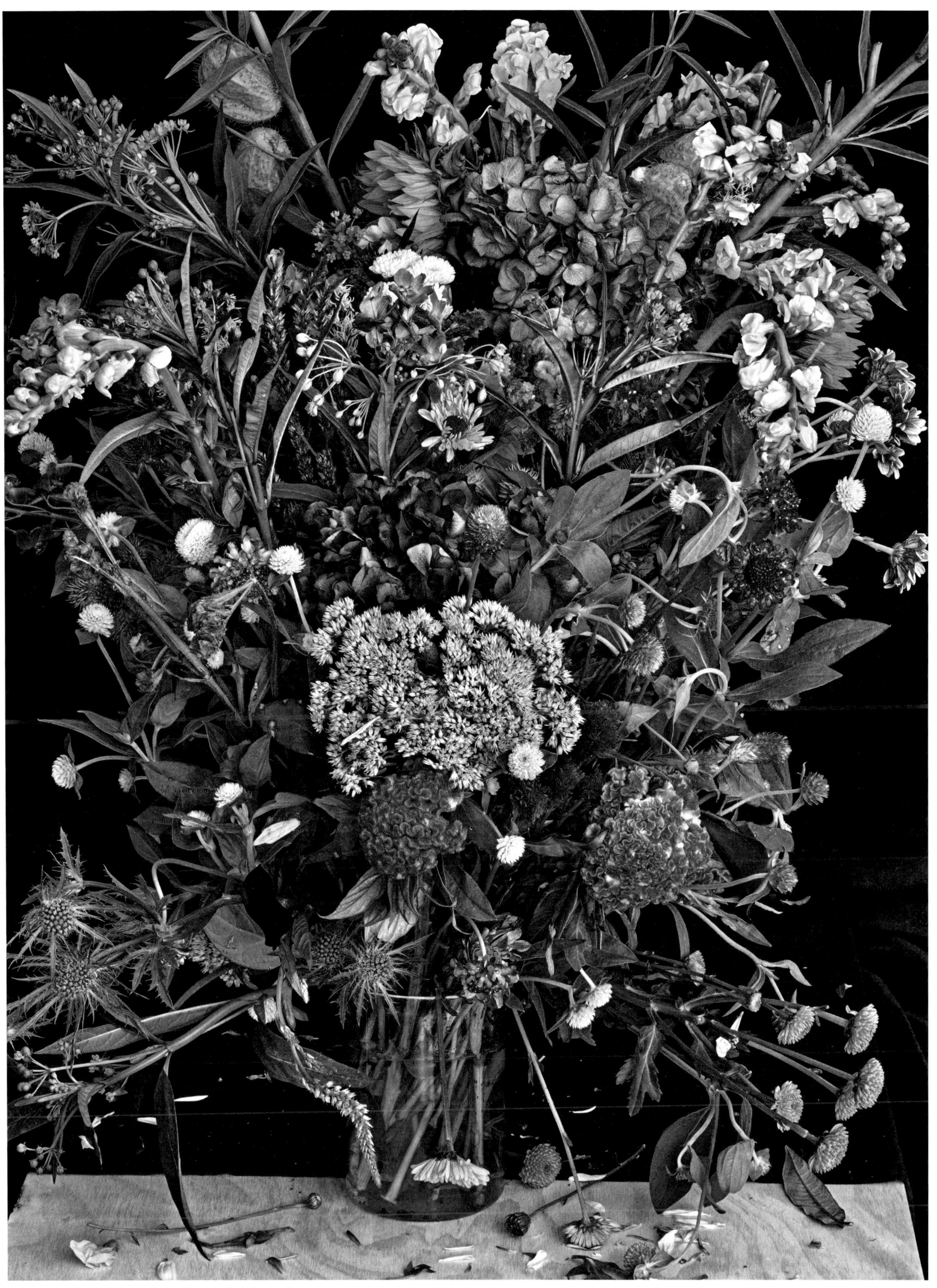

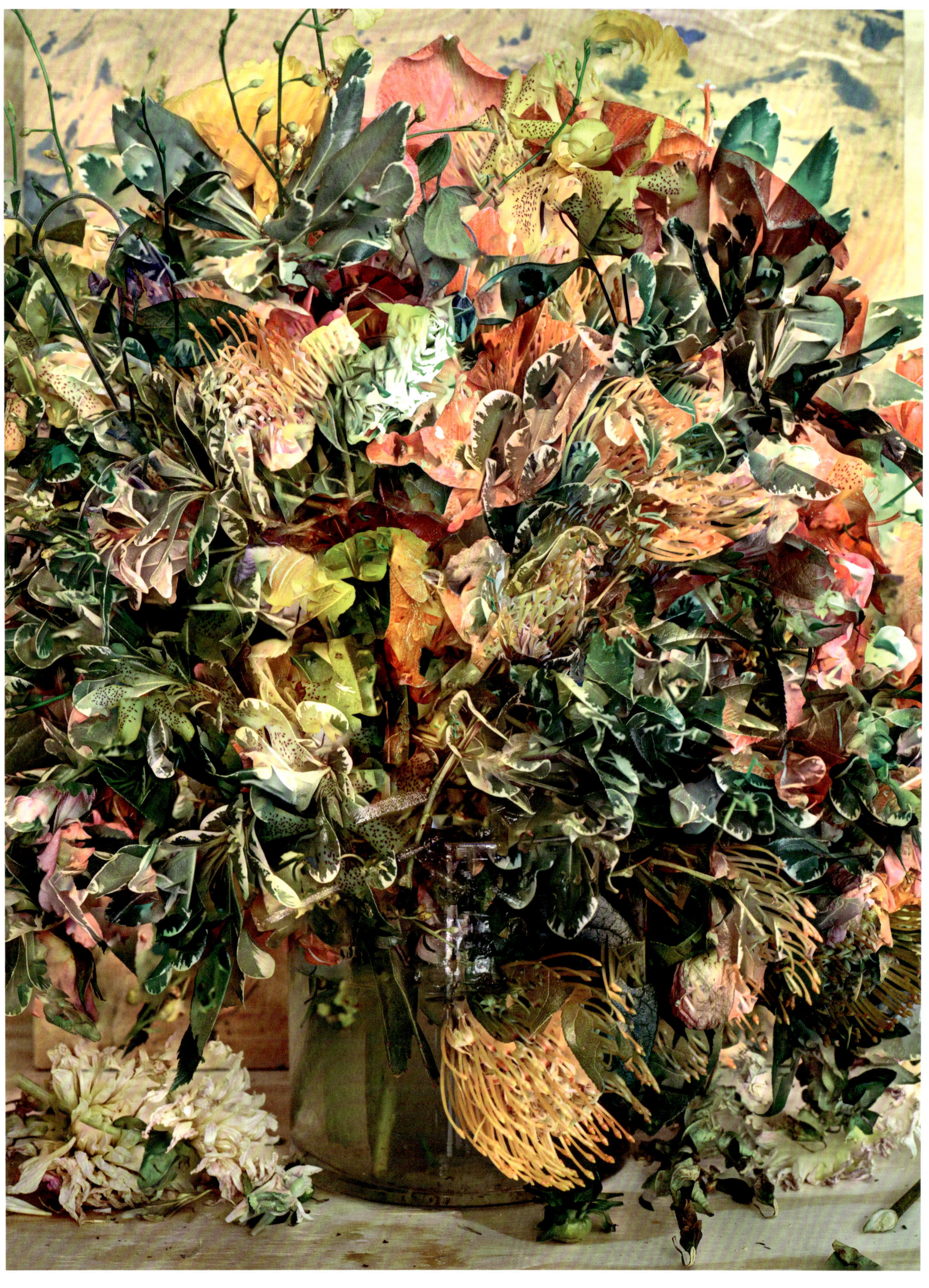

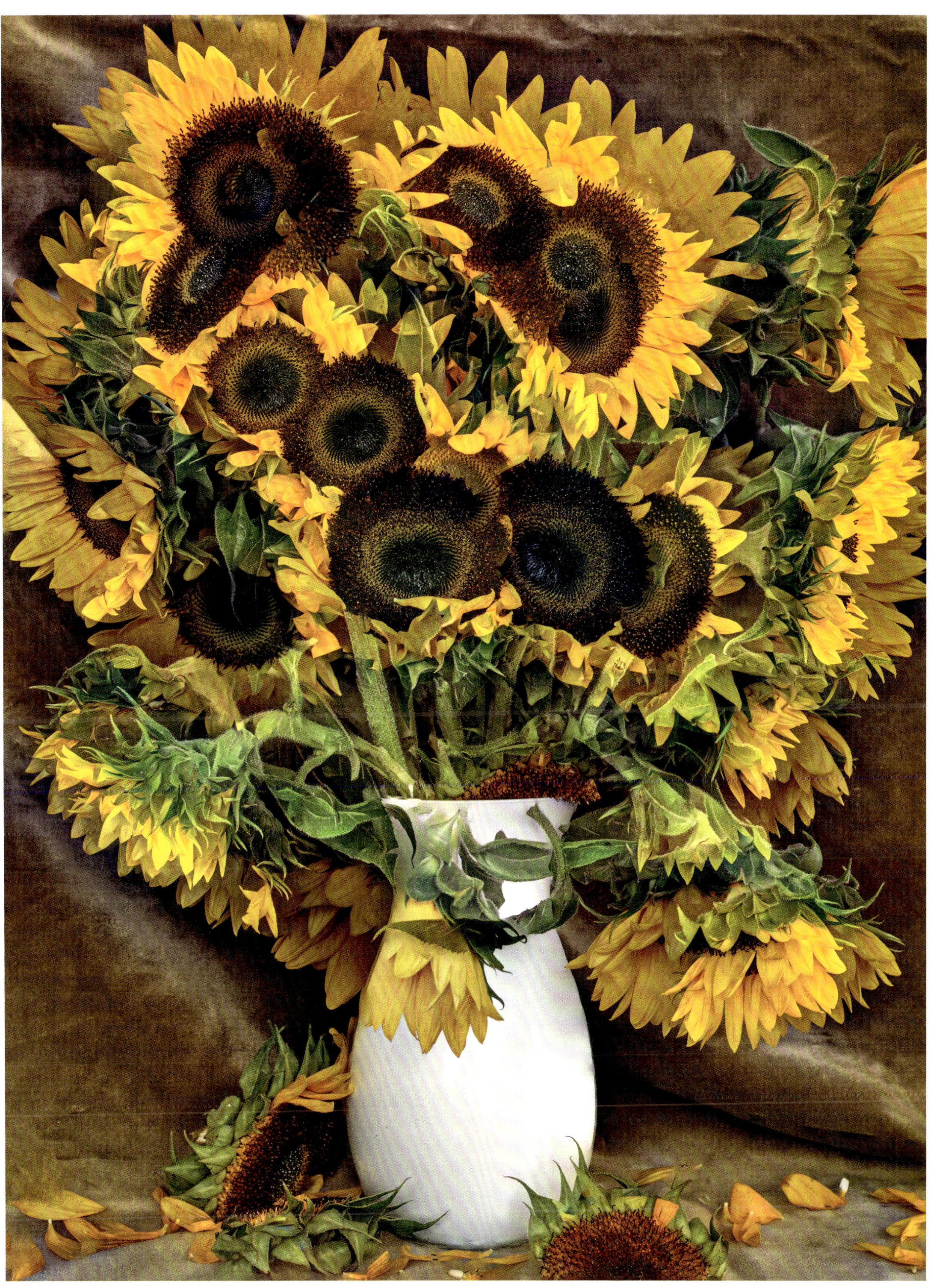

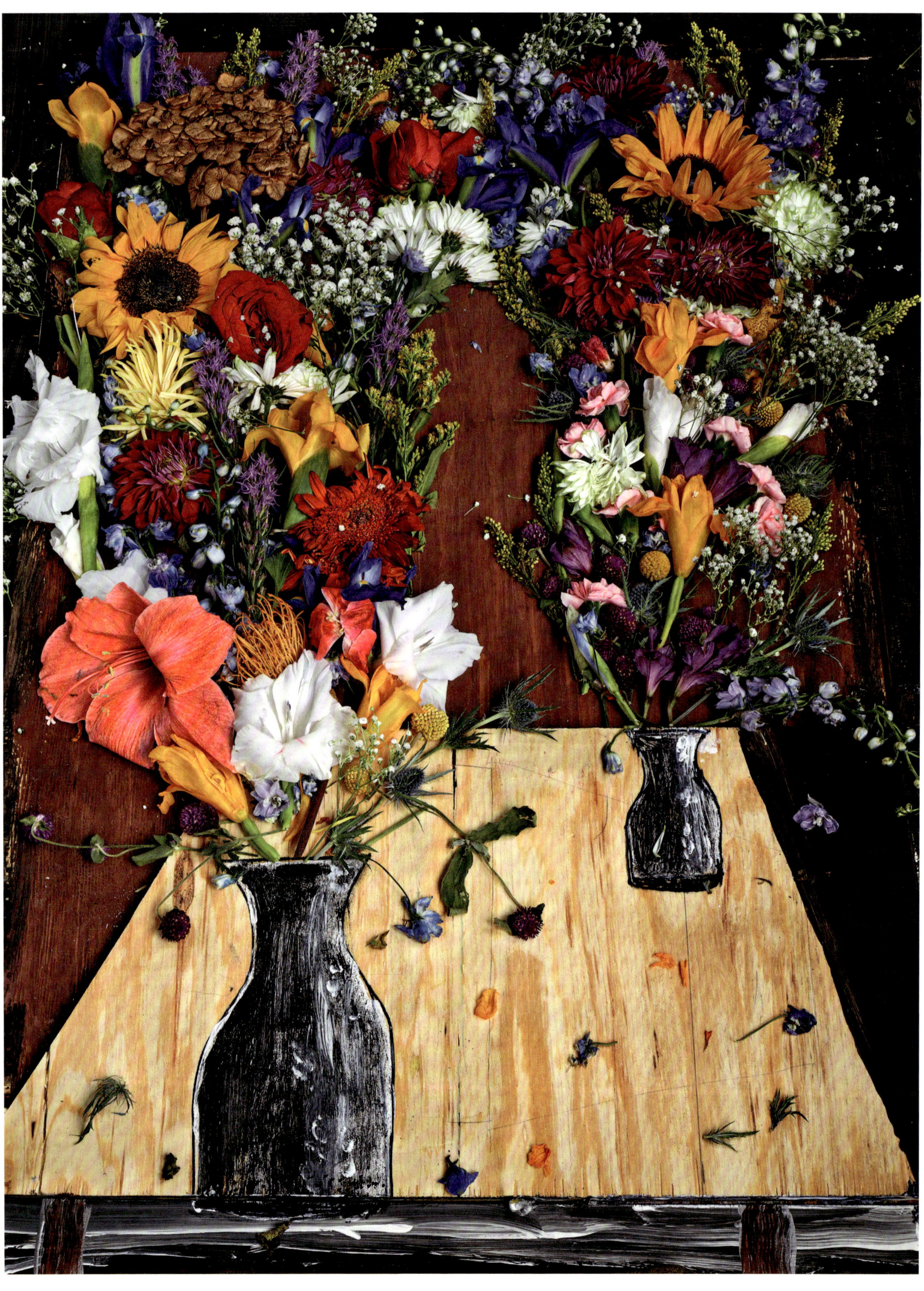

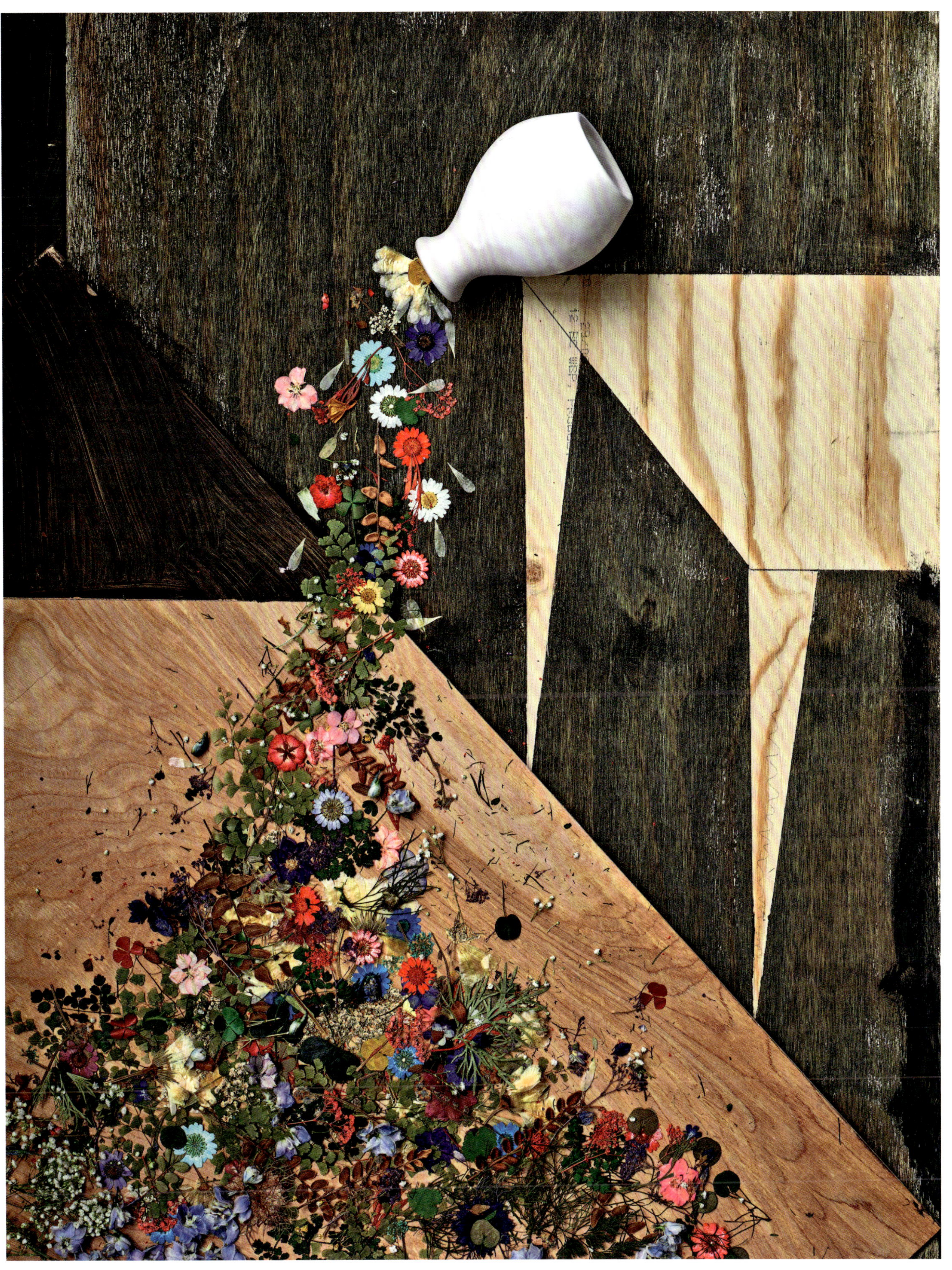

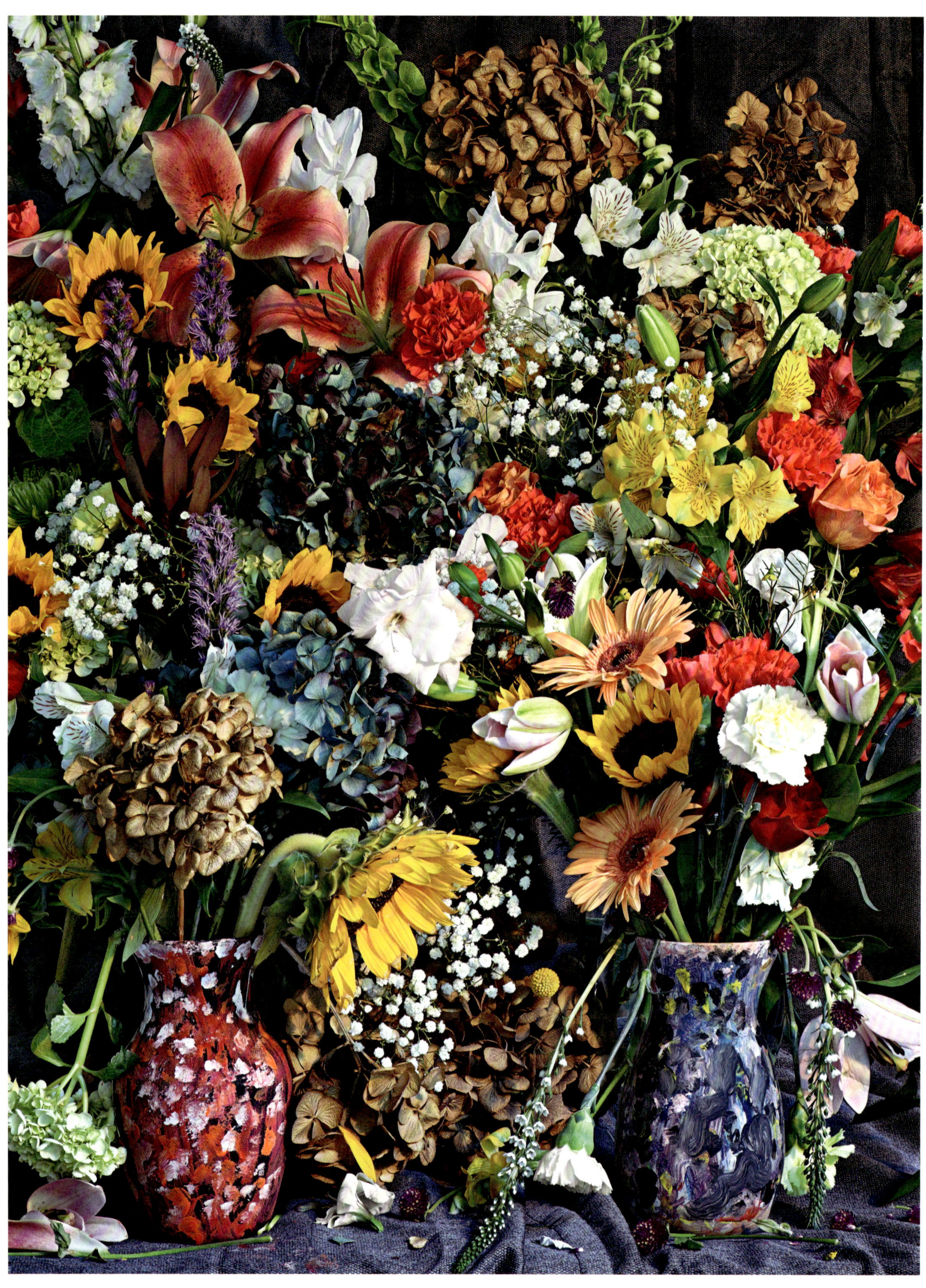

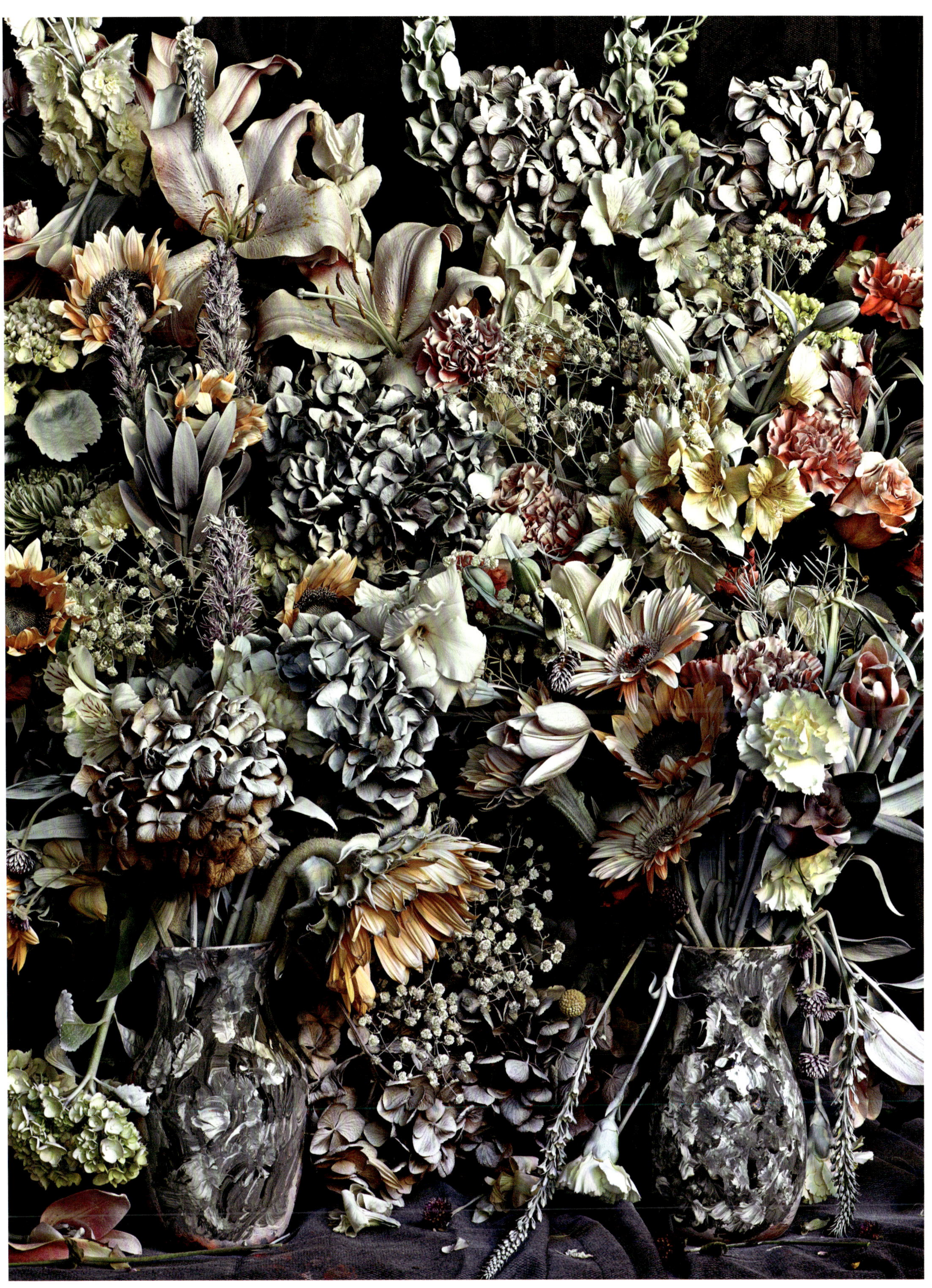

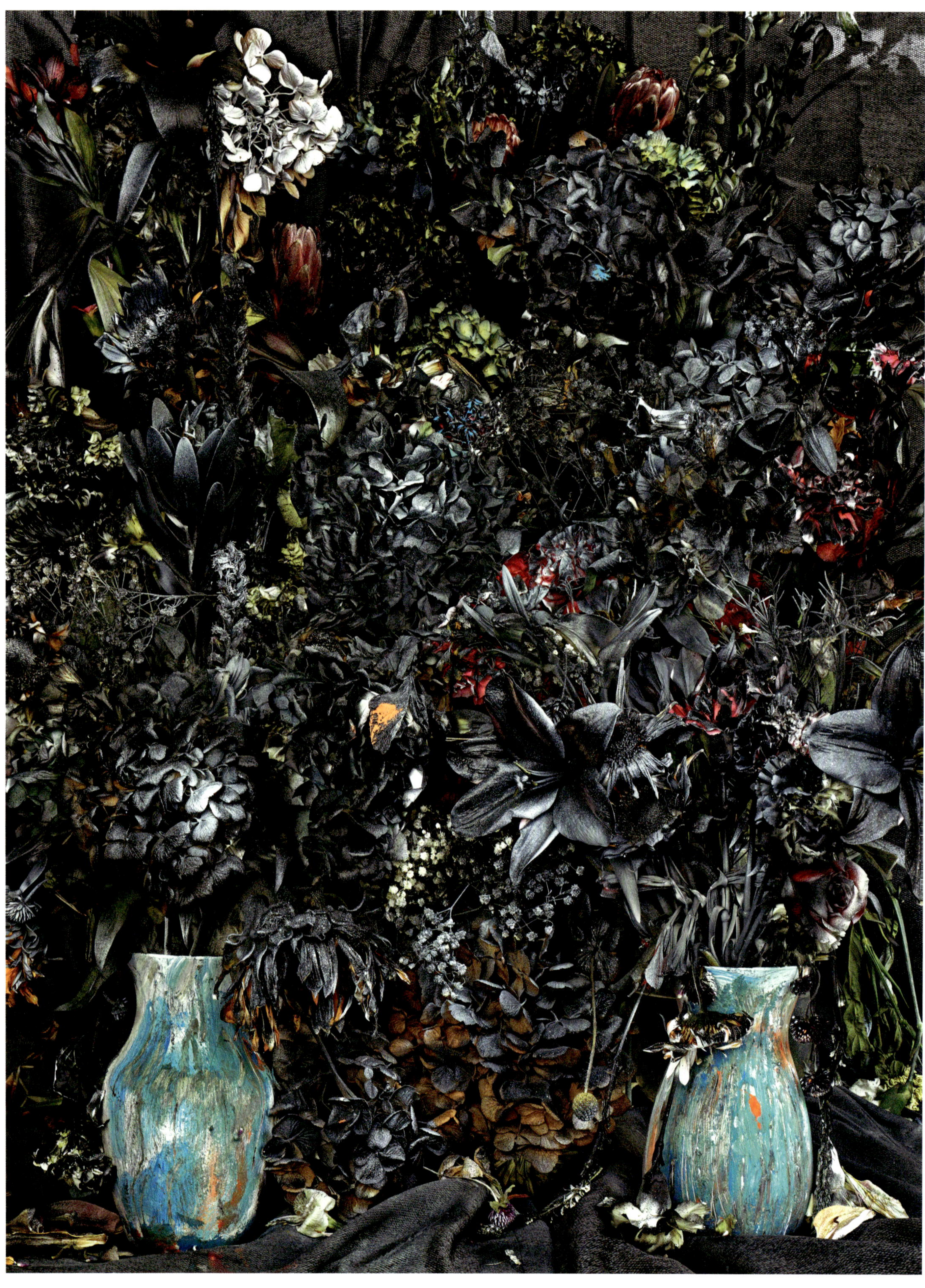

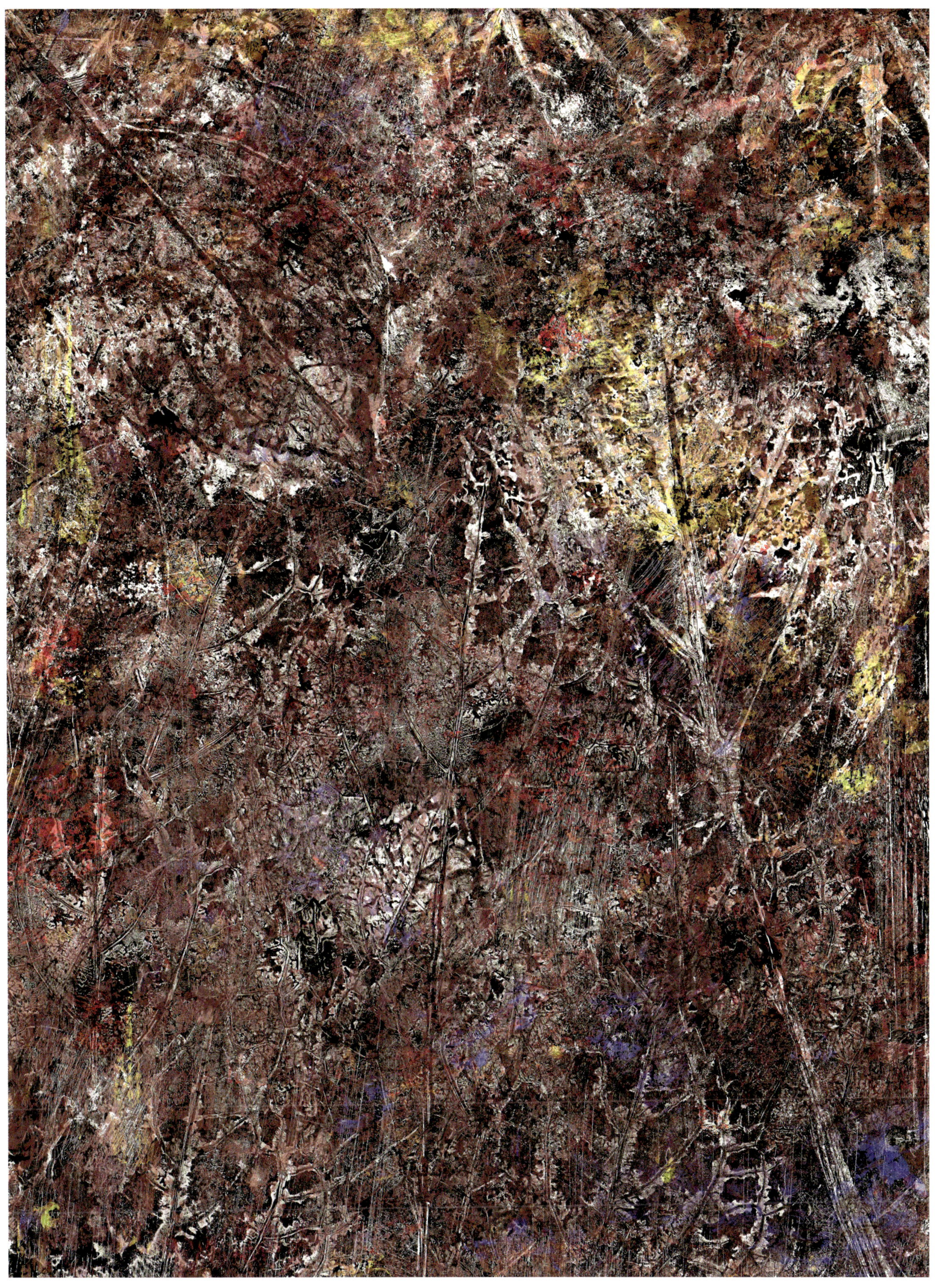

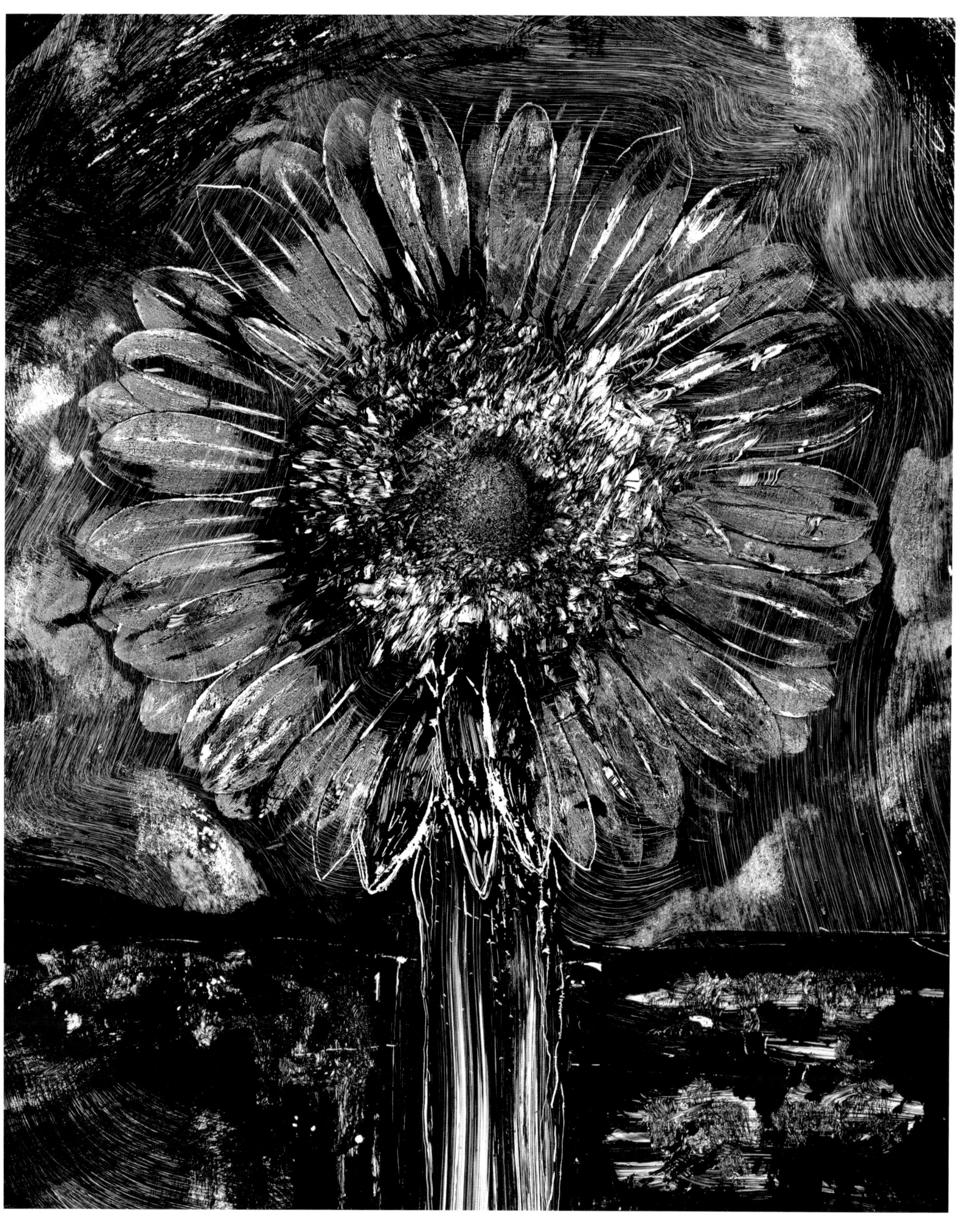

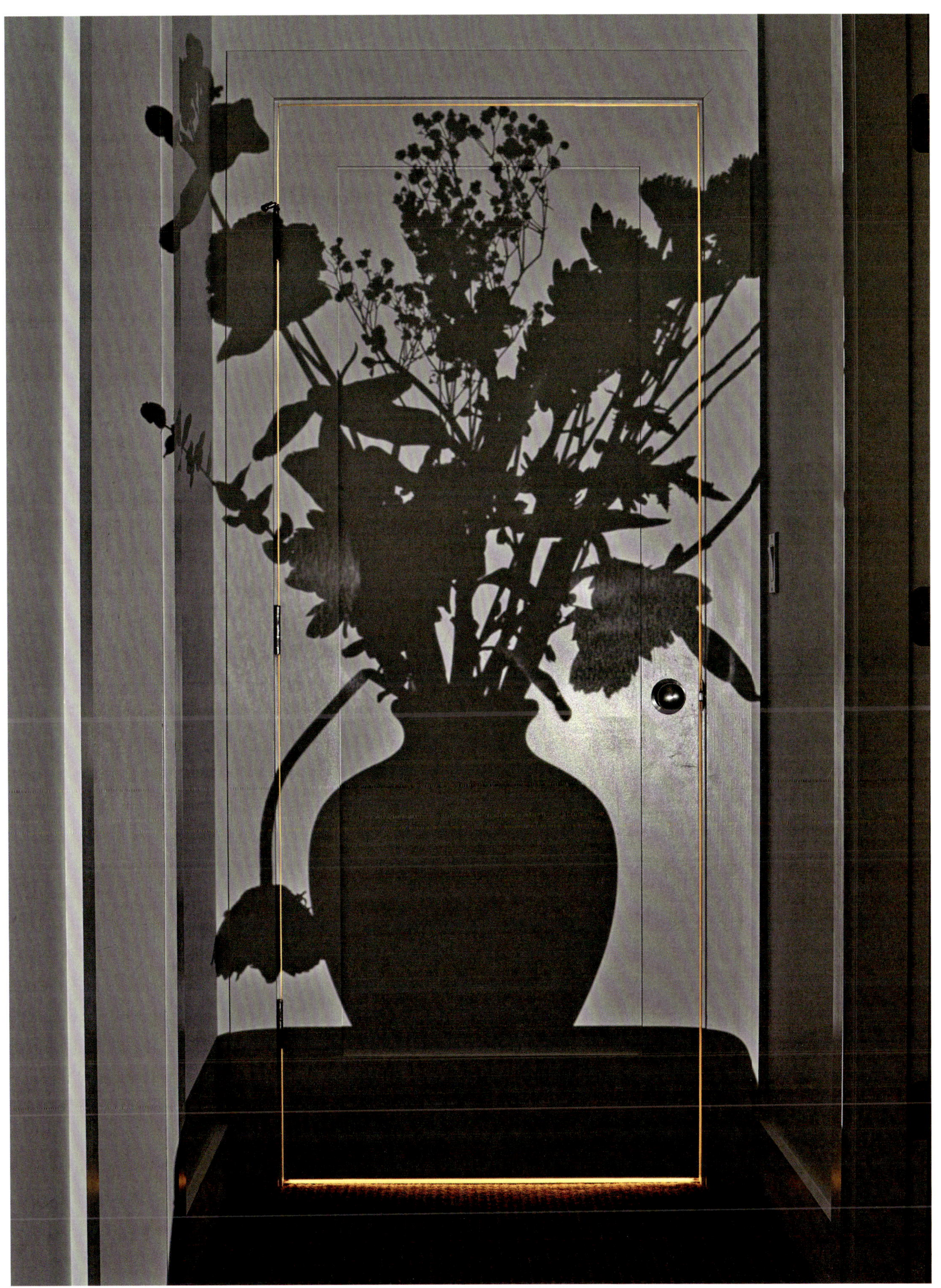

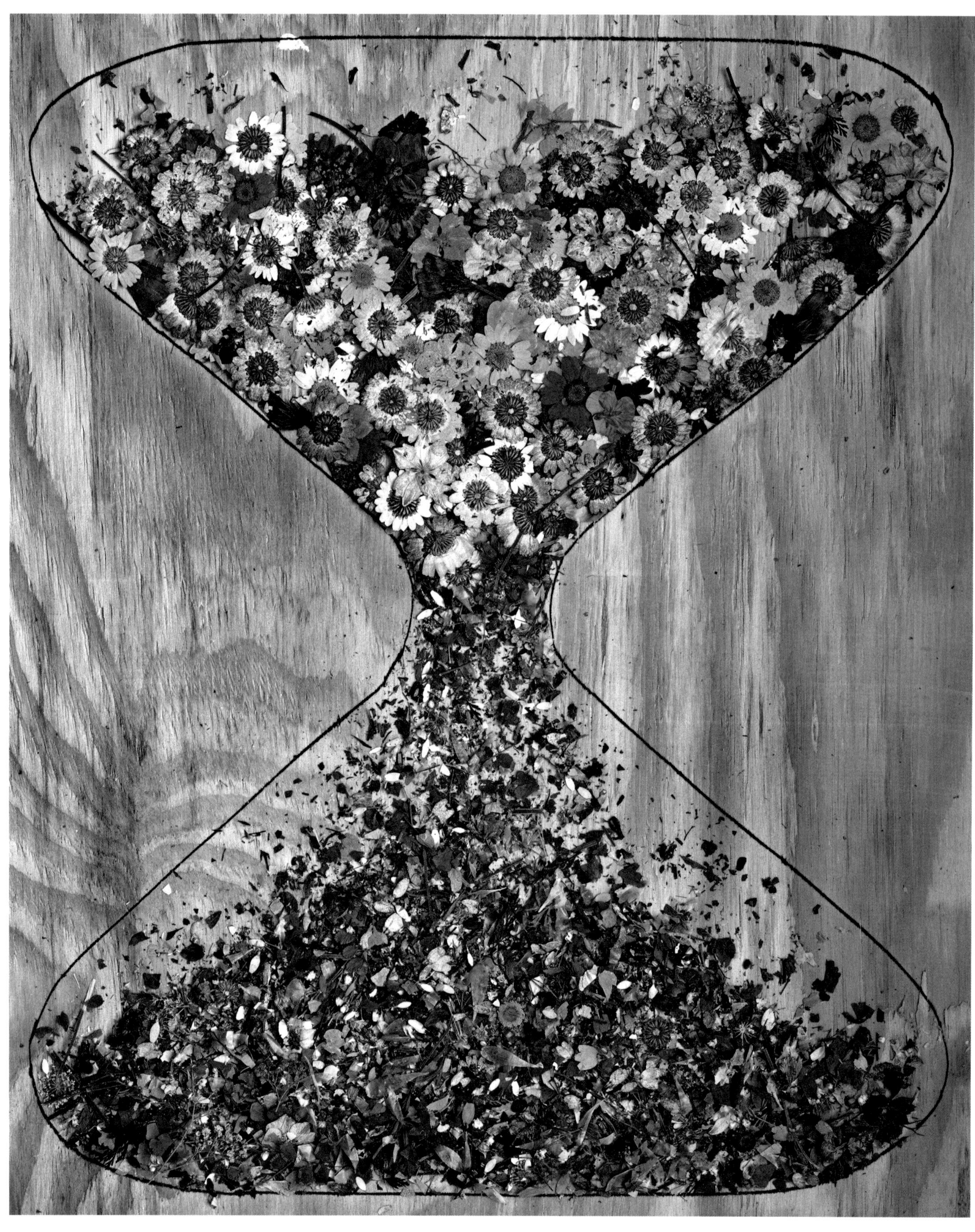

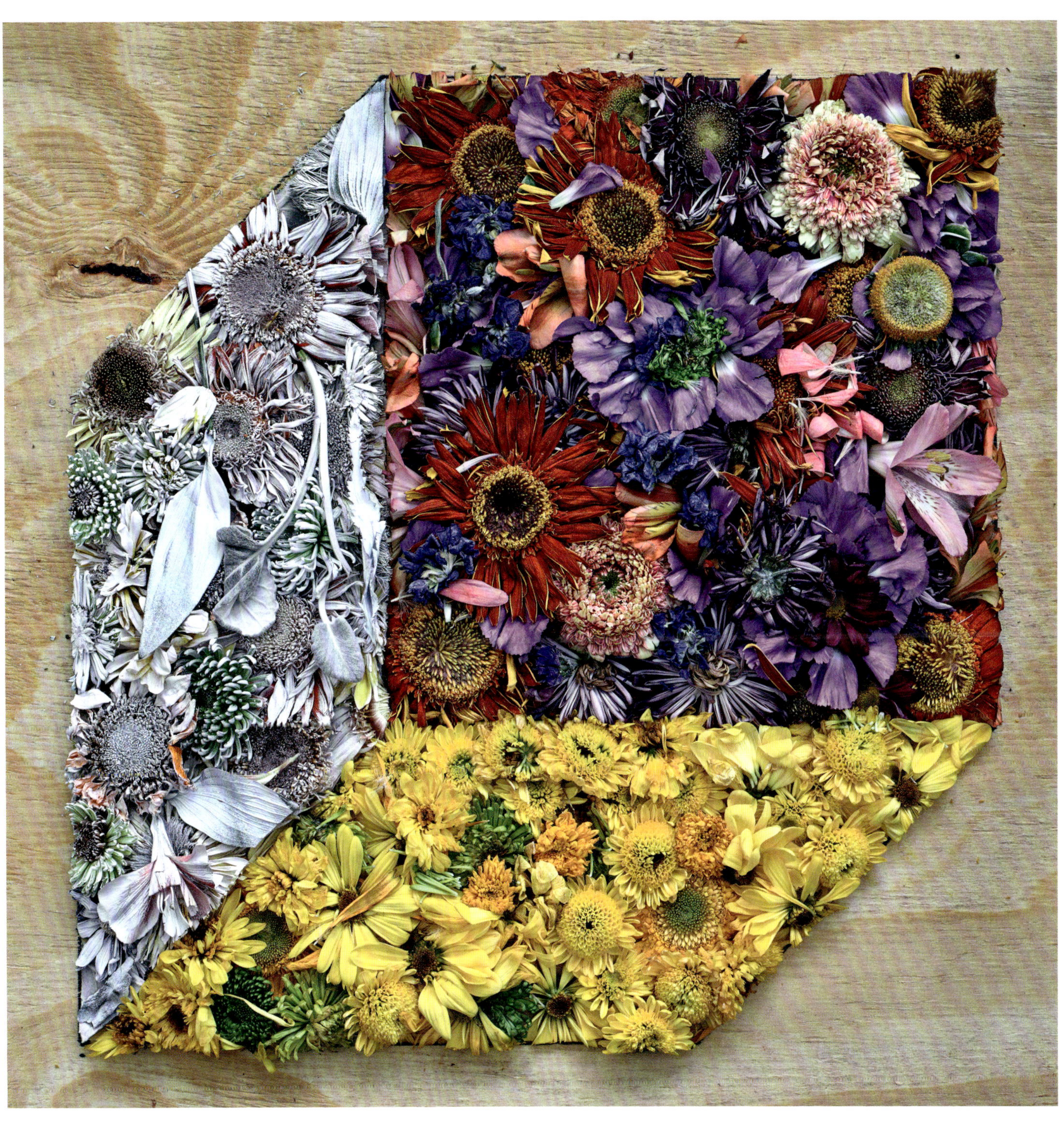

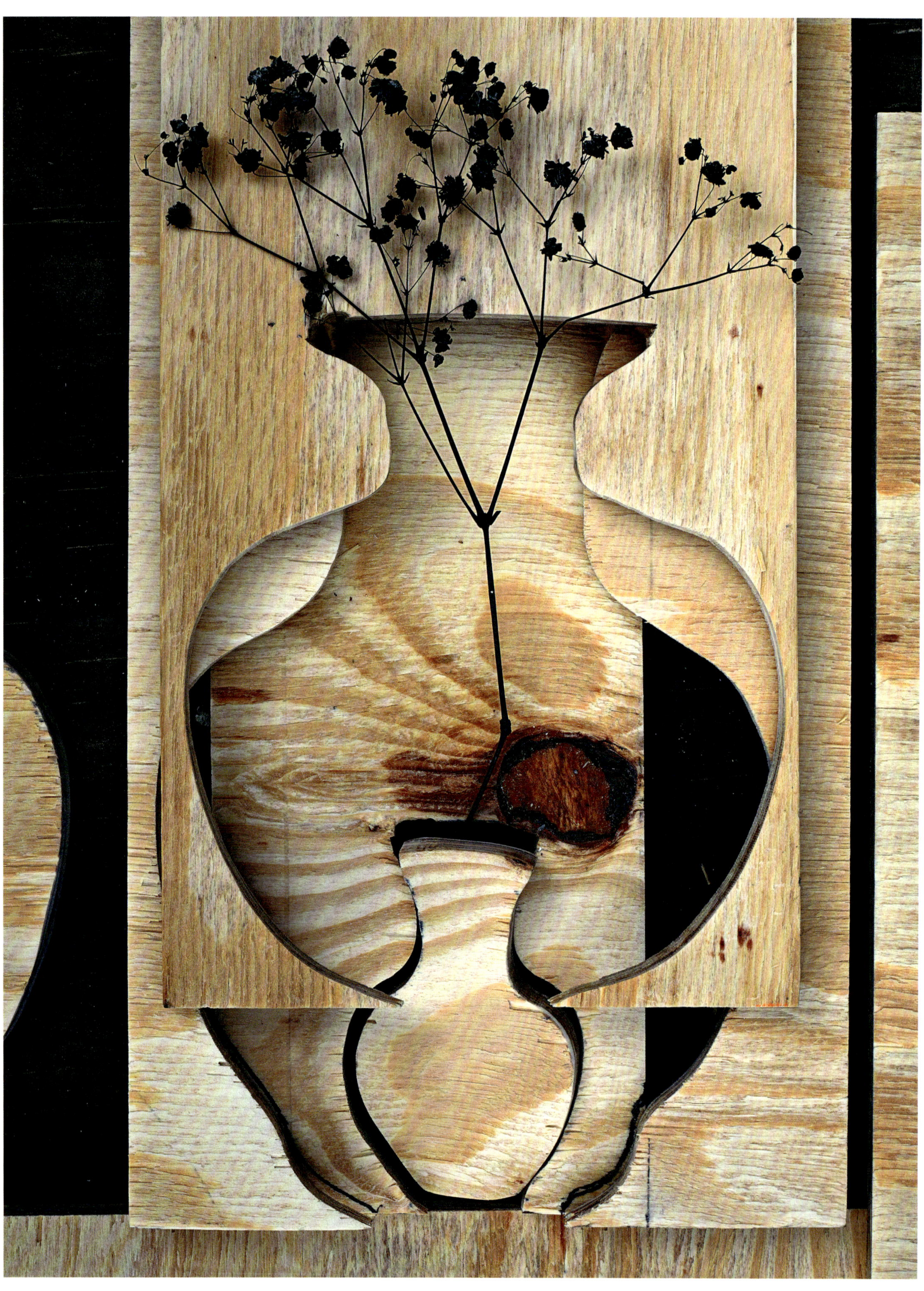

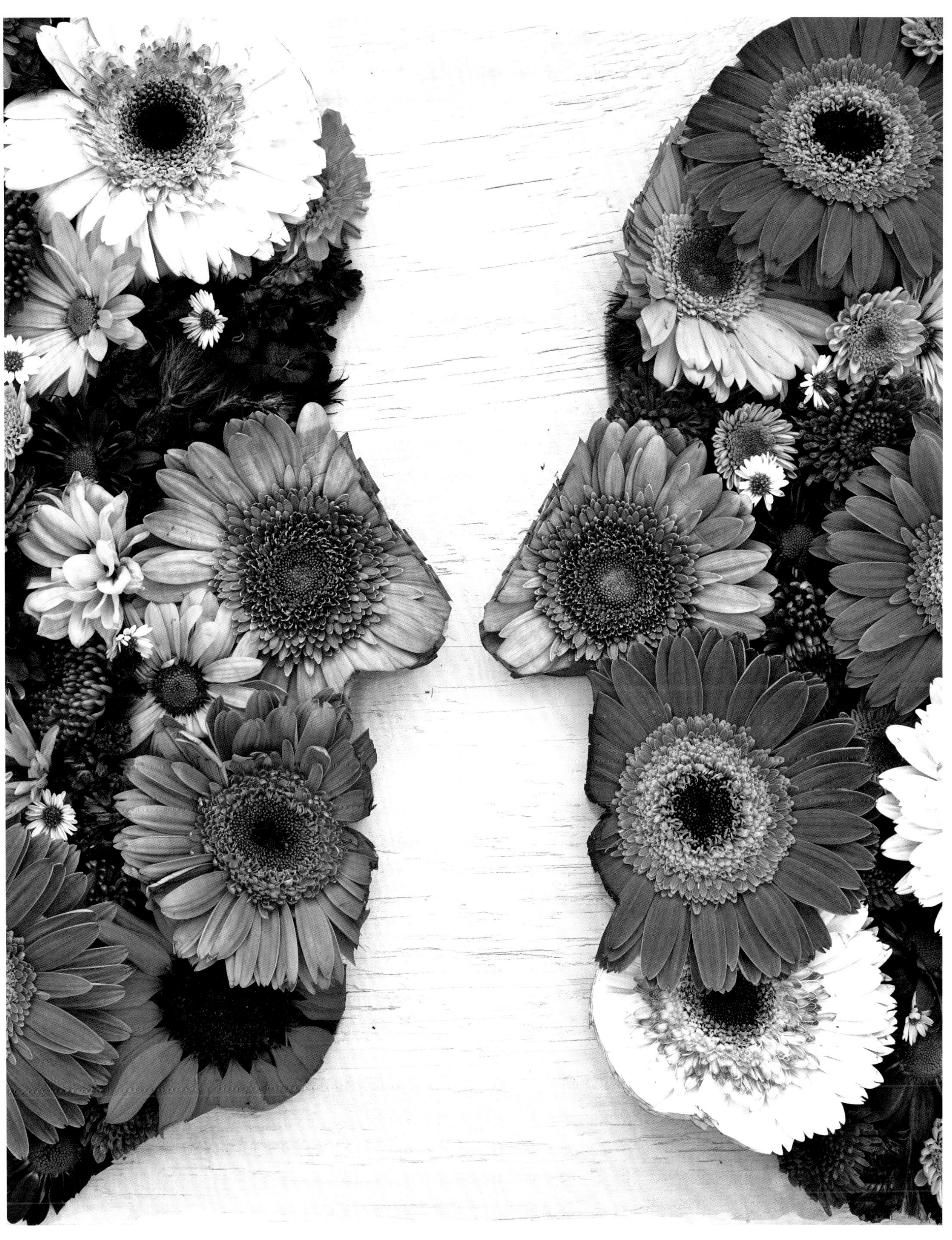

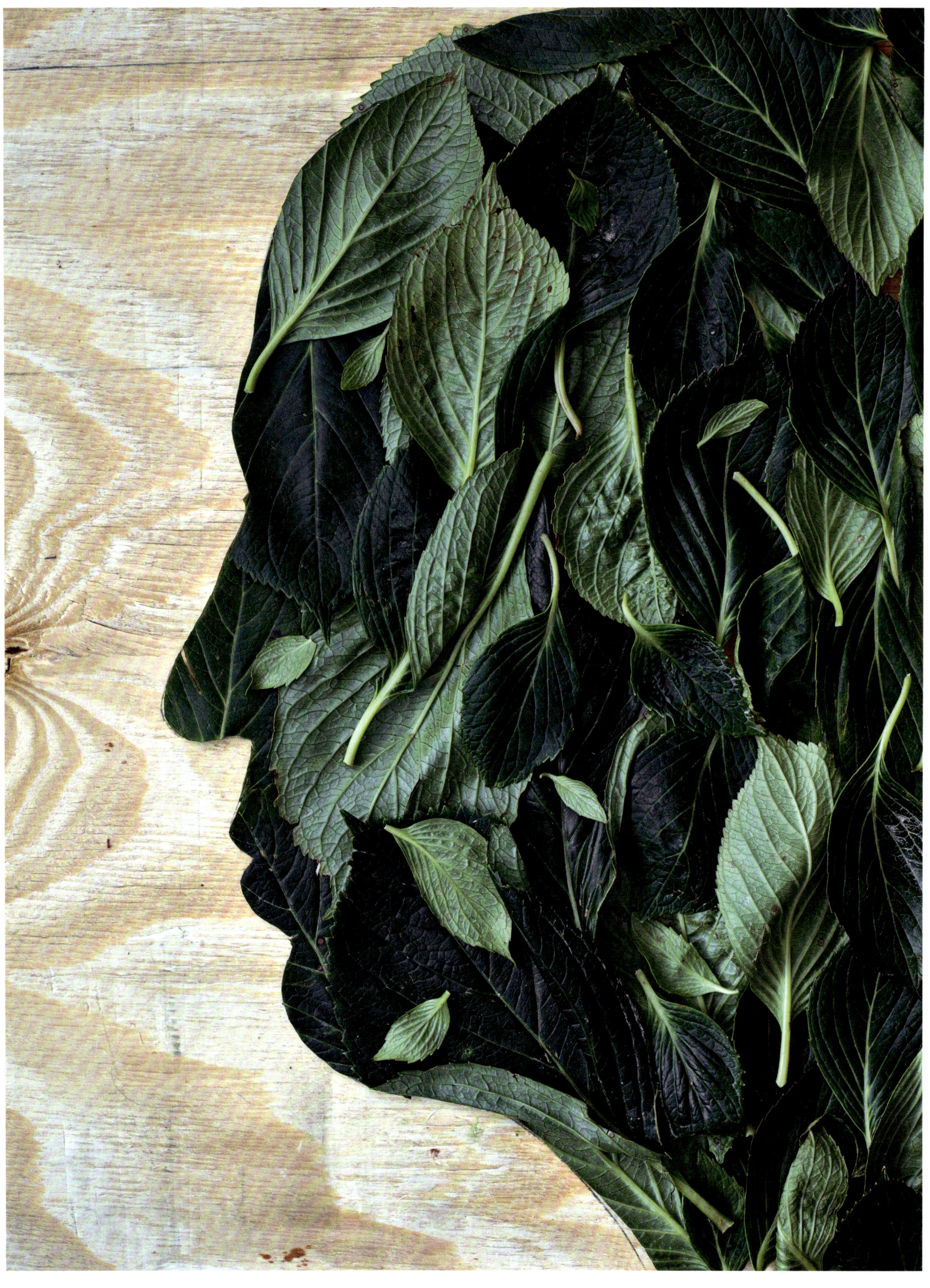

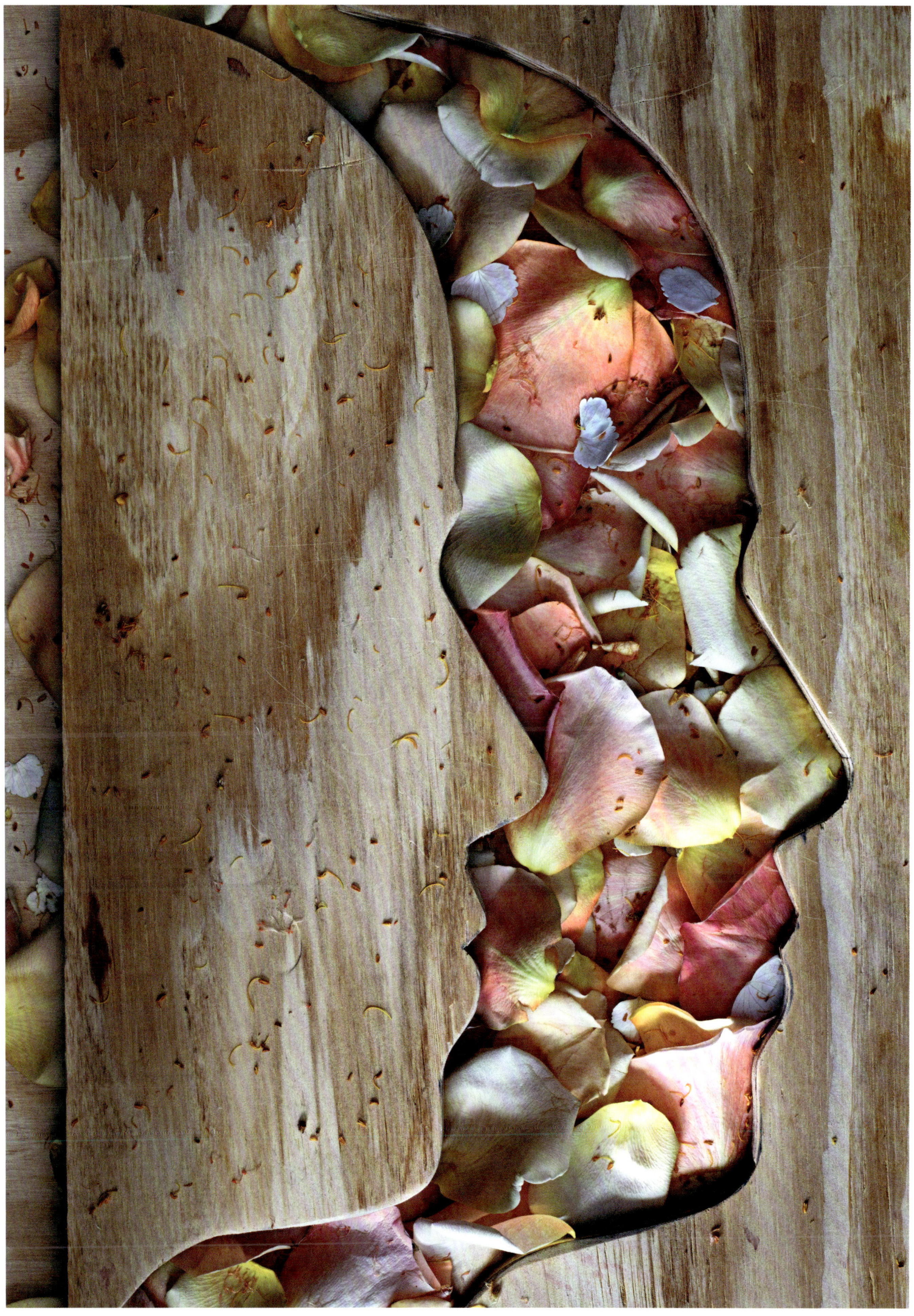

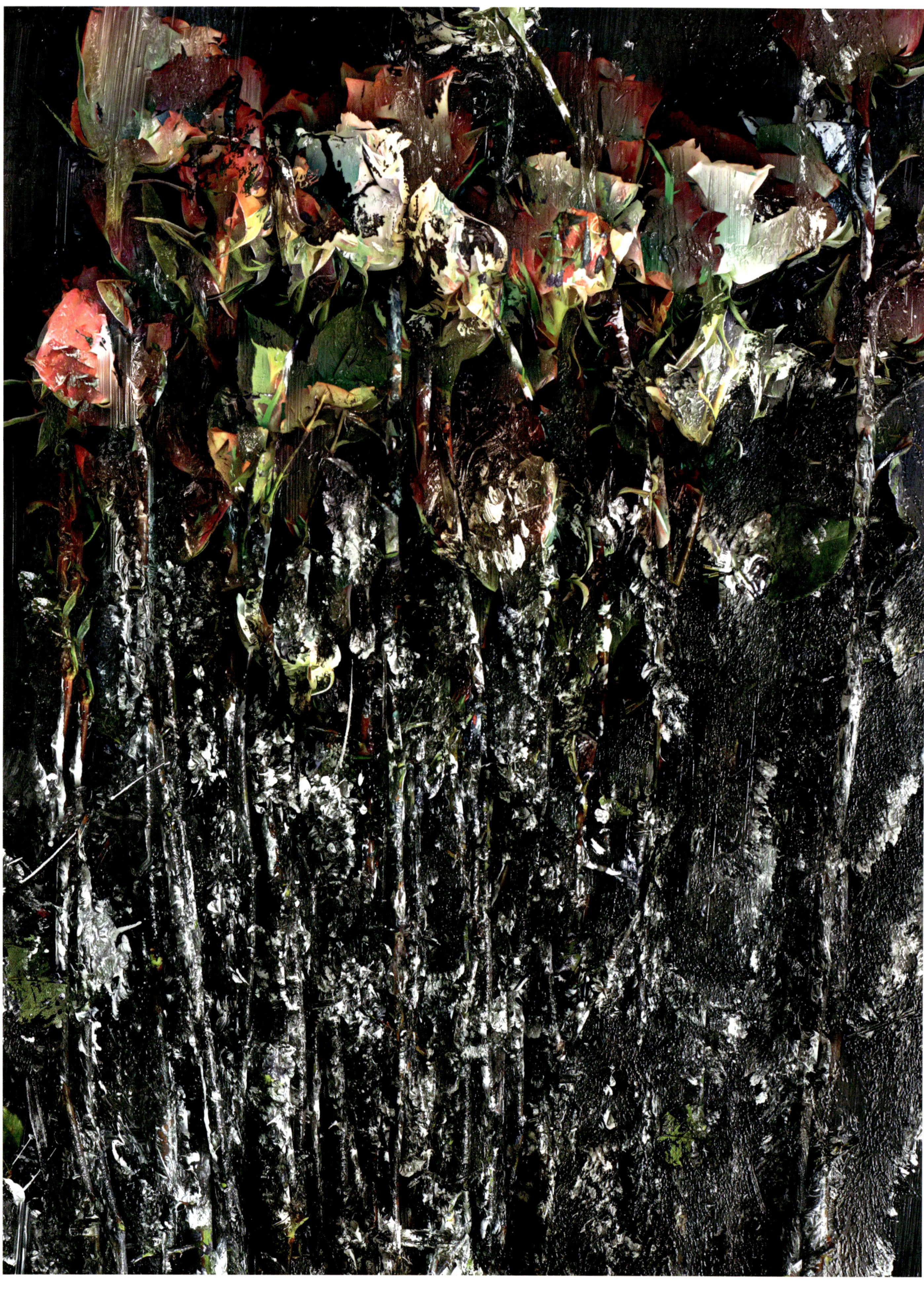

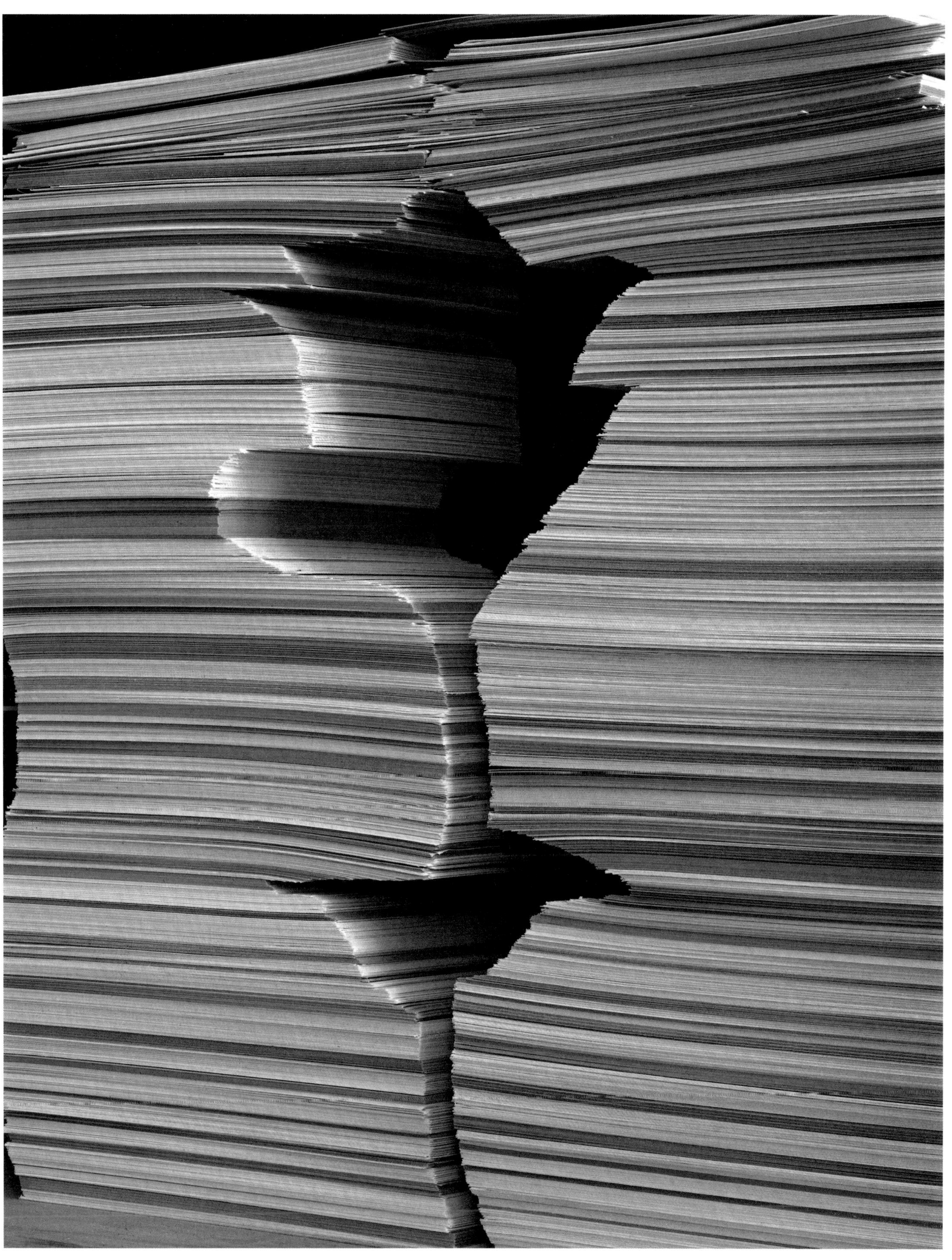

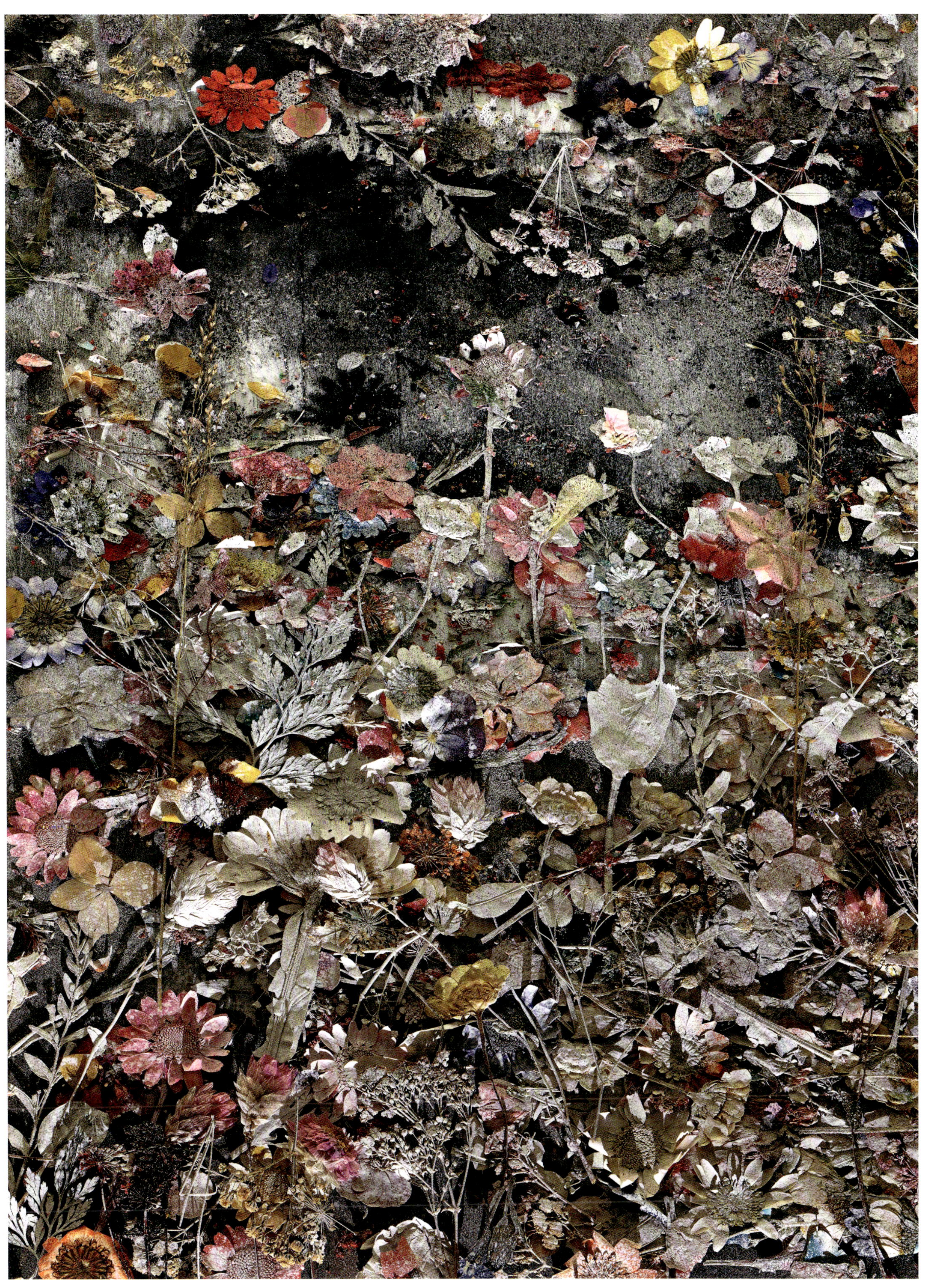

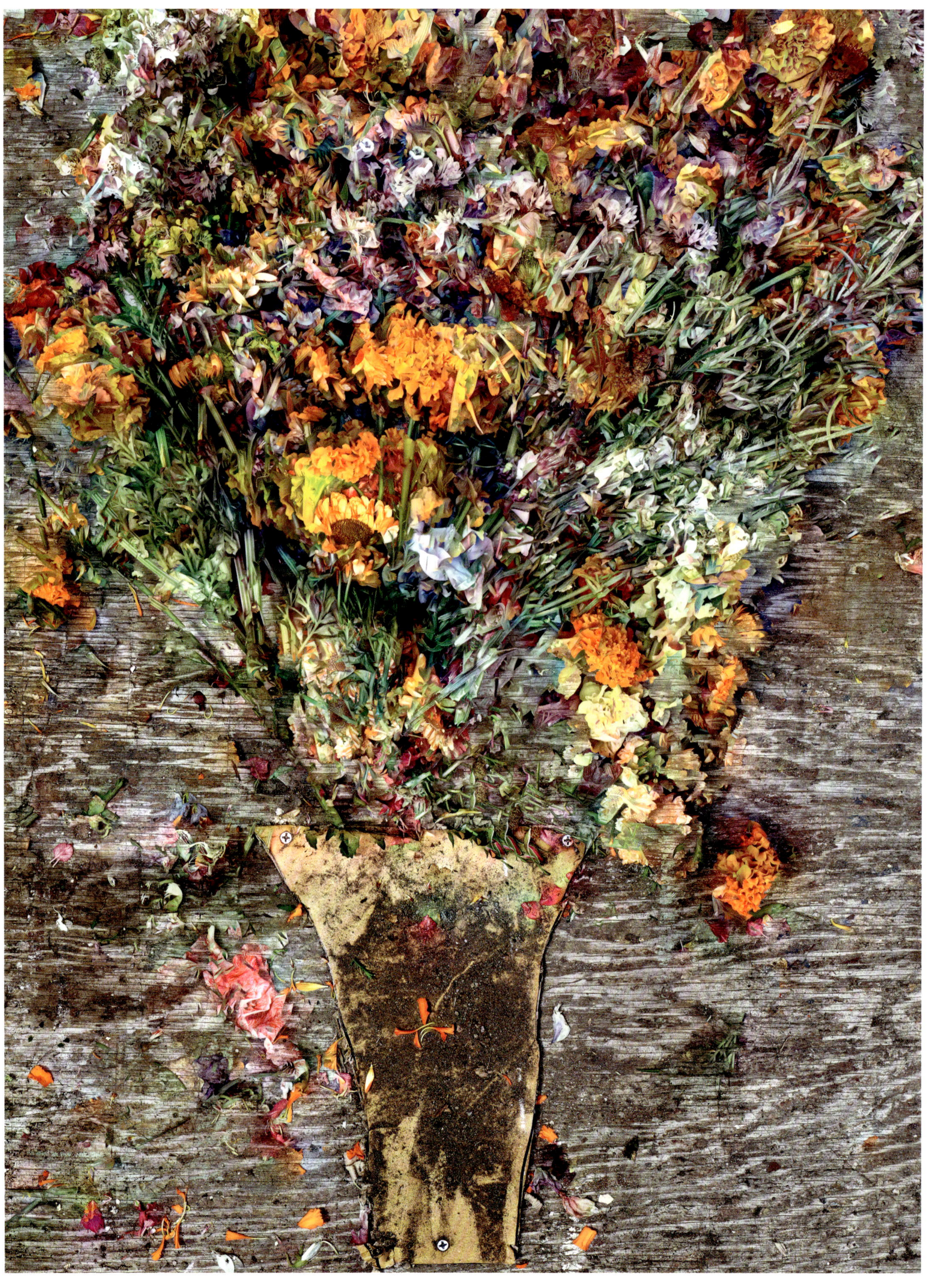

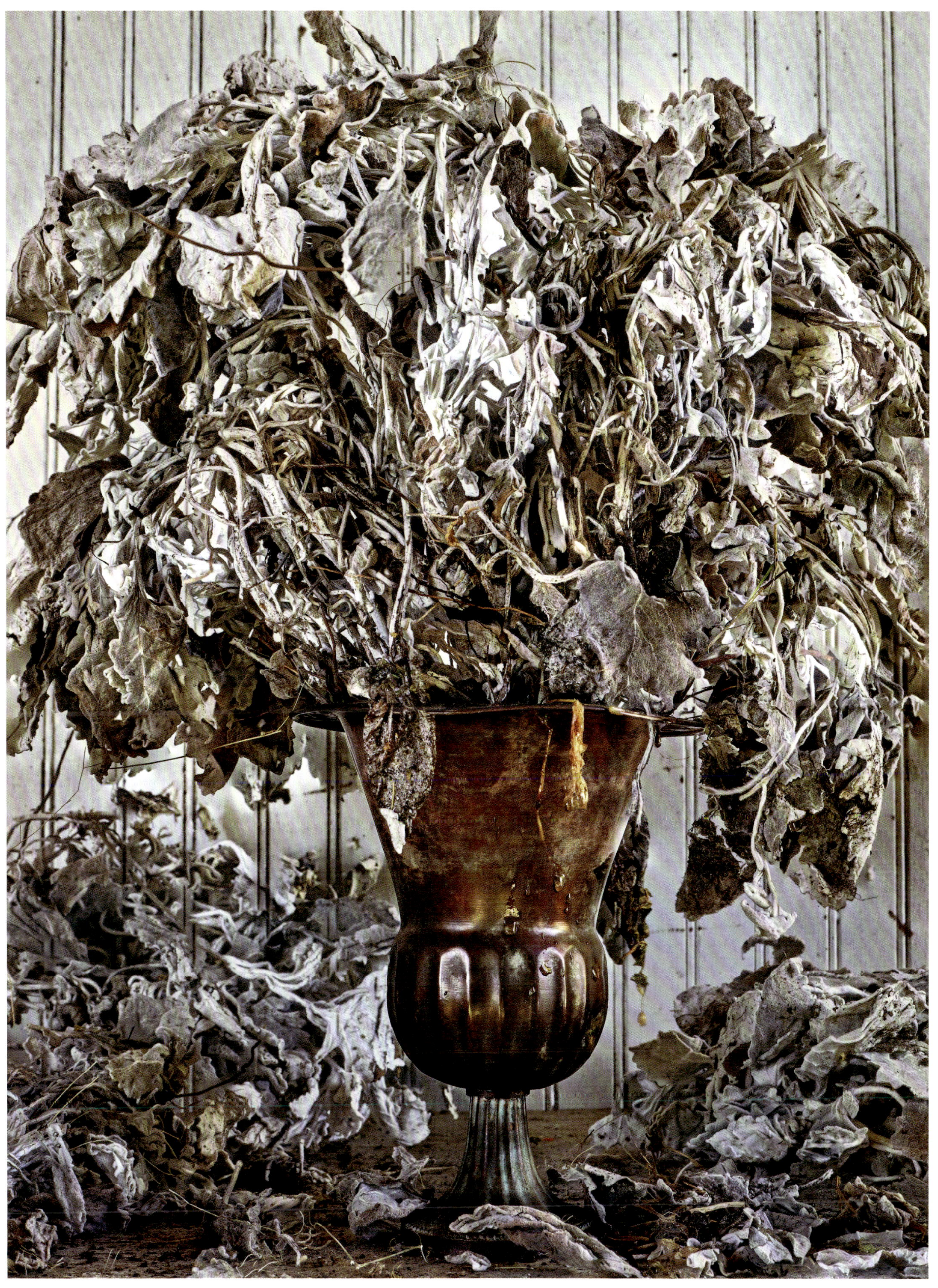

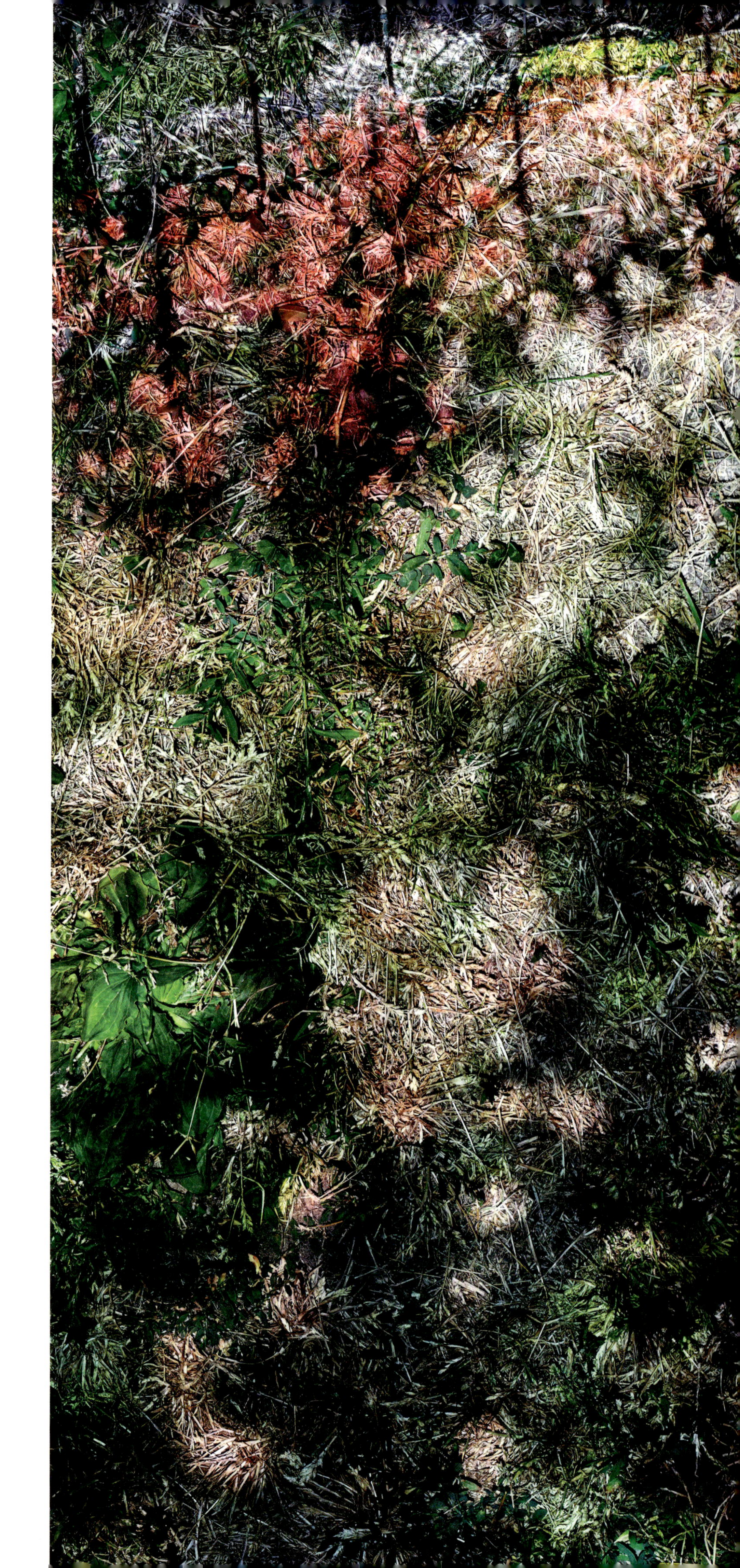

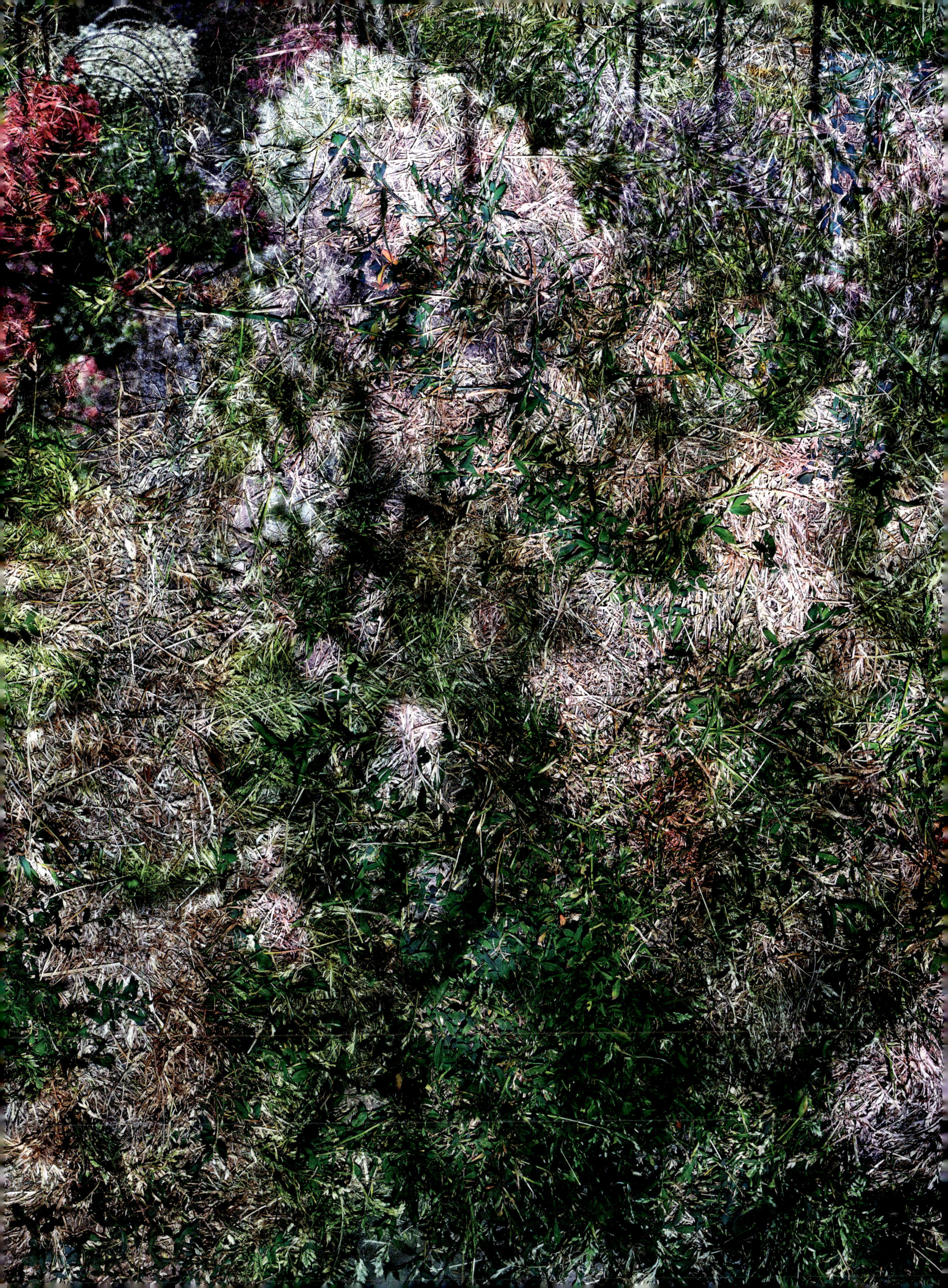

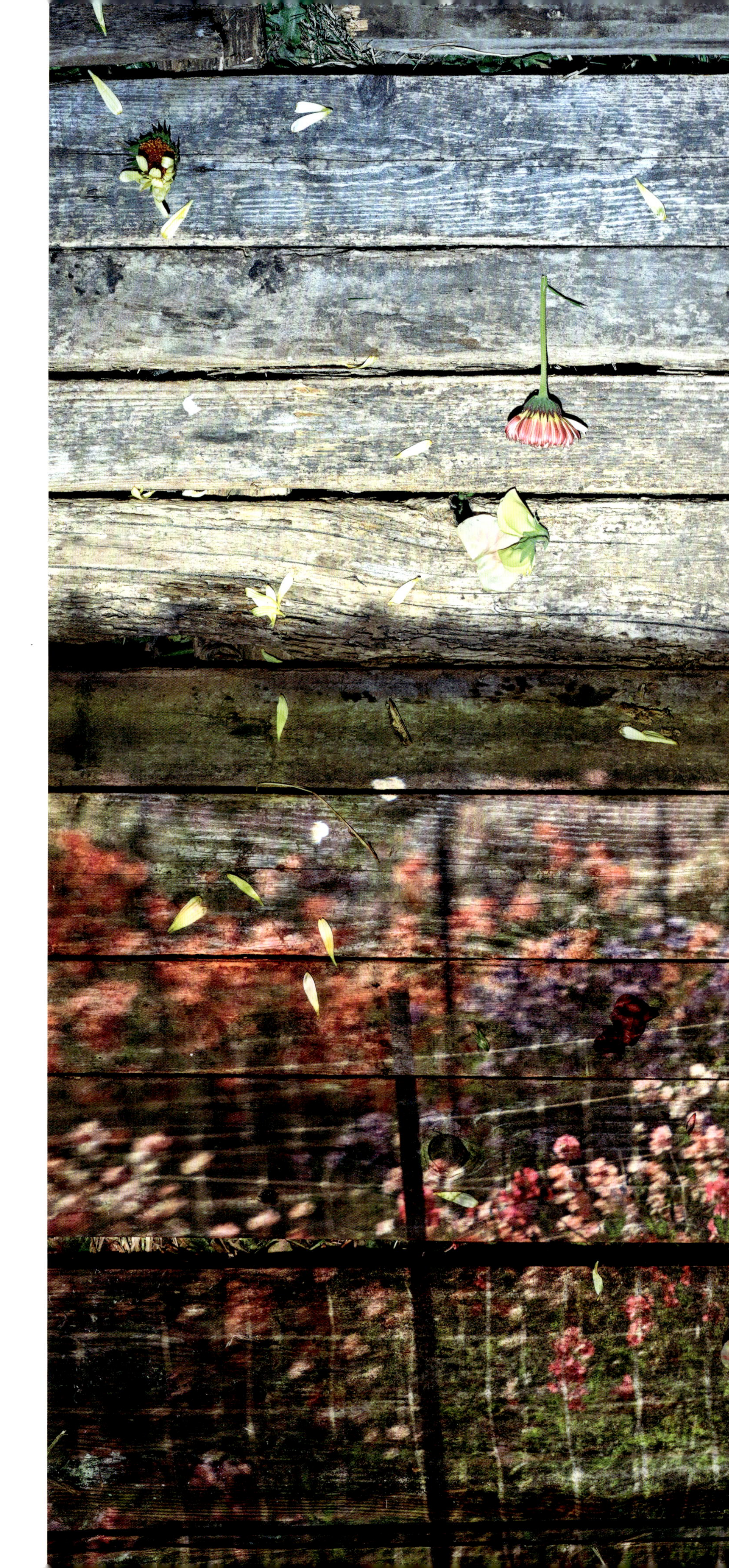

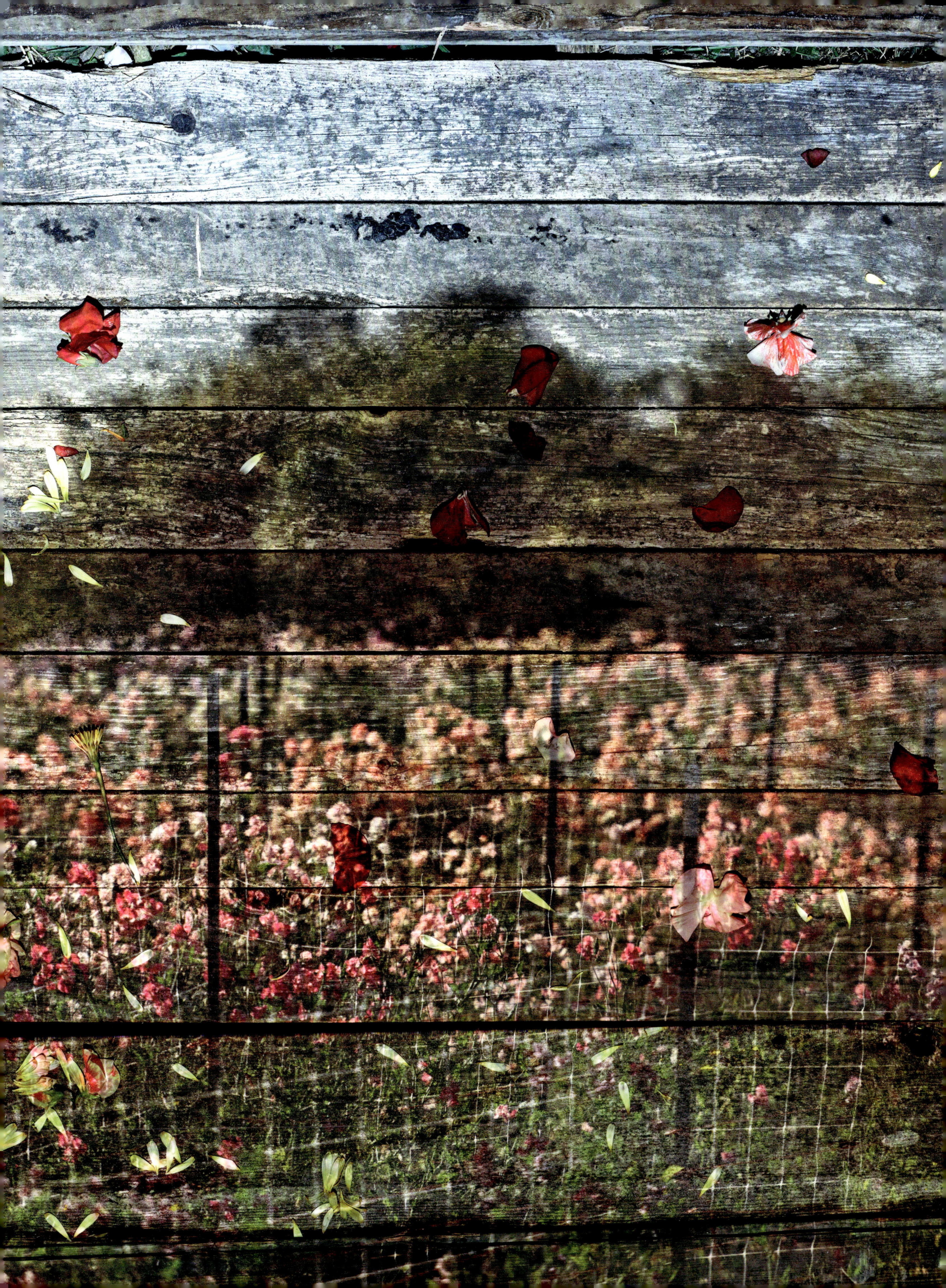

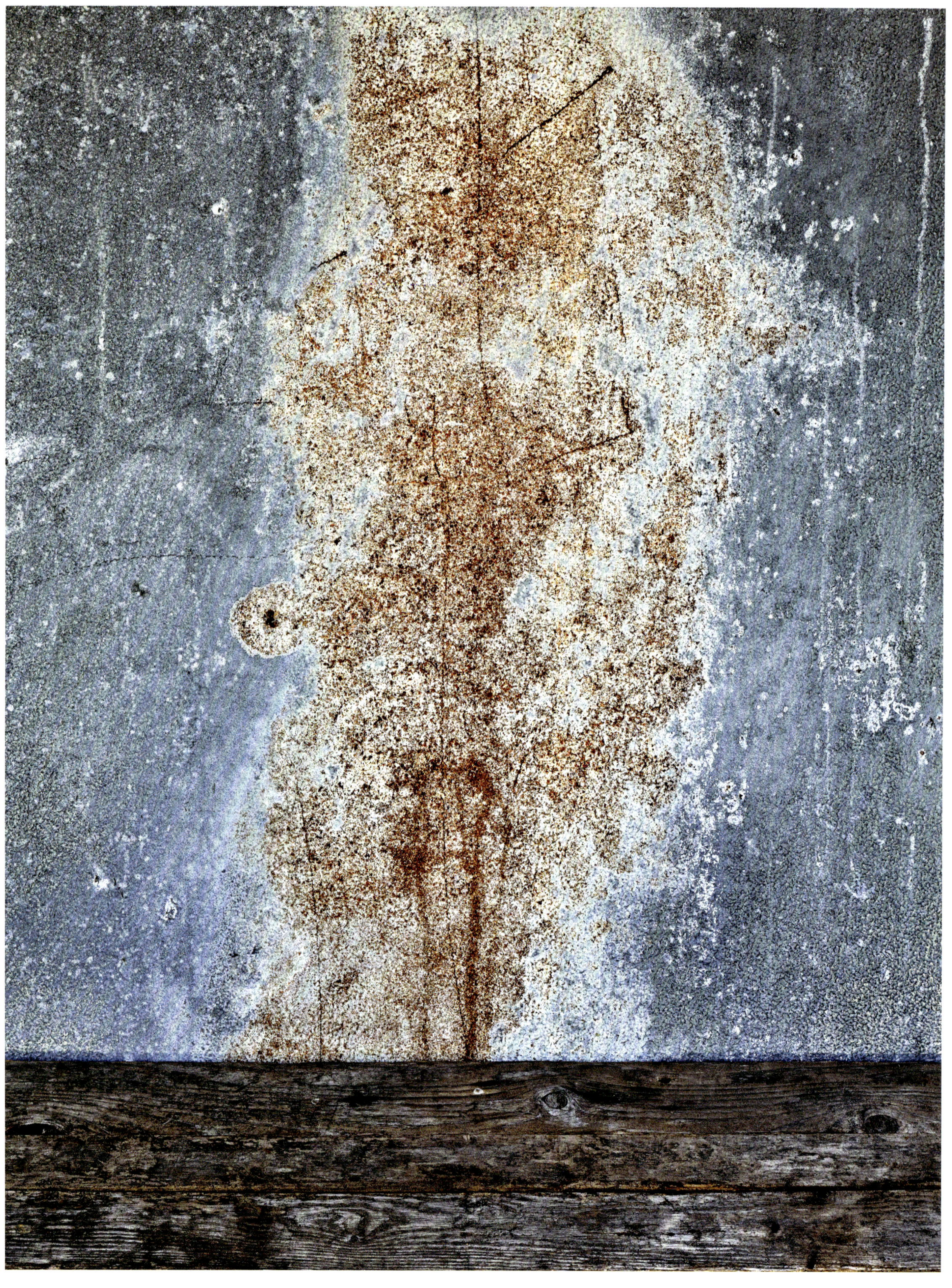

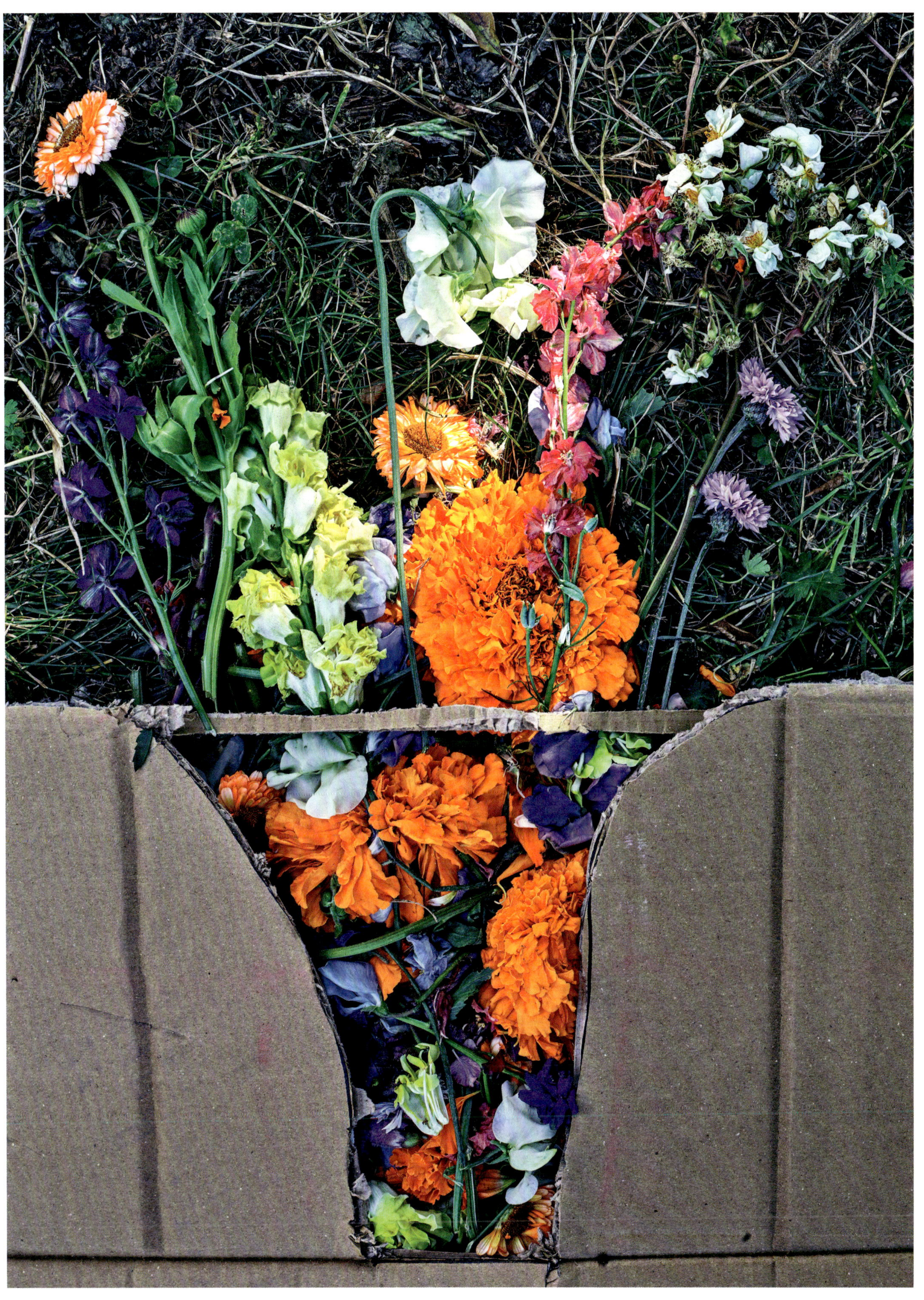

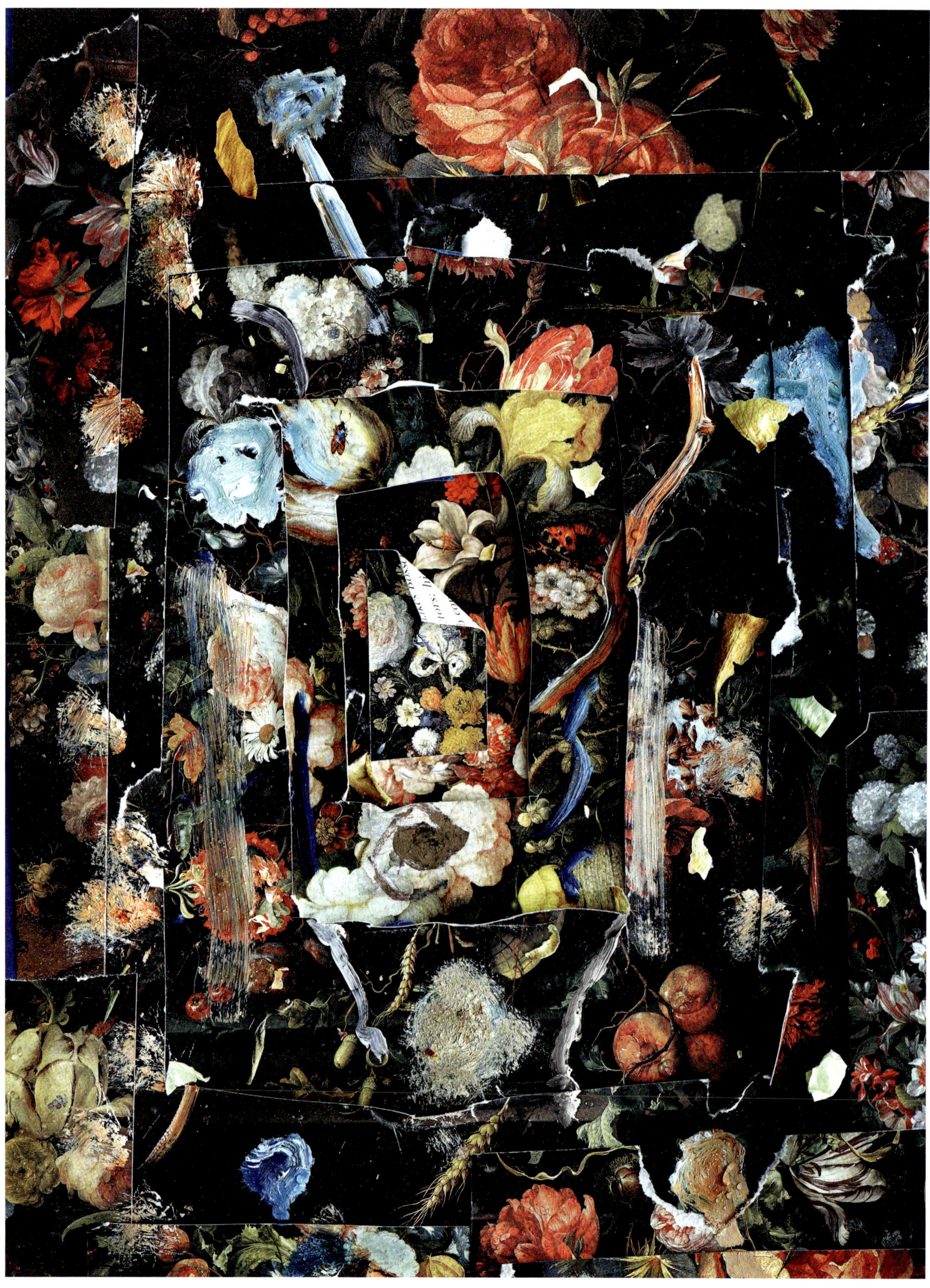

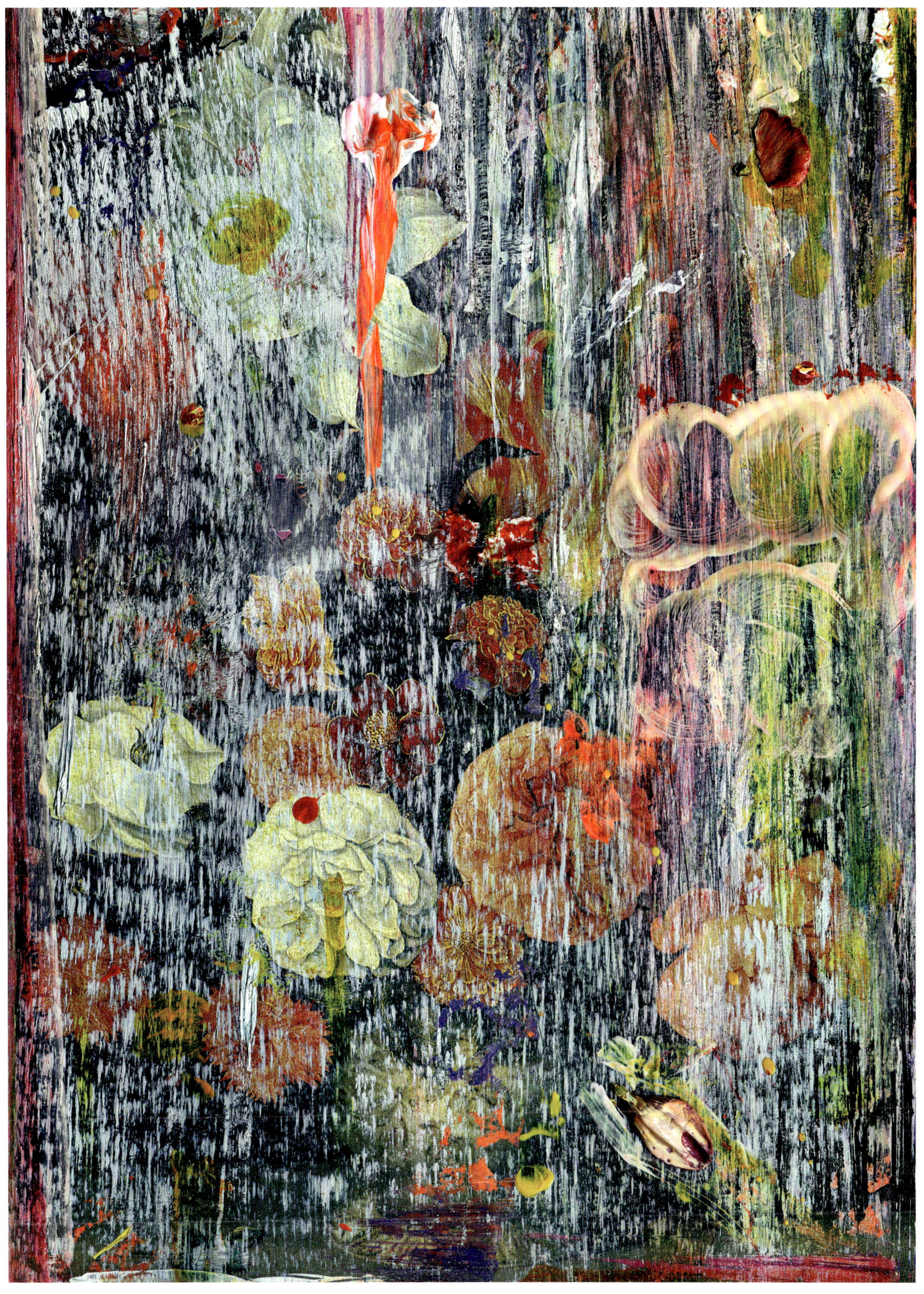

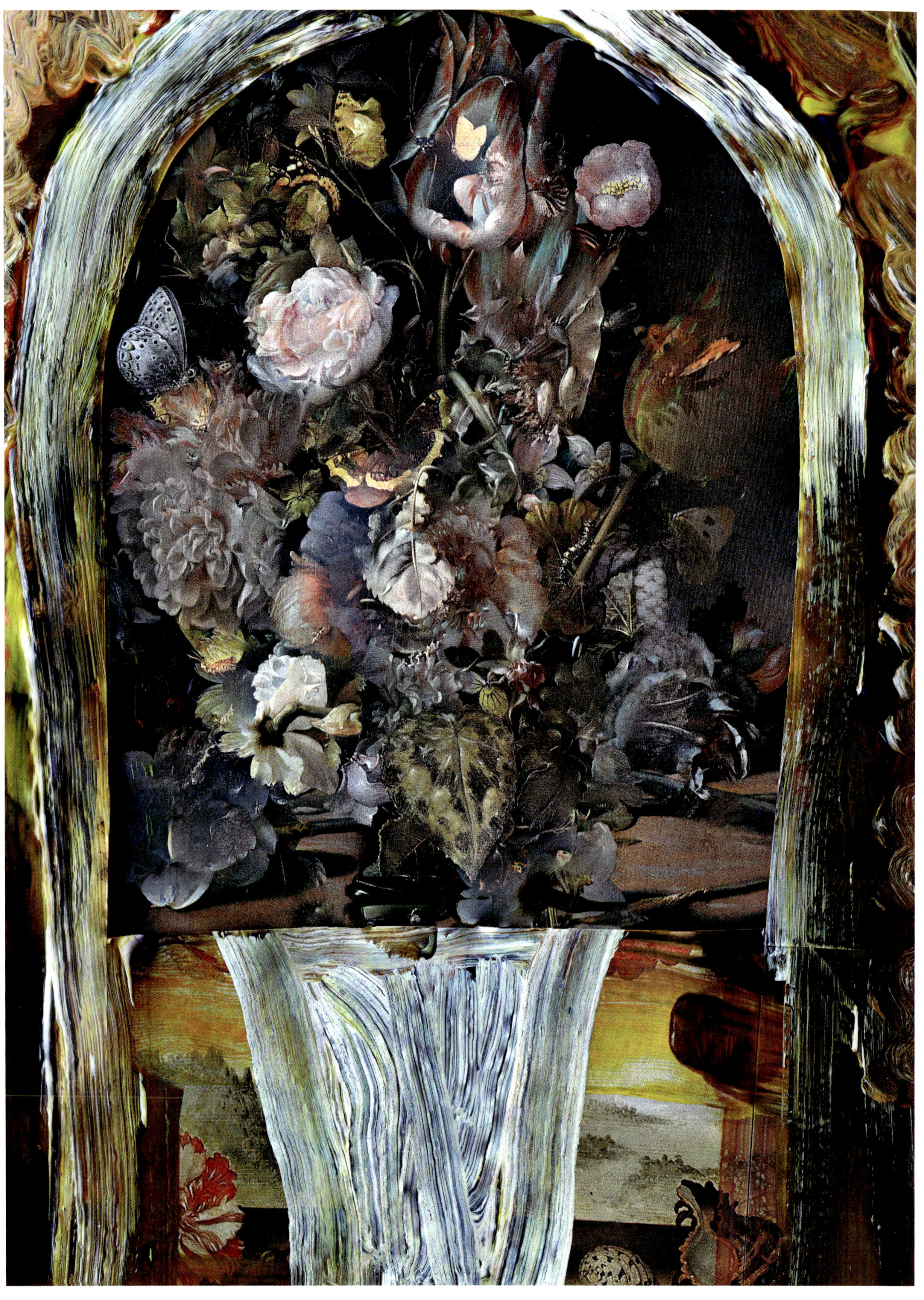

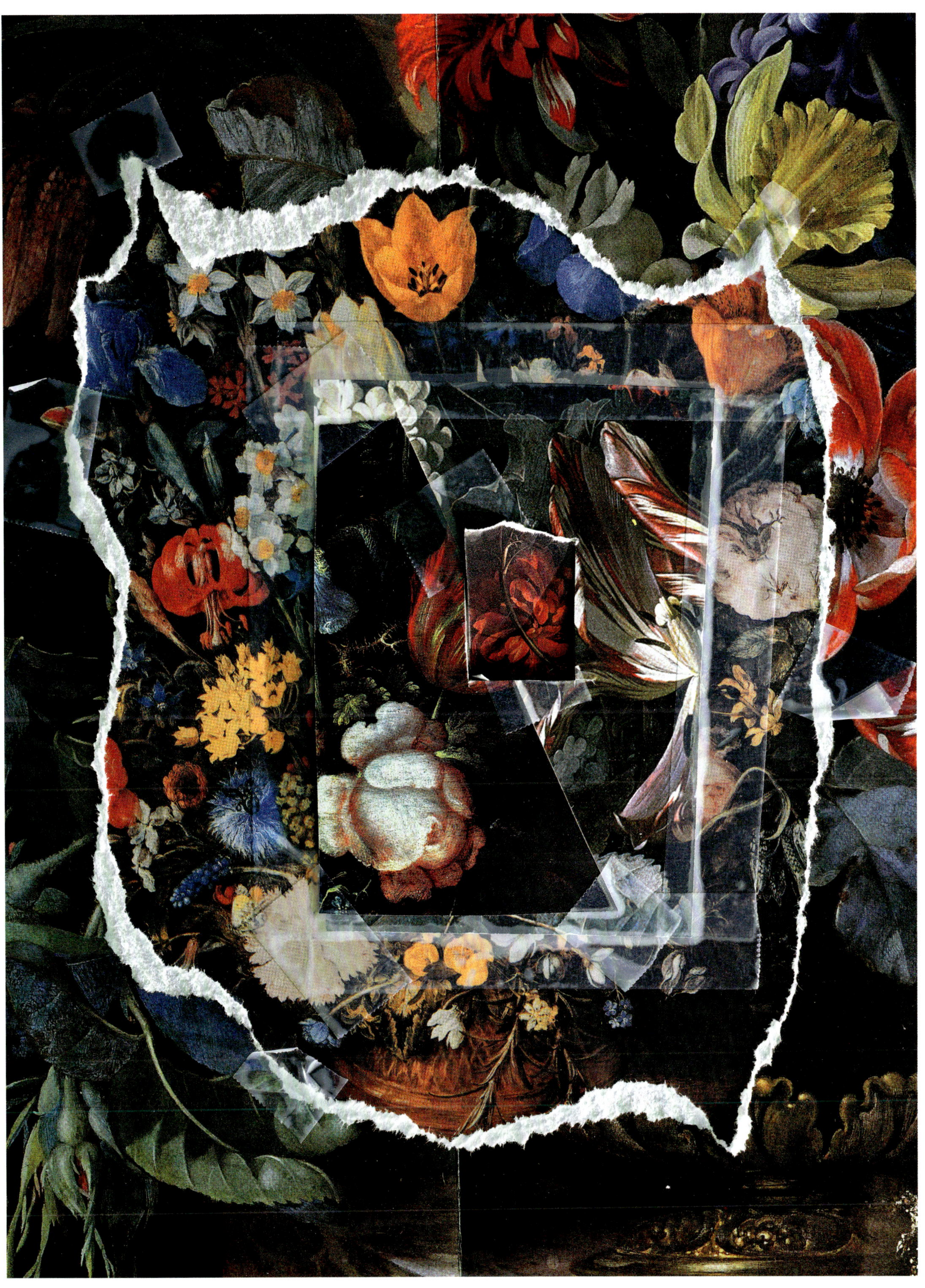

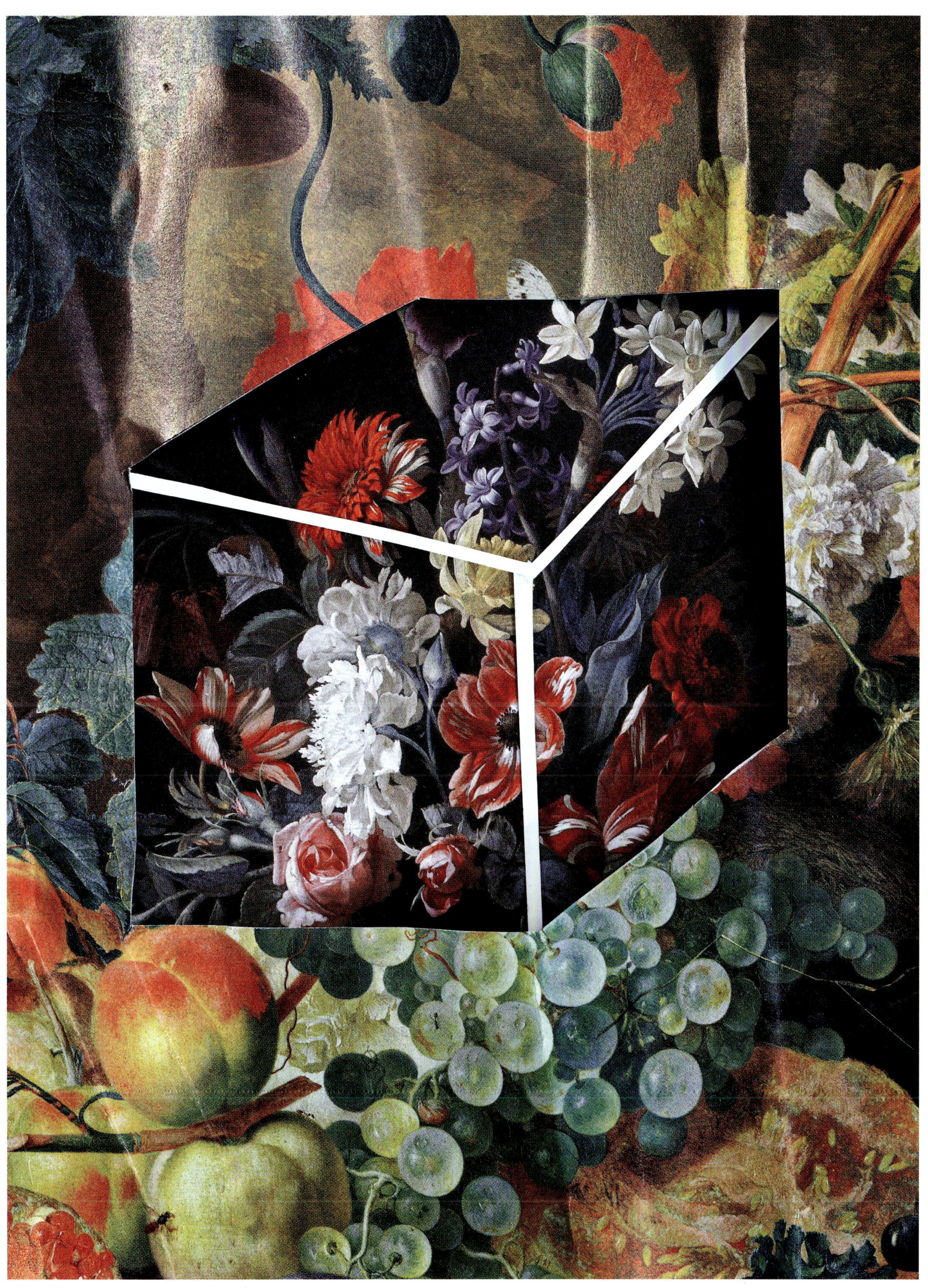

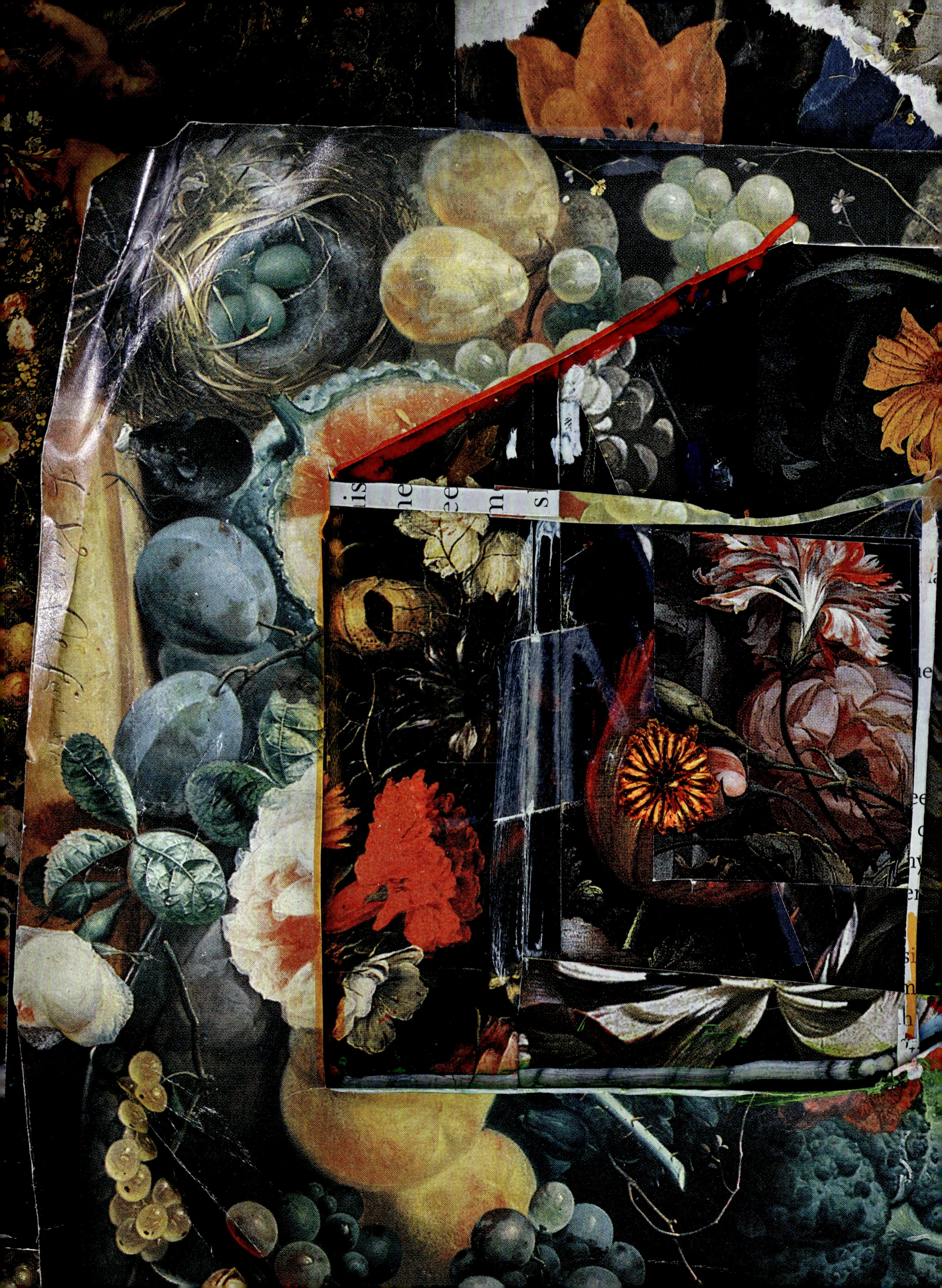

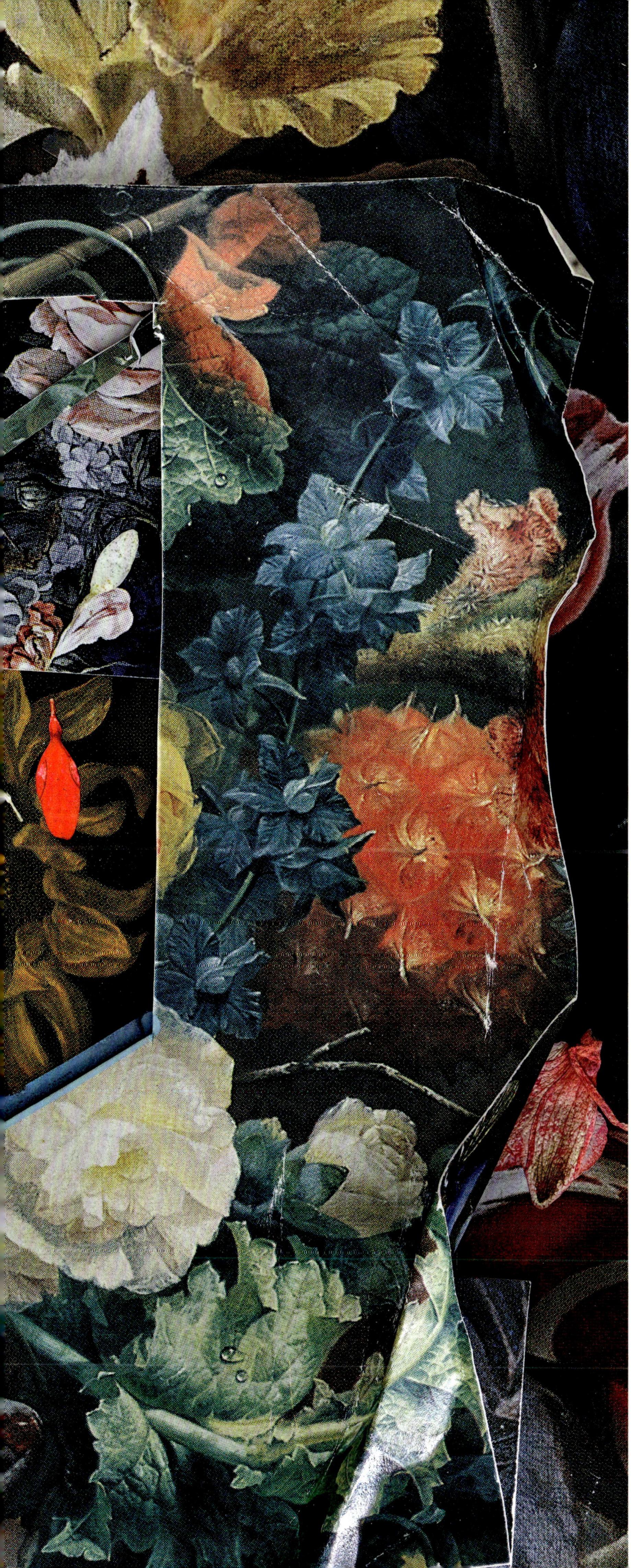

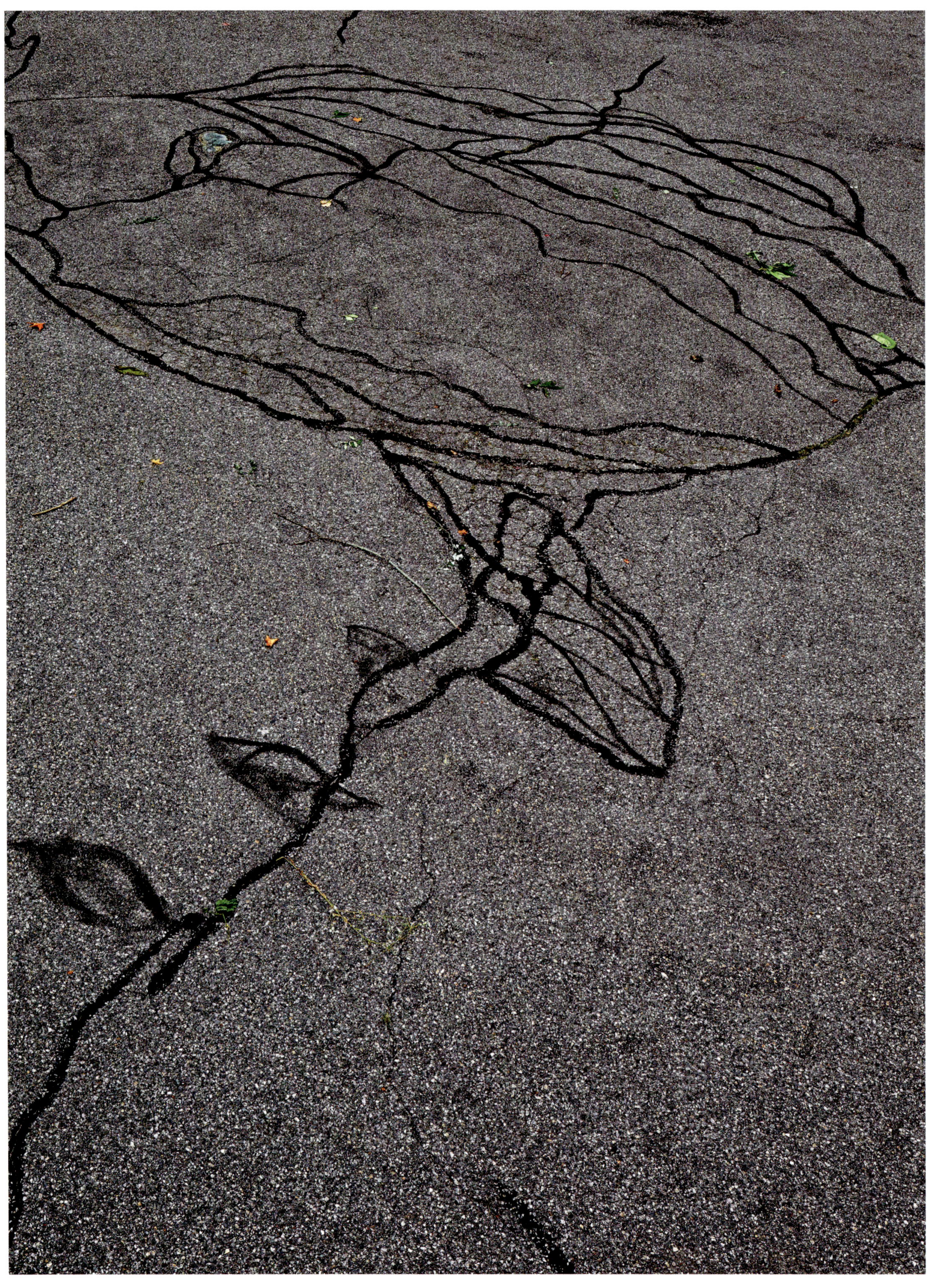

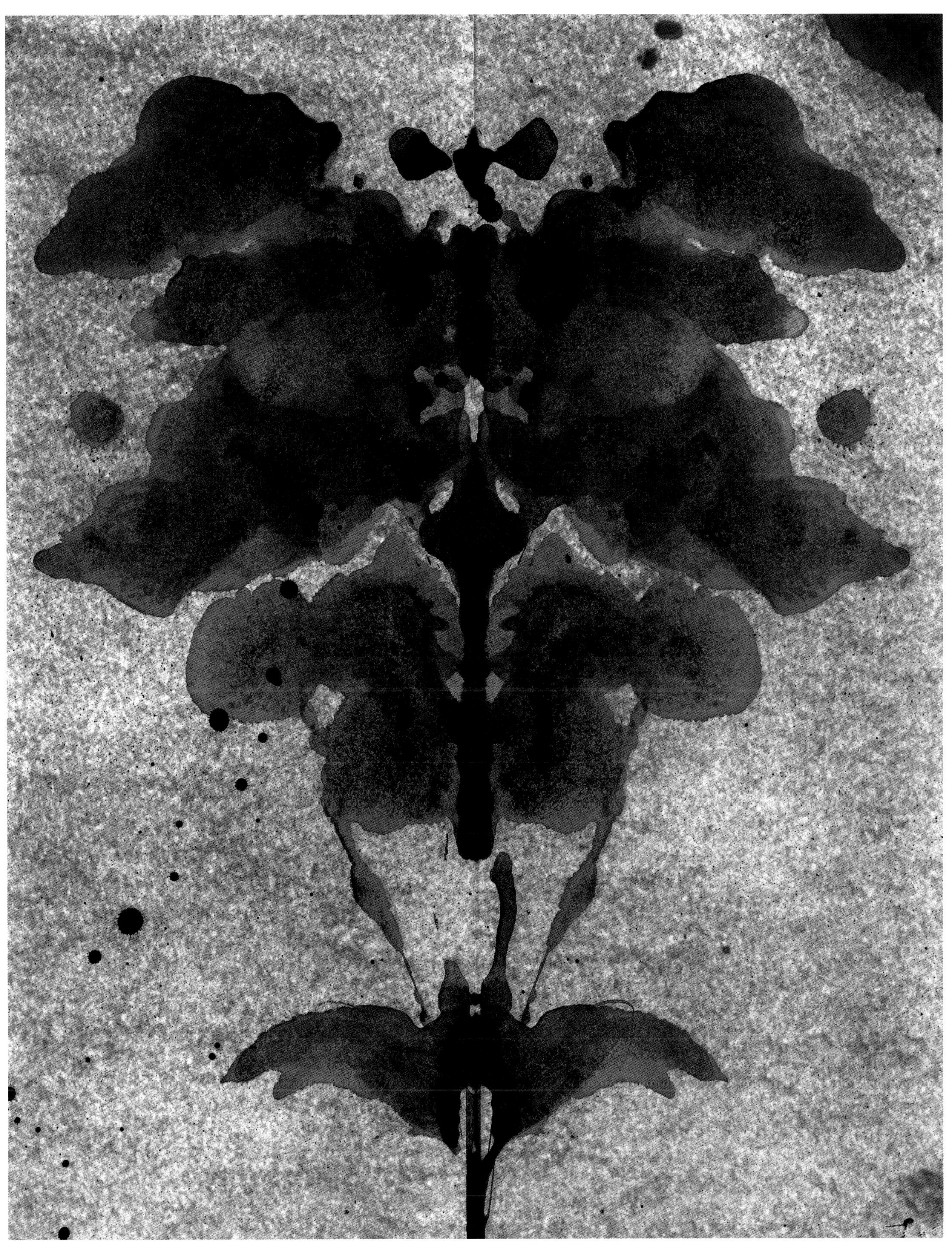

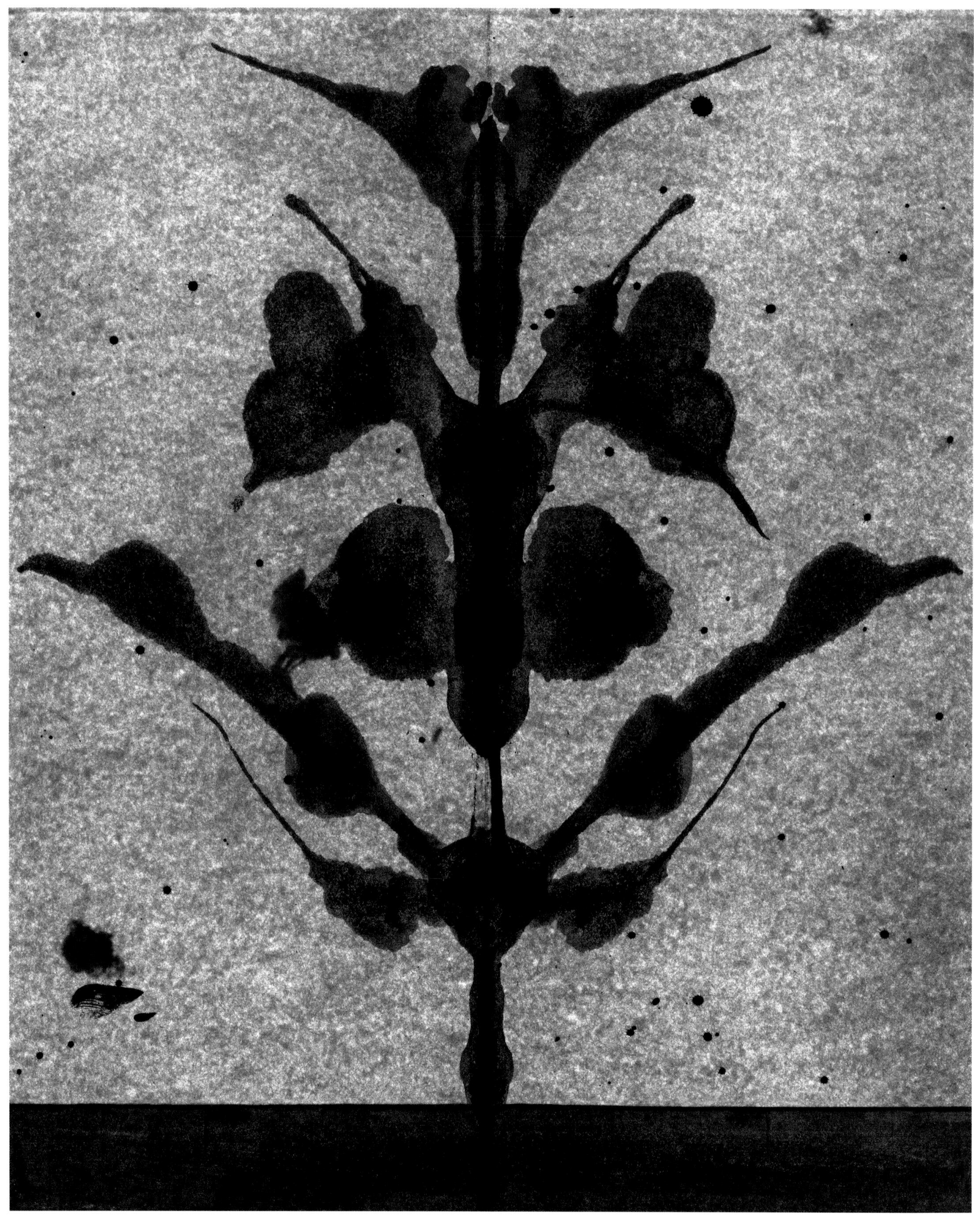

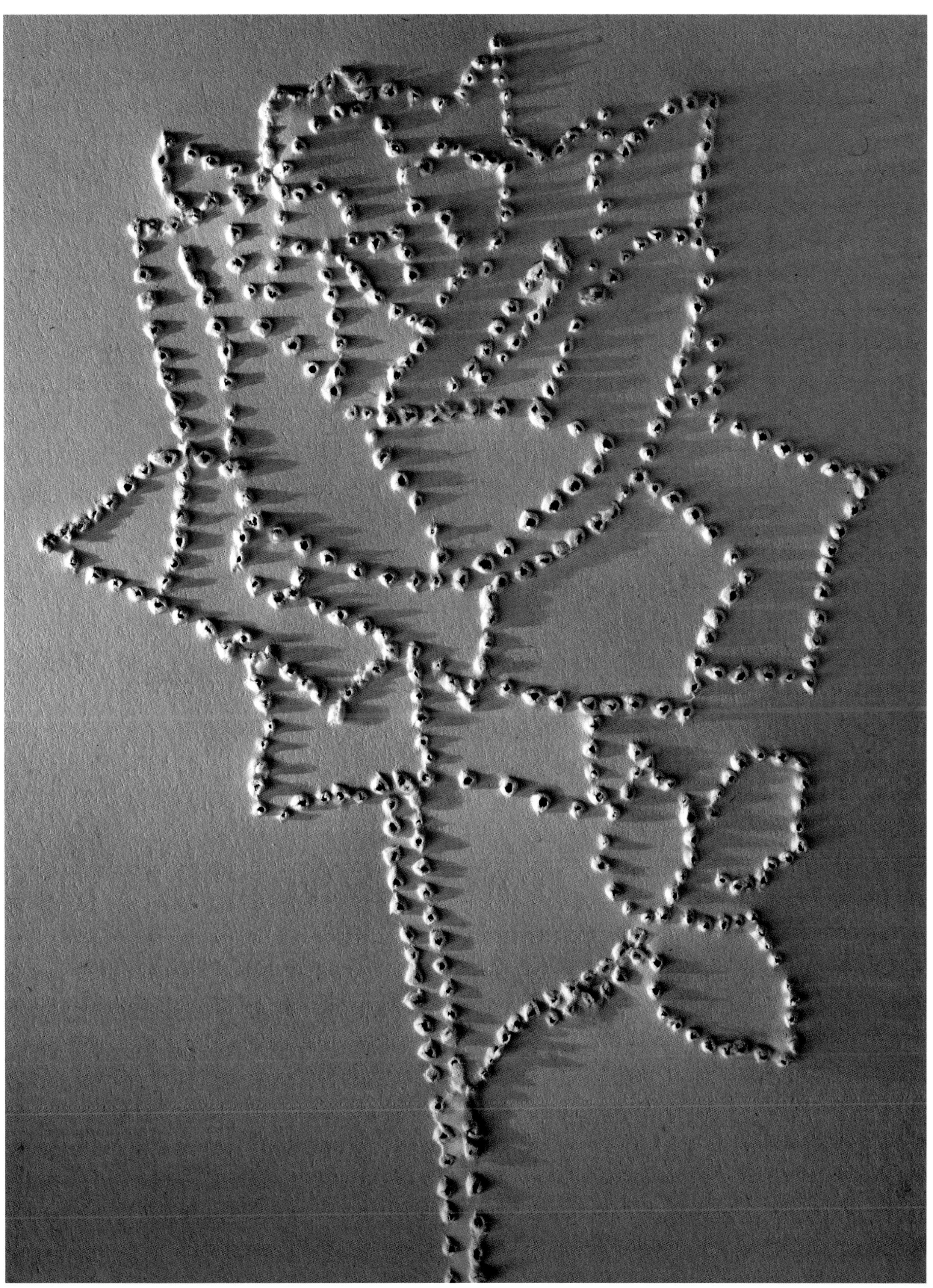

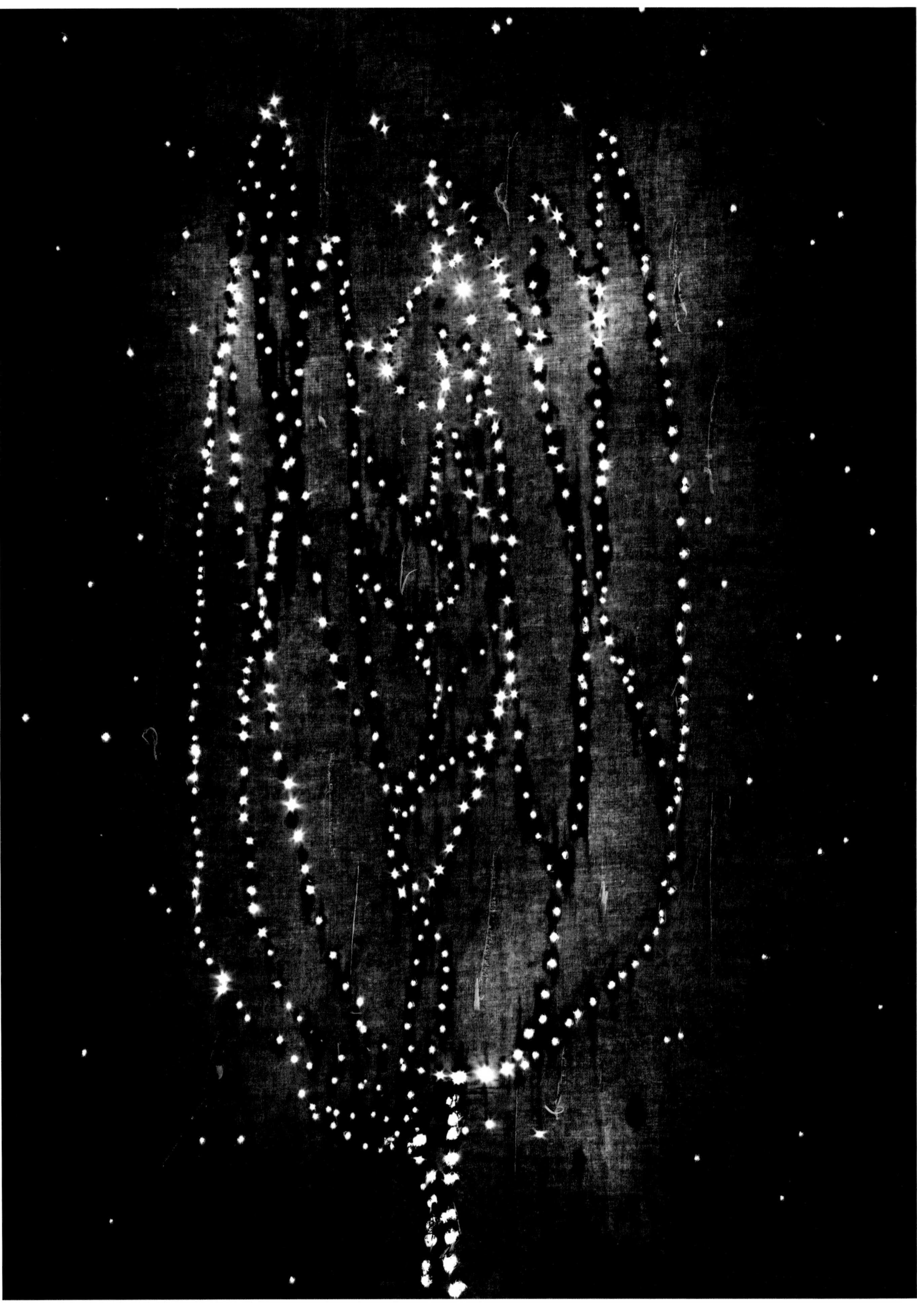

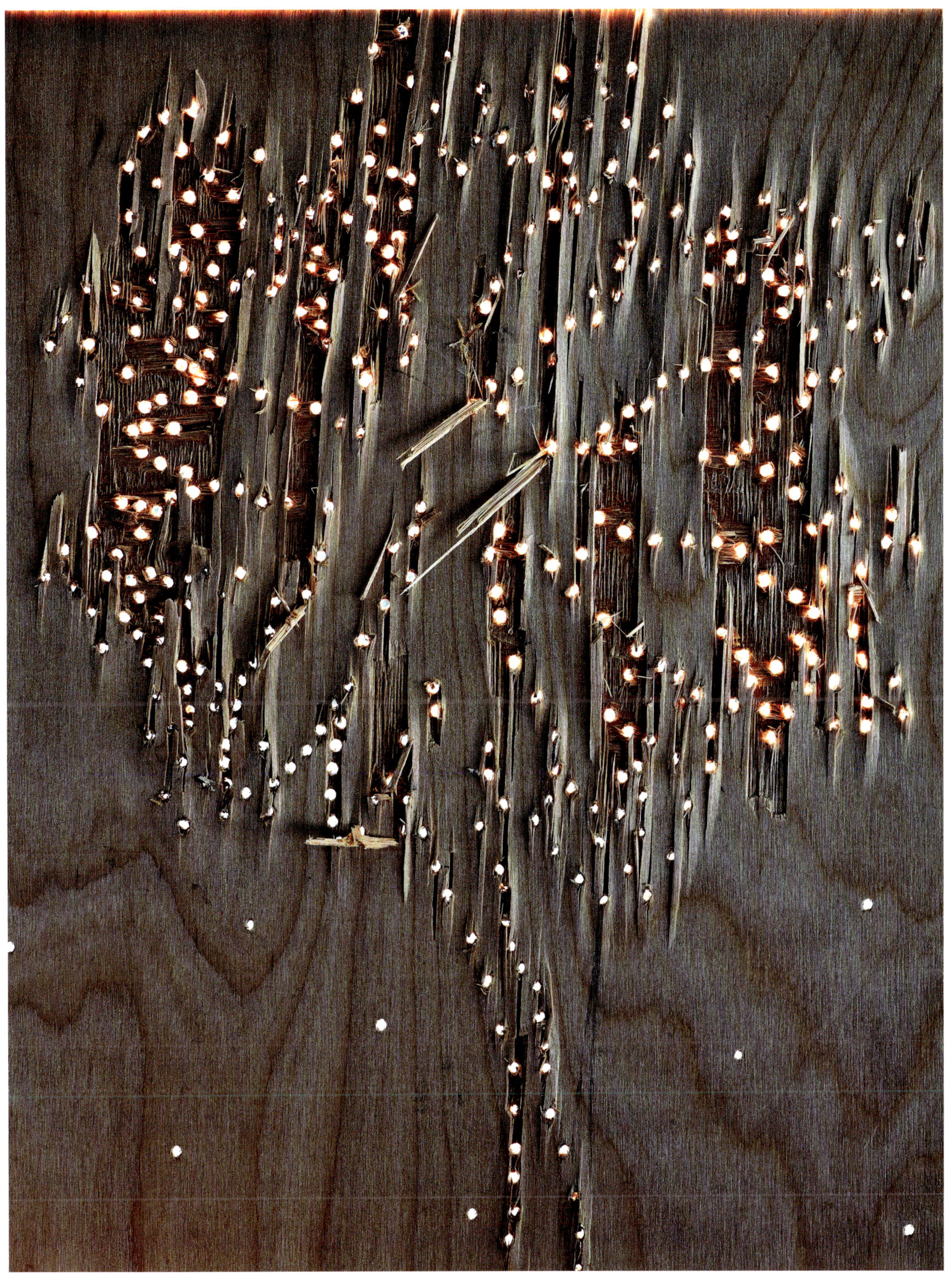

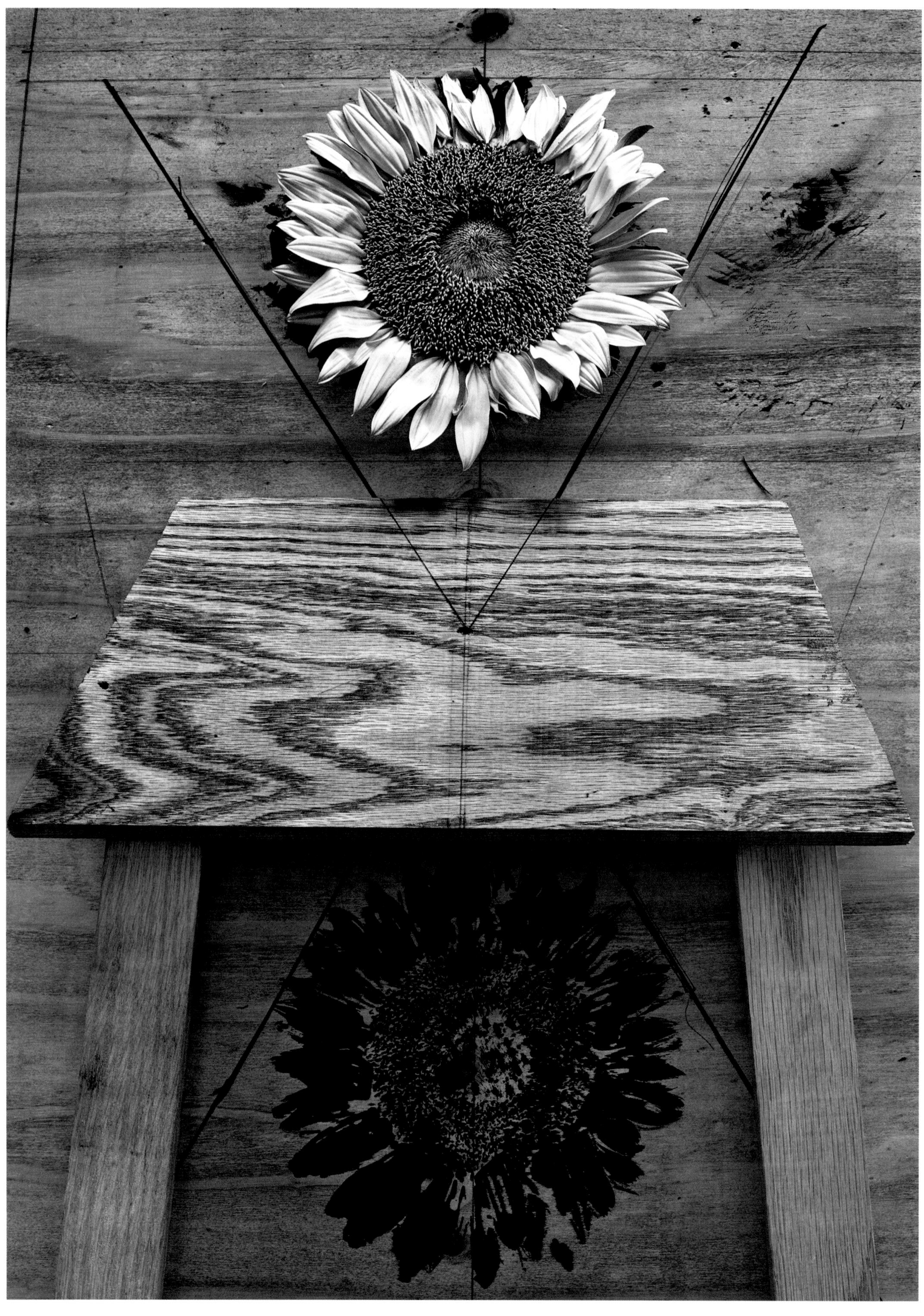

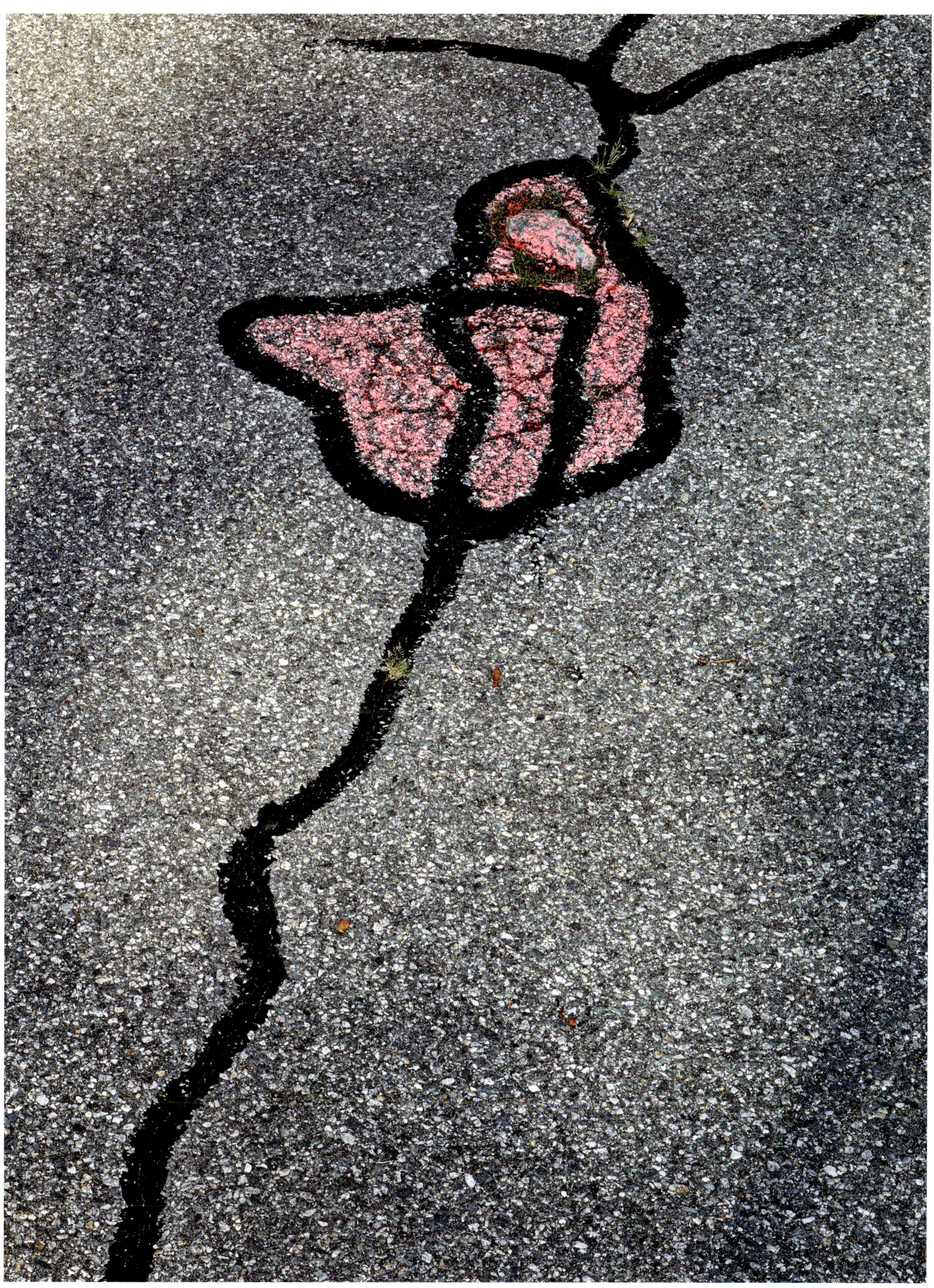

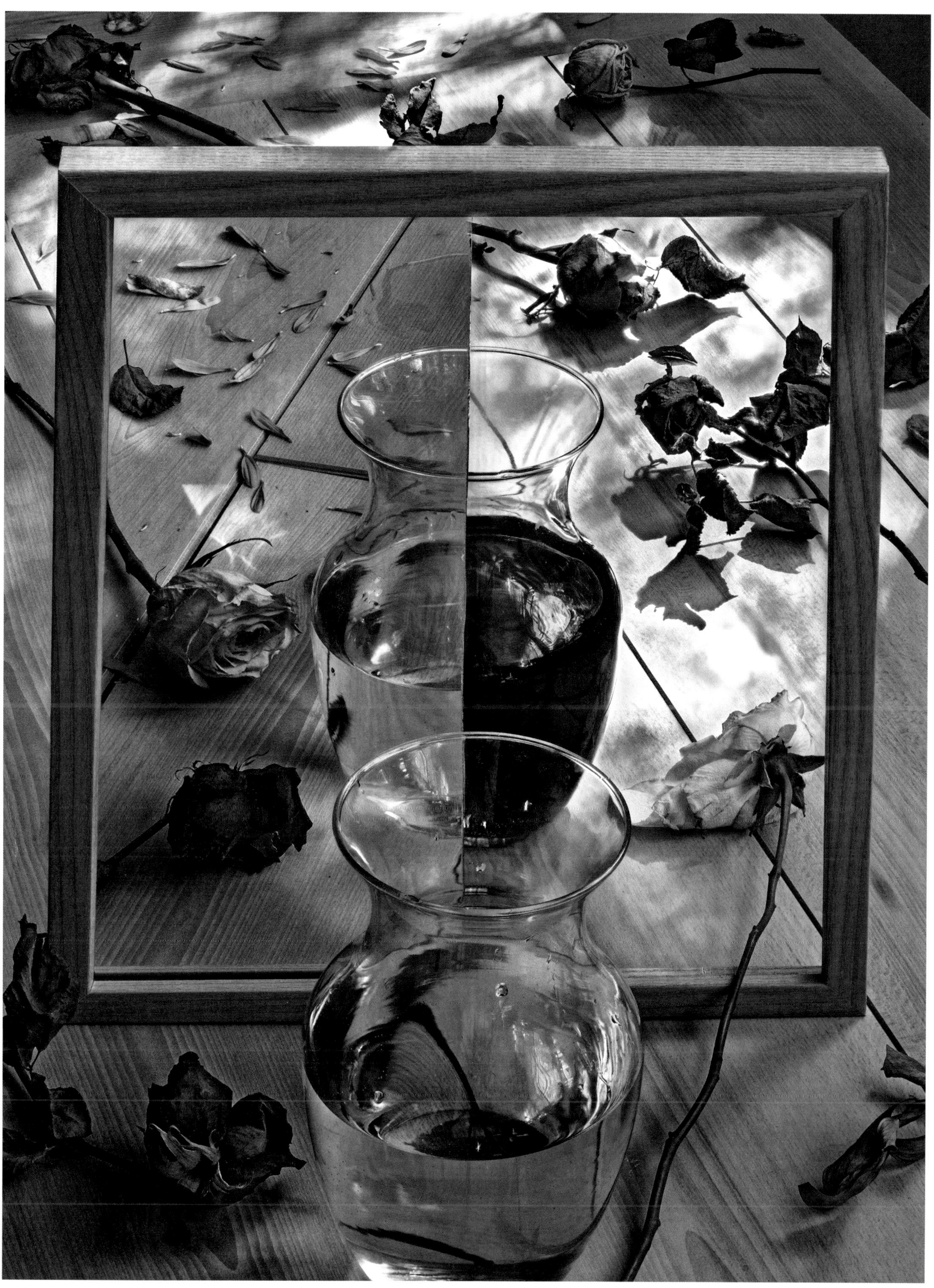

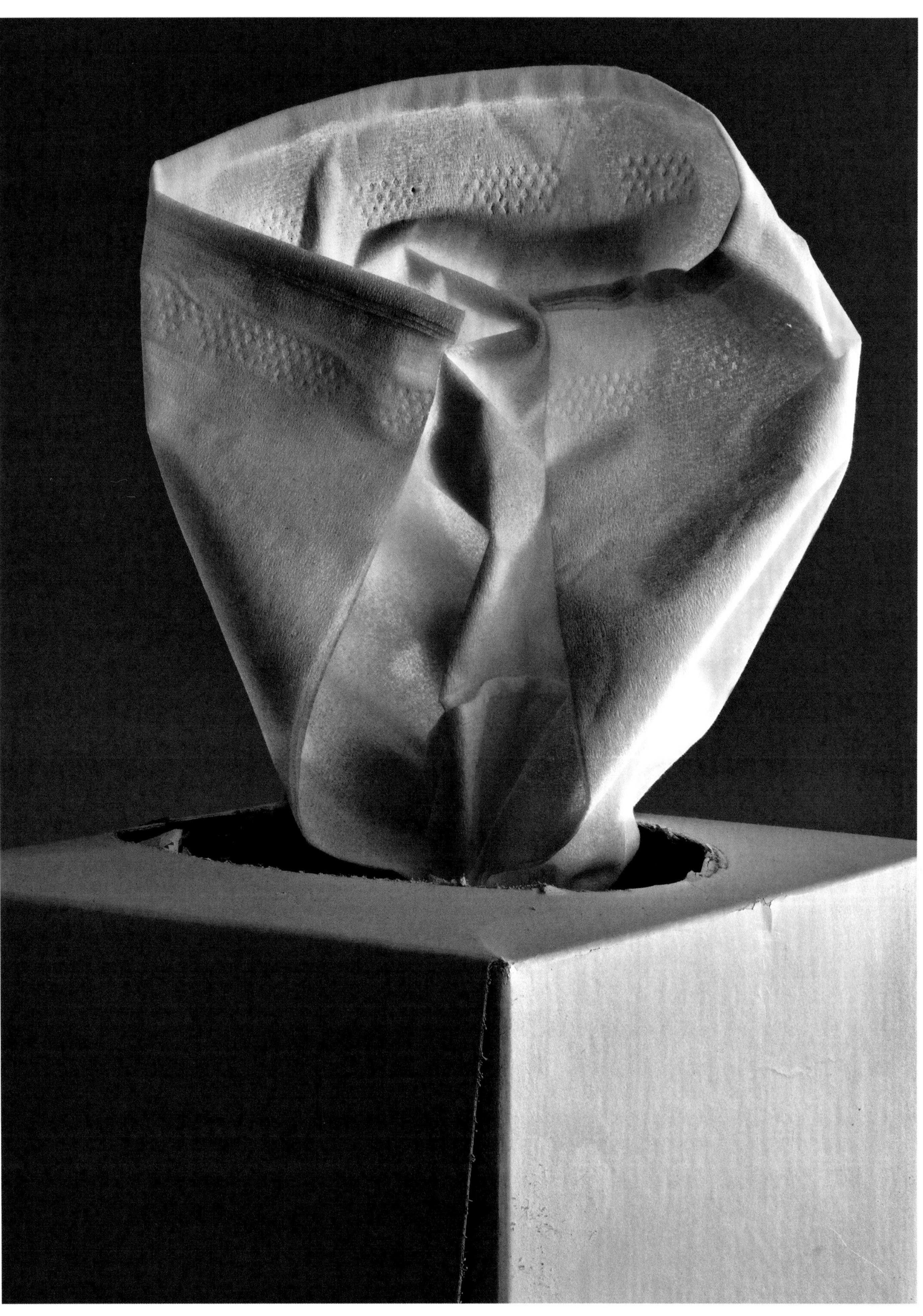

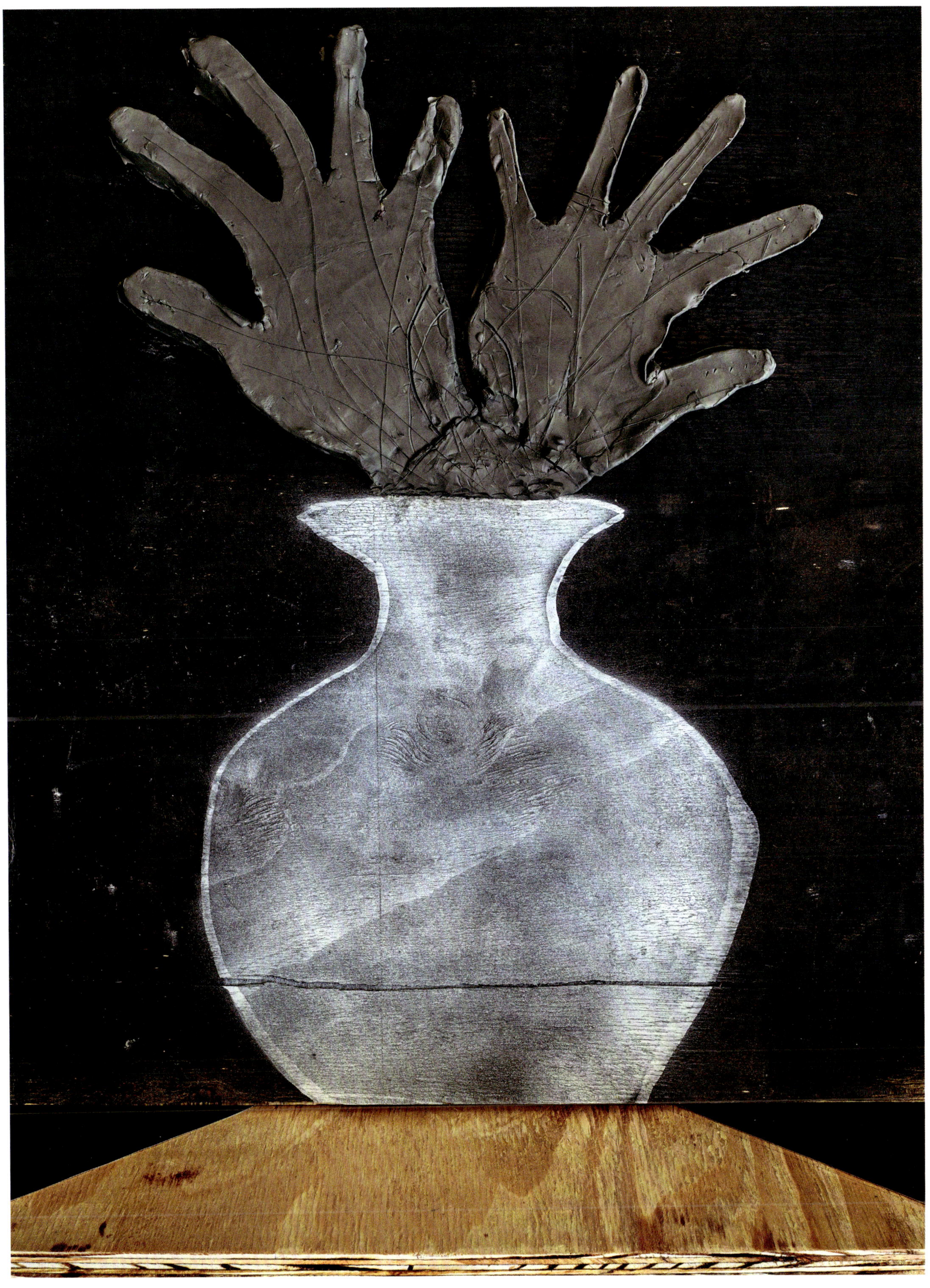

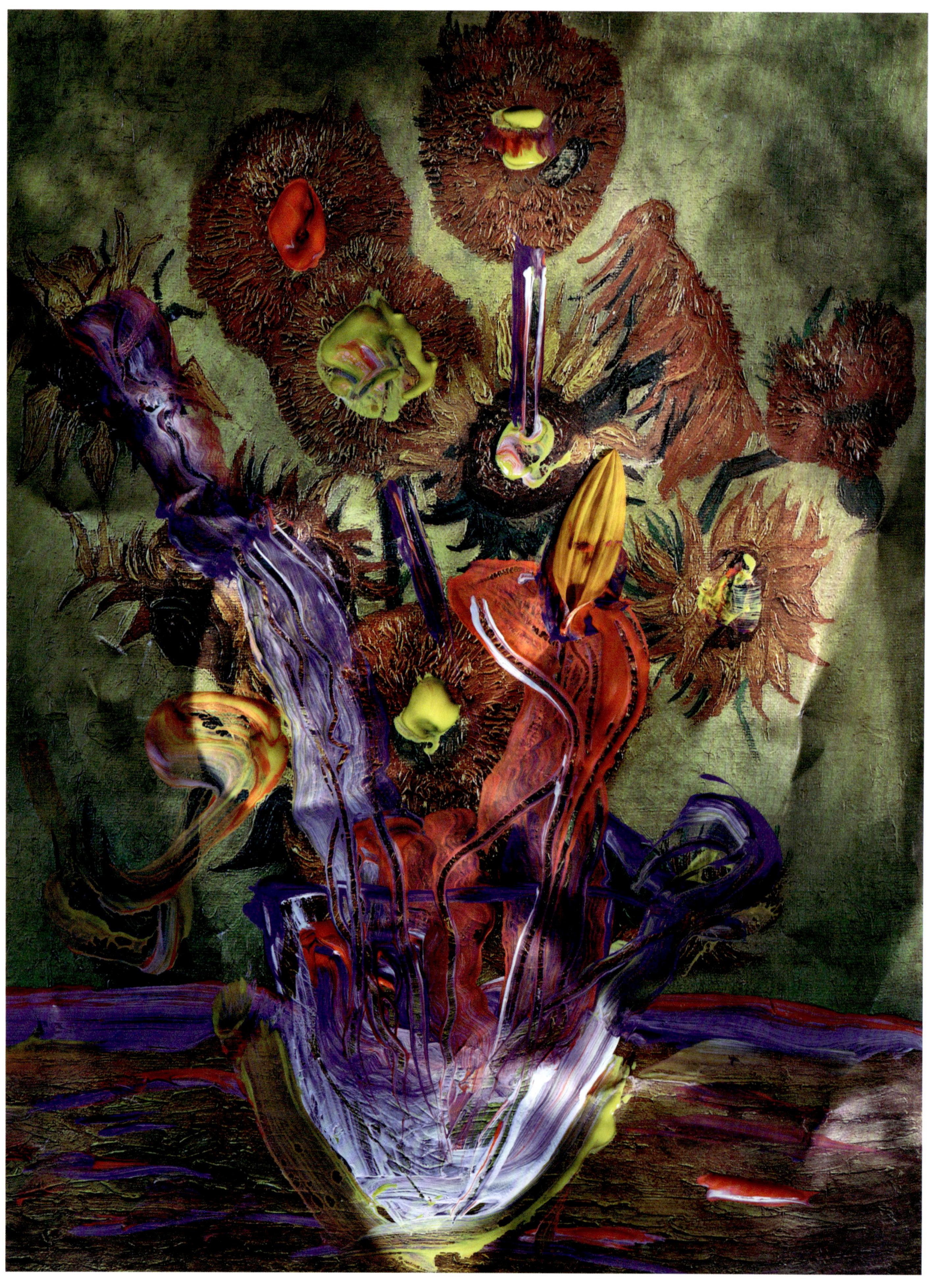

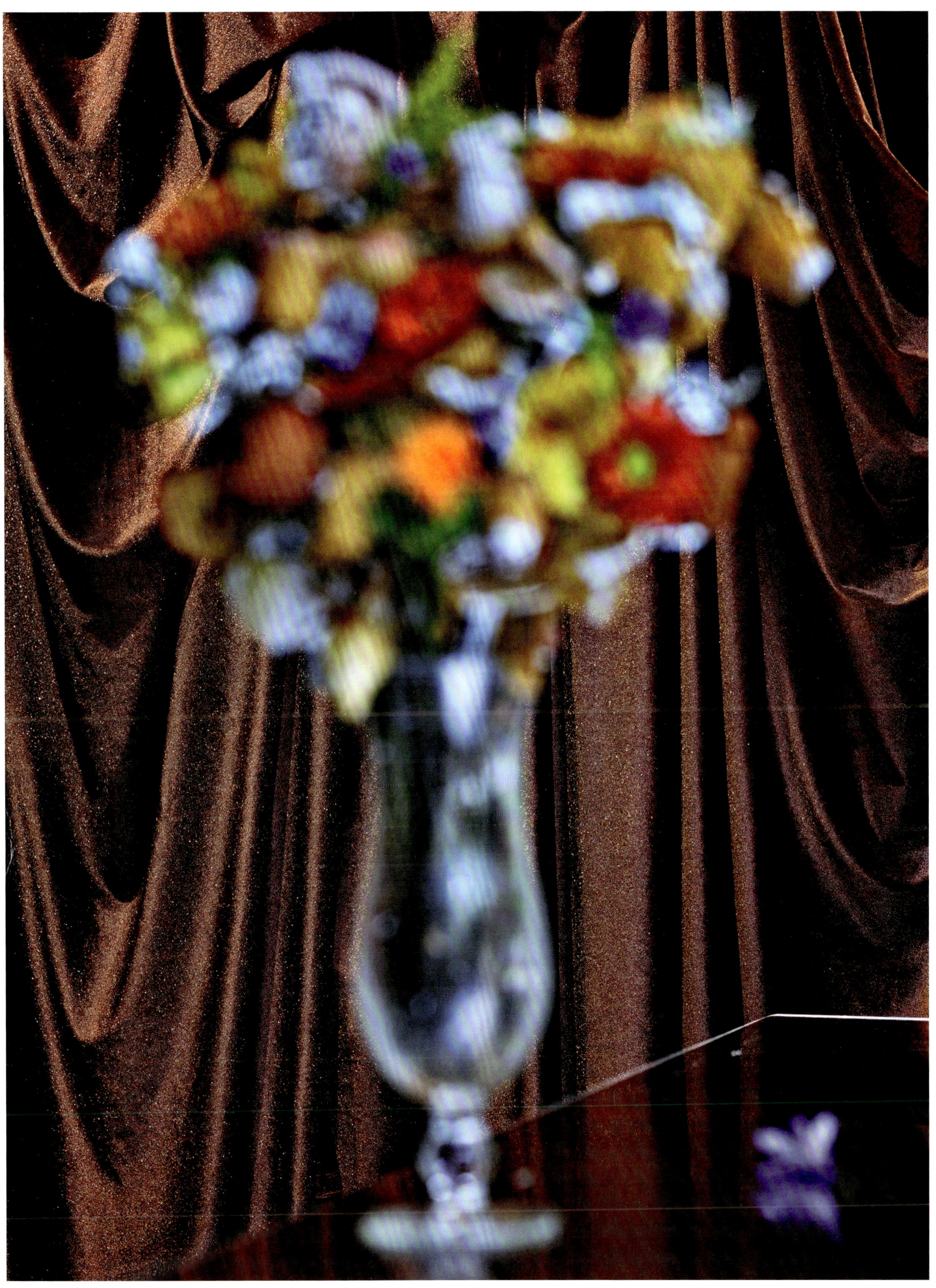

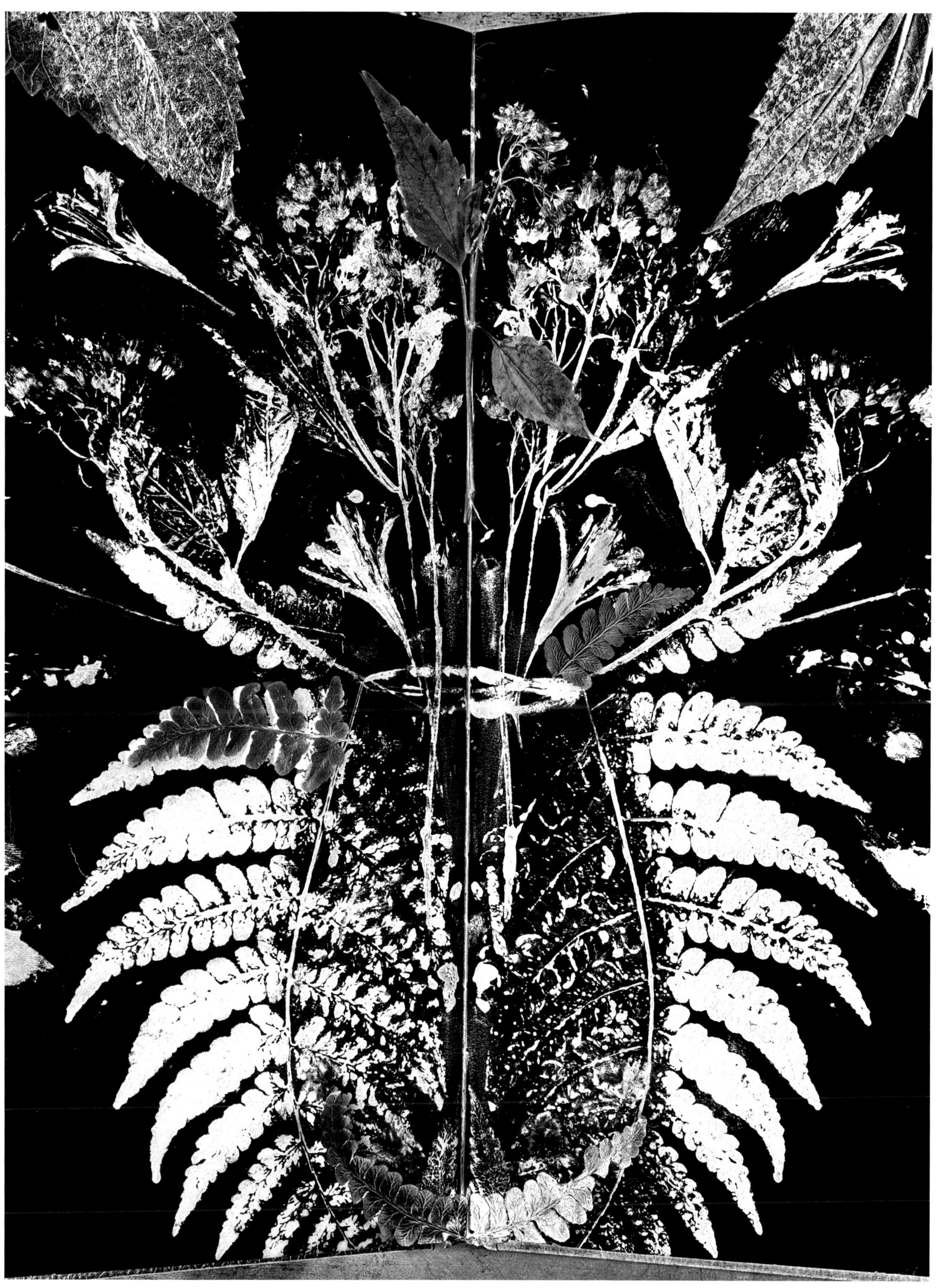

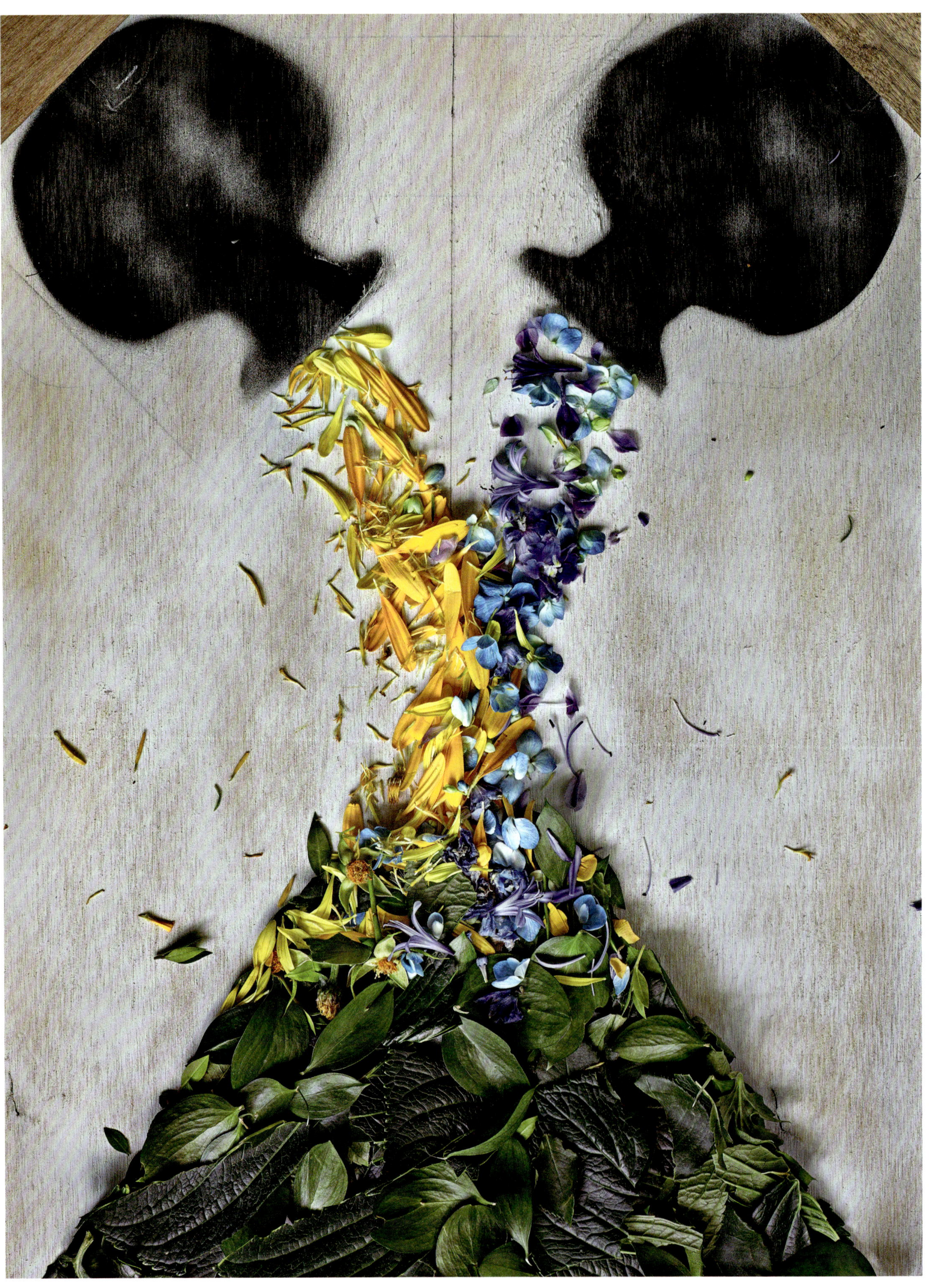

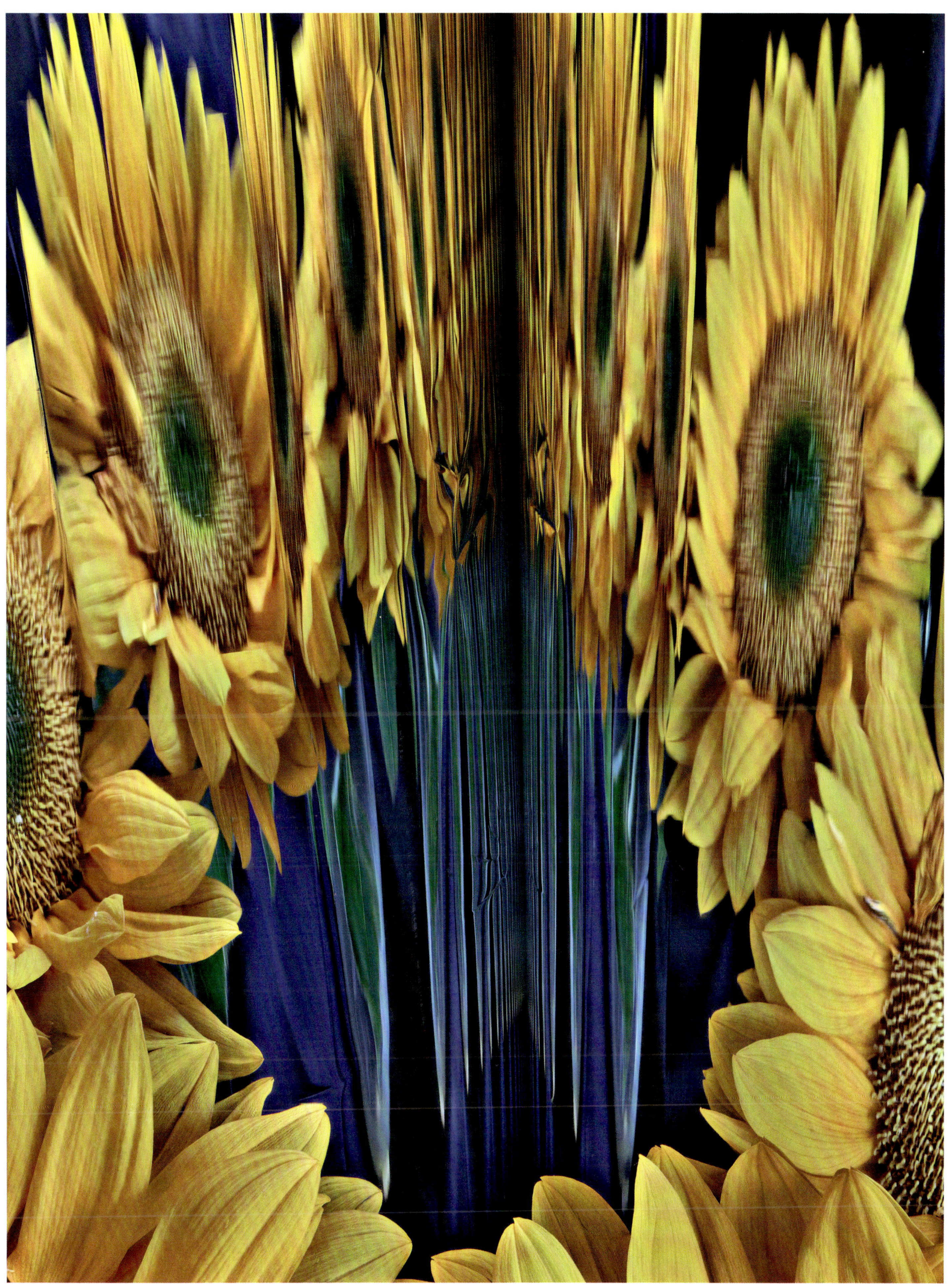

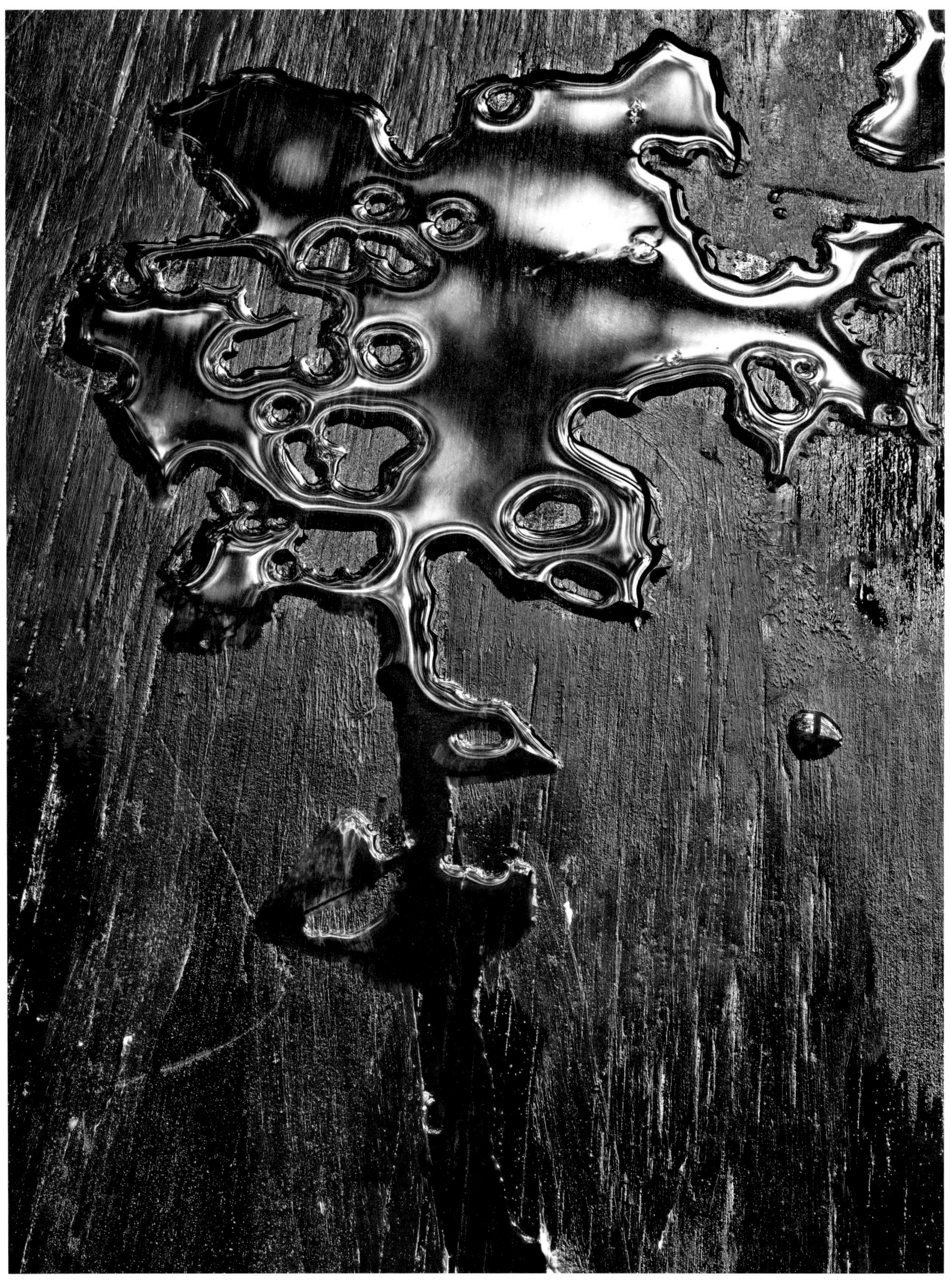

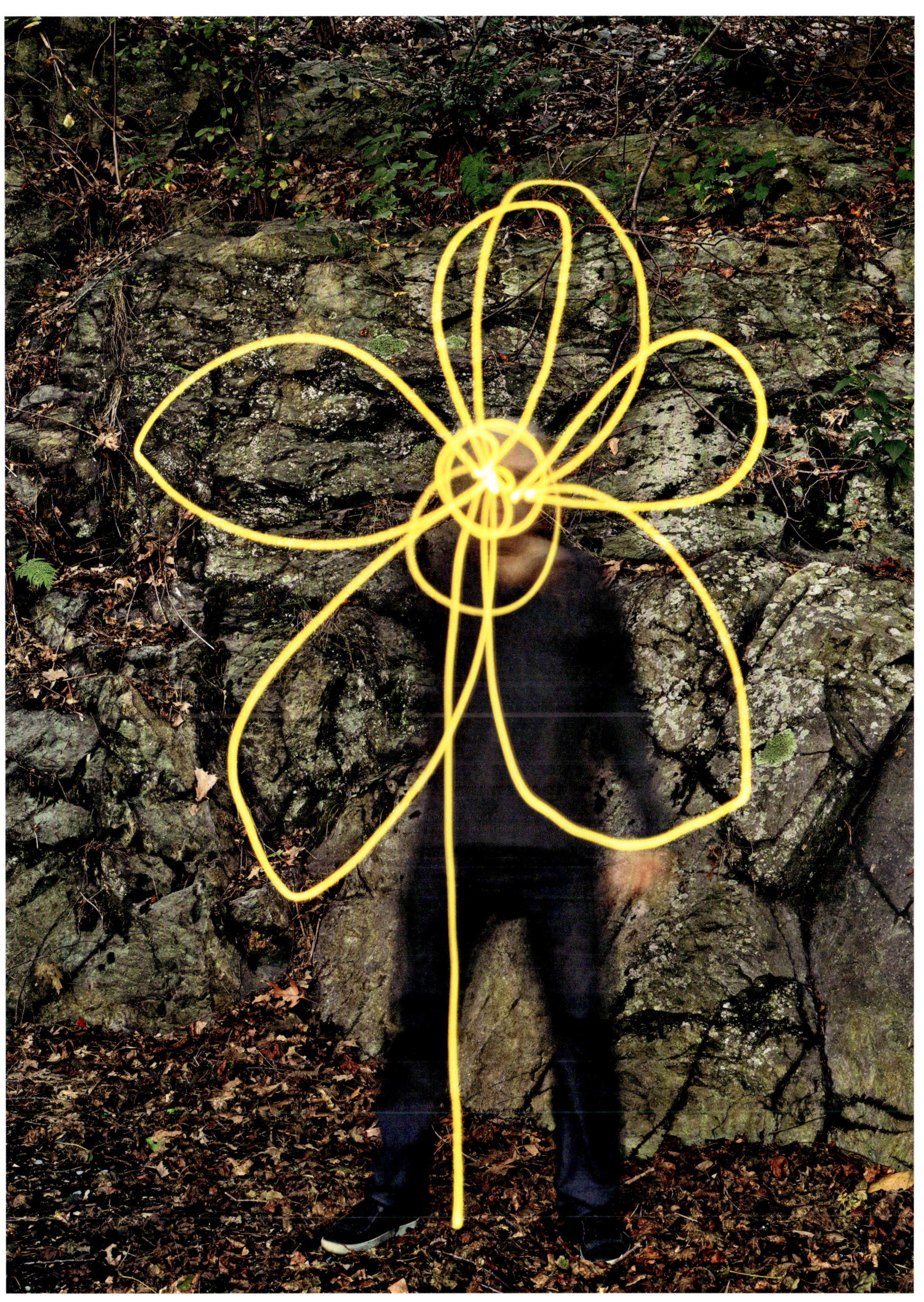

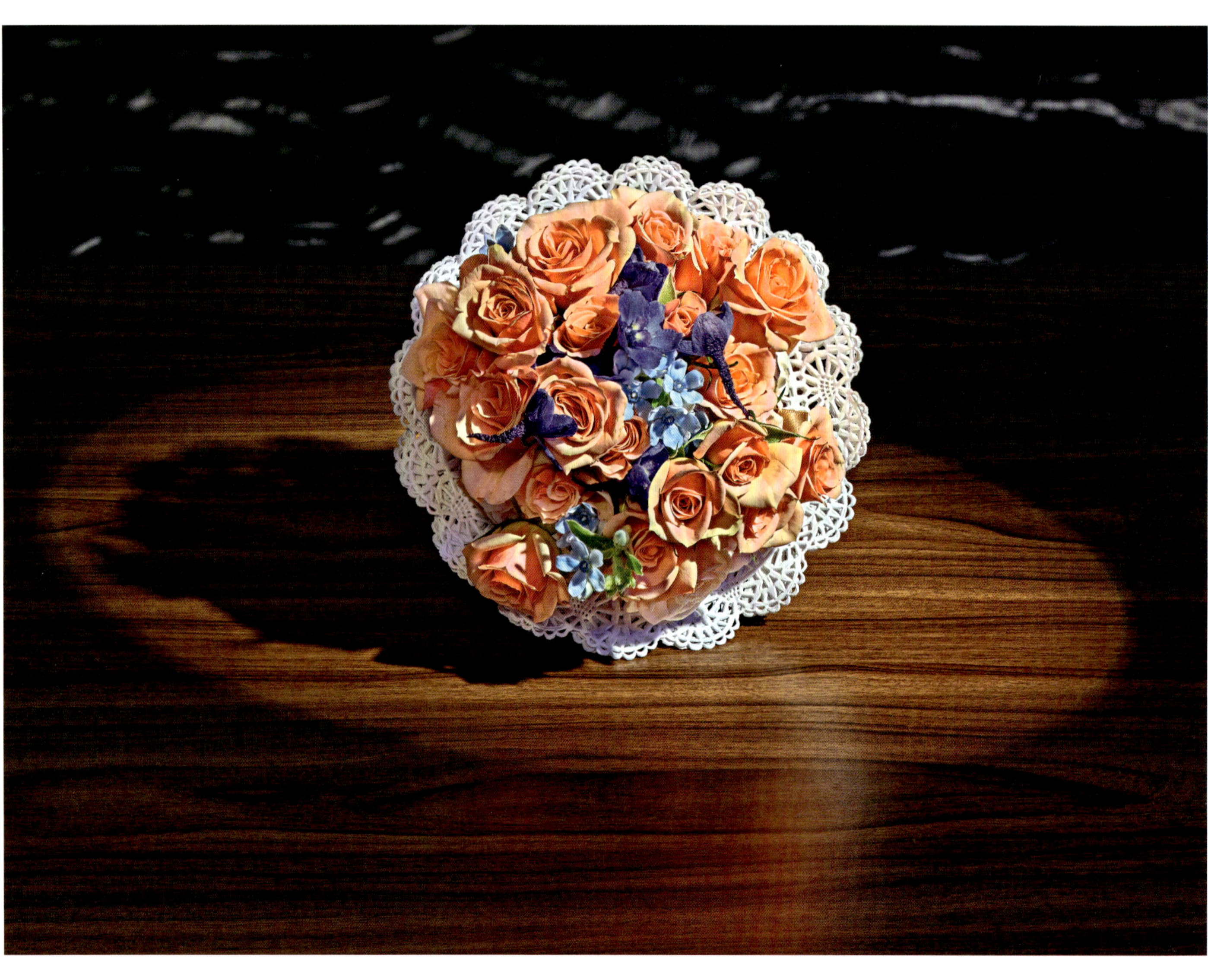

ACKNOWLEDGMENTS

I'm indebted to the assistants who helped me to produce the photographs in this book over the last three years. Talented artists in their own right, they all contributed skill, advice, and patience, in a spirit of collaboration that I will always remember. All of them are graduates of the Massachusetts College of Art and Design, Boston, where I taught for more than thirty years. In chronological order, they are: Robin Myers, Matthew Cronin, Jillian Freyer, Morgen Van Vorst, Alyssa McDonald, and Joseph Ritchie.

The Gifts of Time and Flowers

The artist I live with is not sentimental. Still, on many anniversaries and birthdays, he's brought me flowers. At first, there was the ubiquitous hodgepodge from the local grocery. Then came more expensive mixed sprays from Whole Foods. Eventually, as sales of art began to supplement our teaching and research salaries, there were overpriced arrangements from boutique florists. While I always appreciated Abe's ritual gestures, I often wished he hadn't bothered.

I love flowers. My husband knows that. He has seen me buy them for myself and others, take pleasure in arranging them, and even try to grow them (with rare success). So his thought to bring me something I love always touched me, especially in times when we struggled to be good partners.

But I could never bring myself to tell Abe that I didn't really like mash-ups of different species squeezed into proximity with one another. I preferred my flowers straight up—all of one kind and modernly spare—the better for looking closely at stalks and stems, petals and buds as they slump and dry into a stiff monochrome. I've never had to defend my practice of keeping flowers past their prime or explain how I find their detritus and decay to be as beautiful as their just-cut former selves. Abe is used to living with my disquieting bouquets.

Before Abe decided that alcohol made it hard for him to fulfill simultaneous commitments to parenting young children, teaching full-time, and making art, I used to give him wine to honor special occasions. He never made light of my lack of sophistication in matters of the vine, but I'm pretty sure he saved most of the bottles I gave him for his annual parties for his students.

A few birthdays ago, Abe gave me flowers of a different sort. They came in the form of a photograph, created for the occasion, and it was an image unlike any he had made or given me before. A digital profusion of dozens of exposures fed to a computer for collaboration, the picture rendered a mixed bouquet that I *could* love. It referenced all the elements I relish about still lifes composed of real flowers: time changing the composition, a conversation between parts and the whole, the relationship between a stable container and the shape-shifting nature within. I had a perfect gift of flowers that would last my lifetime.

The pictures that followed *Flowers for Lisa #1* gave me a new lens through which I could see my sometimes-tortured relationship with love and art. The more I looked at them, the more I found myself understanding my husband's entwined passions and preoccupations—his urge to create something as an expression of his tenacious embrace of me, our uncertain world, and life itself.

Abe introduced me to photography. Not long after we met, he took me to the Museum of Modern Art in New York. Our destination was a Harry Callahan exhibition of more than two hundred pictures taken over thirty-five years. Among them were several portraits of Callahan's wife, Eleanor. I couldn't have known then, at twenty, that I would spend my life with an artist, but I was sure I was no Eleanor—ethereal, mythical, comfortable (or so it seemed) on the far side of the camera lens. Still, even as a novice viewer, I remember feeling moved by the relational transaction I believed was taking place in Callahan's rendering of the person he loved. Eleanor seemed to me to be a participant in the picture-making enterprise.

Recently, I paged through the catalog of that exhibition and was struck by an observation John Szarkowski made in his essay. He wrote that the fulcrum of Callahan's work was "located at the point where the potentials of photography and his own private experience intersected." I could say the same about Abe. In this series of images and the many that came before it, it is easy for me to see recurring themes related to exile and a childhood upended by politics; to an imagination let loose by libraries, museums, and music; and to the great release from loneliness that came with a camera. These themes, along with eventful, detailed, and sometimes dark dreams, are what shape the interior landscape that Abe navigates with photography, a medium he loves for its enduring potential to move beyond its apparent boundaries.

It seems to me that photography is a good match for an obsessive thinker. Its technical revolutions in Abe's lifetime, combined with an inner drive to invent, support Abe's photography as a way of making sense of a complex inner reality. The place that relationship takes in the fabric of Abe's creative preoccupations has changed over time, but, like the Eleanor Callahan I imagine, I've always been invited into the artistic process and gradually came to feel comfortable there.

What started as a solution to one year's "What shall I give her for her birthday?" problem turned into a multiyear fixation. Sketches strewn about the studio would suggest images to come. I looked forward to the trial and error, undoubtedly more than Abe did; the struggle to get each image right led to new conversations, to giving each other things to read and looking at the history of art together. Some of the images that resulted evoke aspects of love we seldom celebrate—complexity, darkness, even loneliness. Others suggest the playfulness, reverie, and humor that can form the ballast that sustains intimate connections over time. The pictures illustrate our story.

Early in our life together, I had a different relationship with the obvious third partner in my marriage. Then, art was my beguiling, necessary rival. It had the power to make Abe his best self, to keep him constantly enthralled. It never burdened him with resistance the way I did at times. It waited for him patiently. It's not that it didn't place demands on him; it did, but the pressures felt in the studio never bore the weight or obligation that human interactions do.

In the messy years—when children arrived and friends were lost to AIDS and cancer, when a chronic illness emerged and work that meant so much to me required far more of my dogged effort than my creativity—I was jealous of Abe's art. It offered him escape and nourishment, and he used it for both while doing his part in managing the logistics of our shared, complicated family life. In our marriage's more recent chapters, however, with reflection on how I want to live a hopeful last third of my life, I find myself accepting my husband's essential preoccupation in ways that make me happy, in ways I could never have predicted.

When the *Flowers for Lisa* series began, I was wrapping up a second stint in graduate school and was in an internship as a psychotherapist. I had my own ongoing obsessions, and Abe could certainly see that. *Flowers for Lisa #59* and *#60* feel like faux Rorschachs, and while not a tool I will ever use in the work I do related to early attachment, I felt Abe's reference to a psychological instrument in his photographs signaled his joint attention to matters that are important to me.

As the *Flowers for Lisa* pictures grew in number, I began to worry about the day when the stream of surprises would stop. What would happen when Abe felt he'd said all he had to say about flowers and love and the inevitable impermanence that surrounds us? Would it matter to him that I had come to depend on the ritual reflections he was making visible? His experimental ruminations on love were something I did not want to end.

There were almost daily delights as iterations of final versions piled up. Abe would bring me sketches, drafts, and many almost-but-not-quite-right attempts to extract from his imagination the image that would eventually land in a frame. I recall many nights pulling in from work and wondering what new rendition of flowers might be waiting. I have to pass by Abe's work space to get to our apartment, and as the flower pictures were emerging, I know I initiated more than my usual number of studio visits. I didn't want to wait for the frequent invitation: "Hey, babe, can you come take a look?" And I began to be more assertive in my suggestions for photographs to come. I love the paintings of the German pre-expressionist Paula Modersohn-Becker. "Couldn't she inspire a picture?" I remember pleading more than once, but to no avail. He tried, but Abe was never able to make an homage to Modersohn-Becker that felt right to him. Her frequent use of sunflowers, though, is something Abe incorporates in this series.

The intimate colloquy Abe and I were having as he made his flower pictures felt like an unanticipated reward for having paid our dues. It made me wonder what our lives would be like now had I walked away that time when our firstborn was not yet one and I fled with him to my parents. A rift growing from ruptures Abe and I didn't know how to repair pointed us down a road we did not take, and I'm not sure why. I don't think our choice to remain together was totally conscious, and the terms of our continued engagement weren't especially well navigated. Still, they held us in each other's hearts fervently enough and long enough to withstand what could easily have done us in.

Perhaps not surprisingly, even in the equanimity of the connection we have now, Abe and I still perceive many things differently. *Flowers for Lisa* is no exception. I think that, for Abe, beyond the impetus to make love visible, his project is the manifestation of an artistic dare he posed to himself. With each new idea or technical discovery, through painstaking trial and error, the pictures let Abe delight in what he believes is photography's transforming power to show something new about reality.

I, on the other hand, see *Flowers for Lisa* as evocations of particular passages in our co-biography. To me, they are less still lifes than the portrait of a shared life, a narrative still in the making. To my eye, number 7 is about the year our daughter sang Stephen Sondheim's *Into the Woods*—ad nauseum. Number 3 captures what it felt like to walk nighttime streets in Maine the winter we first met. Number 30 is about a painful argument; number 29, about an argument just starting to be resolved. Number 18 transports me to the artist's residency in Umbria after years in the parenting slog, when the simple joy of eating together outside made stored resentments evaporate. And so on.

While I imbue each image in the series with a sterling memory or weighty resonance, their creator approaches them as exercises in devotion. I see them as keepsakes, proof positive that what connects us is real; Abe treats them as tools for tending the fields of love and commitment. At the crux of things lies perspective, our separate takes on the time we've spent learning to be better together.

The Magnetic Fields is a group of indie musicians whose 1999 triple album, *69 Love Songs*, was a favorite in our household. Stephin Merritt, the group's leader and composer, said in an interview that the songs were actually not about love at all; rather, they were about *love songs*. With seventy-six pictures in my possession now, and as delighted as I am with the objects themselves and the years of shared reverie and close looking that they recall, I know that they are more than *Flowers for Lisa*. As much as they are sincere tokens for me and reflections of many of Abe's passions and idiosyncrasies, I see that they are also carefully created tributes to photography and the expansive place Abe keeps for art in his mind and heart. It is a space I feel happy and lucky to share.

I have no comparable gifts for the person I love. These pictures, what they represent to me, to him, render the ineffable. I can only say that I am grateful, not just for the images and the impetus behind them but most of all for the man who made them. His uncommon vision, his unquestioning acceptance of me and of my aspirations and preoccupations, his faith in us—unwavering always—have been the true gifts in all the time we've shared.

Lisa McElaney
Newton, Massachusetts, October 2017

NOTES ON THE PHOTOGRAPHS

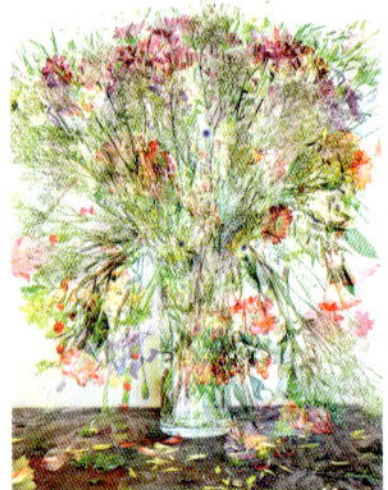

PAGE 31

FLOWERS FOR LISA #1, 2014

I made this first flower photograph to give to Lisa for her birthday. At the time I wasn't thinking of making an extended series on this subject, but I did want to impress her with something that had a bang to it. I experimented with putting together many different renditions of flowers to see what would happen. In traditional film photography, the technique I use here is called a double or multiple exposure: Two or more negatives are sandwiched together to form interesting composite prints. Some of my favorite examples of photographs using this process were made by Harry Callahan.

For *Flowers for Lisa #1*, I shot twenty different small bouquets separately. For each exposure the vase stayed put and I replaced the flowers with a new bunch.

In digital photography, multiple exposures materialize in very unpredictable and strange ways. One stem ends abruptly, to be continued by another; solid-looking petals give way to transparent ones; and new types of floral combinations are created. I welcomed the chance to experiment with this new technology and let it come up with unimagined results. It turns out that in the process I became a watercolorist, too!

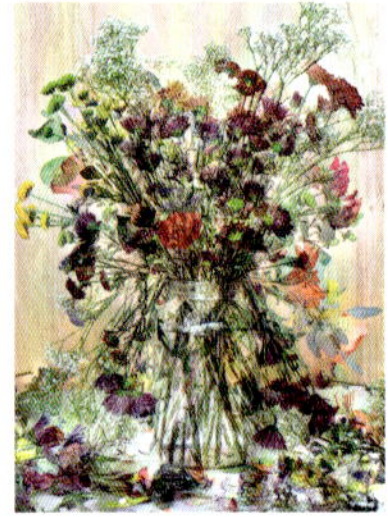

PAGE 32

FLOWERS FOR LISA #2, 2015

Same as number 1 except that I wanted more of an autumnal feeling. And flowers falling under their own weight and age.

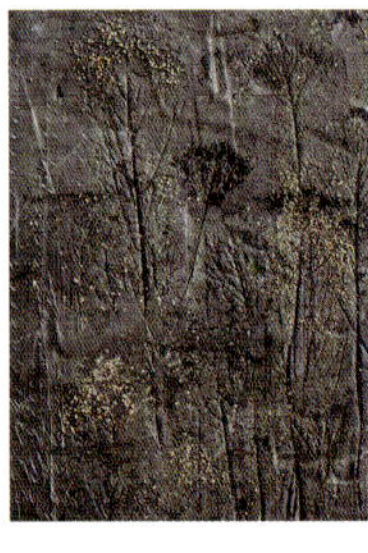

PAGE 33

FLOWERS FOR LISA #3, 2016

I have always admired printmaking. I like how a scratch on metal or wood can leave its ink replica on a paper surface; it's transformative and directly related to the way photography works. For this image I pressed shards of flowers and plants into putty on a board. This style of mark-making reminds me of the petrified ancient fossils and plants that appear in old rocks, giving us a visual trace of the past. With this third picture, I became sure that more image experiments with flowers would follow.

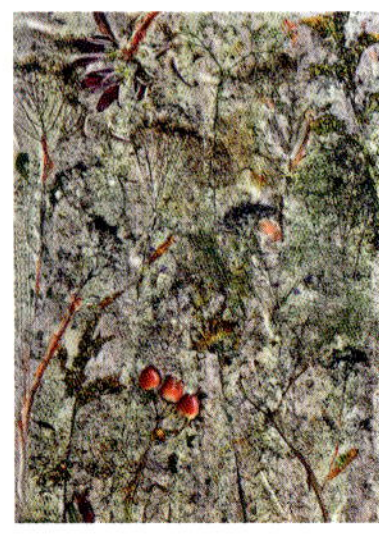

PAGE 35

FLOWERS FOR LISA #4, 2016

Same as number 3 but here I used lighter-colored putty to vary the intensity of color.

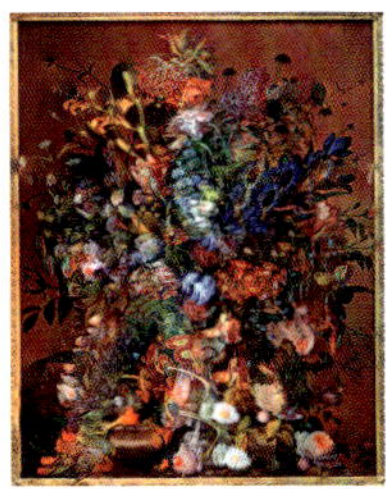

***FLOWERS FOR LISA* #5, 2016**

I used the multiple-exposure technique to play with a painting by Severin Roesen that I photographed at the Philadelphia Museum of Art. When all the separate shots of the painting came together, I loved how the frame remained in place but is now challenged by a number of "escaping" flowers.

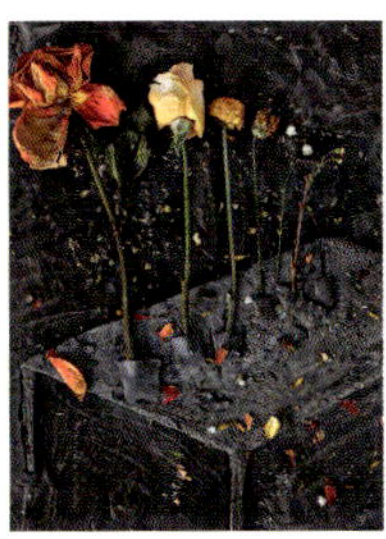

***FLOWERS FOR LISA* #6, 2016**

If I were to make a painting of flowers, I think it might look like this picture. Using my elementary and rough sense of perspective and drawing, I wanted to simulate a child's version of a still life. Playing with perspective shows up a lot in my pictures. This image is the result of a battle between what a lens sees and what an eye tells a hand to draw. Visual awkwardness is something I was after.

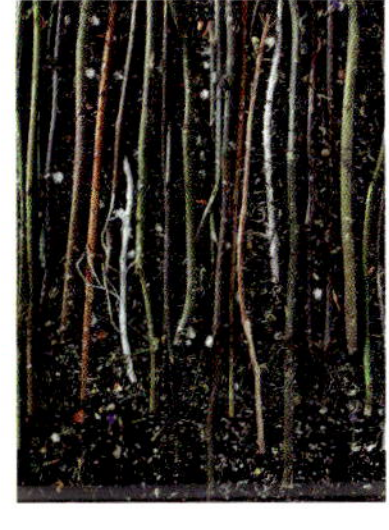

***FLOWERS FOR LISA* #7, 2016**

This image evokes the woods in a fairy tale. I like how flower stems become tree trunks. Illusions like this one are often key in stage design; we know these shapes are not trees, but we convince ourselves that they are. The picture is influenced by certain children's books, especially those of Maurice Sendak, as well as by opera set designs by David Hockney, Robert Wilson, and William Kentridge. Lisa thinks that this photograph looks like a scene in Stephen Sondheim's *Into the Woods*.

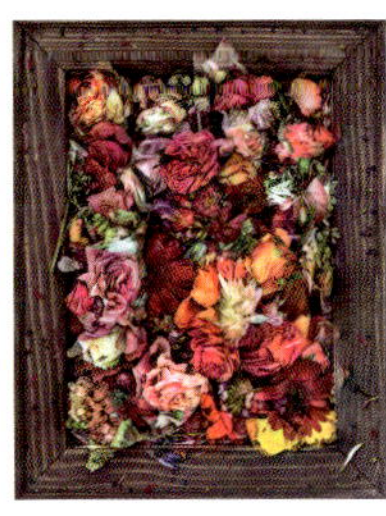

***FLOWERS FOR LISA* #8, 2016**

Numbers 8, 9, and 10 form a set. I wanted to pay homage to trompe l'oeil painters such as Pere Borrell del Caso and William Harnett, whose paintings fooled the eye with exceptionally real-looking objects, so apparently real that the viewer is tempted to touch them. The three photographs are also a nod to William Morris's wallpaper designs. All are the result of just a few multiple exposures, because I wanted the effect to be subtle and painterly. There is no doubt a funereal theme at work in the set. They are conscious attempts to quote from our lives, from when we lost Lisa's mother and my father.

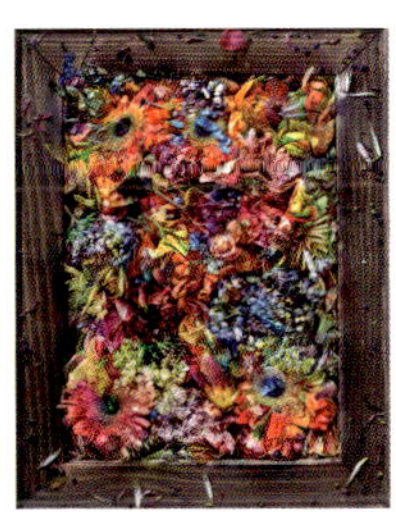

***FLOWERS FOR LISA* #9, 2016**

See number 8.

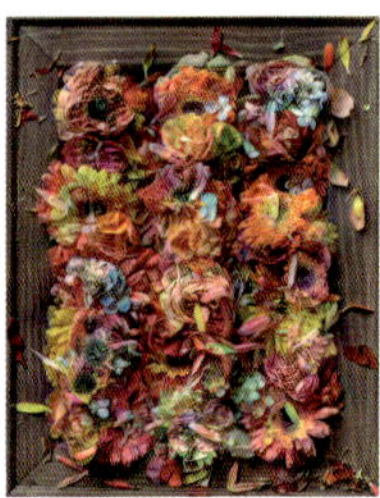

PAGE 42

FLOWERS FOR LISA #10, 2016

See number 8.

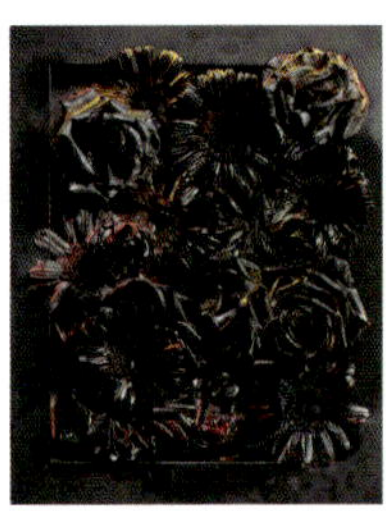

PAGE 43

FLOWERS FOR LISA #11, 2016

I hadn't intended this picture to be part of the set formed by numbers 8, 9, and 10. Looking at it now, though, I find it to be the perfect conclusion to them.

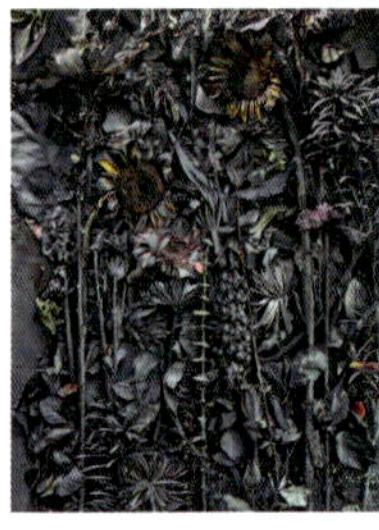

PAGE 45

FLOWERS FOR LISA #12, 2016

British Symbolist painters such as Dante Gabriel Rossetti influence the palette here—it's a picture about nostalgia, the bittersweetness of life and light, and dying. I aimed a small flashlight at the upper left corner to rake the light, to suggest the moribund effect of the sun's going away. It's the half-light of melancholia you feel when you are blue.

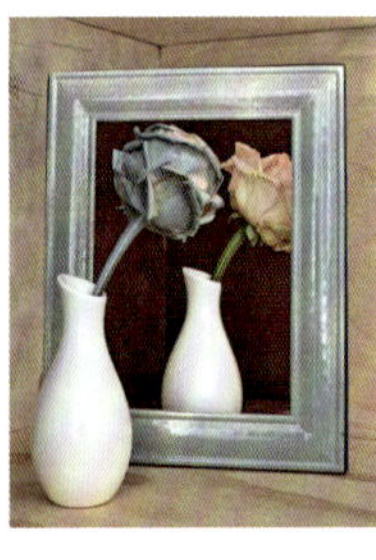

PAGE 46

FLOWERS FOR LISA #13: AFTER RENÉ MAGRITTE, 2016

René Magritte is one of my favorite surrealist painters, mostly because of how he includes everyday objects in his paintings to ask philosophical questions about perception, language, and meaning. For my pictures I borrowed the visual disconnection in the Magritte painting entitled *Not to Be Reproduced*. I placed vases on both sides of a frame to create the illusion of a mirror. There are a few clues that give the illusion away, such as how the rear reddish-painted area makes little sense and the fact that the flower stems don't match. What I like is that the perceived reality of this picture remains a vase looking at itself.

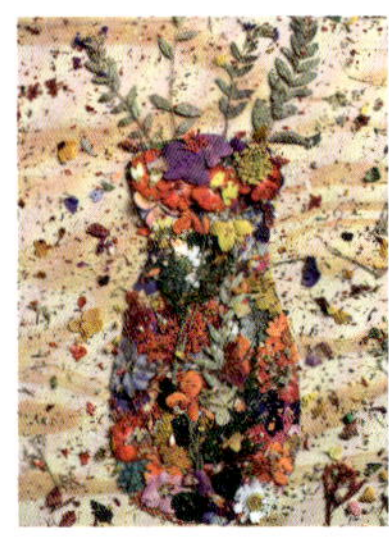

PAGE 47

FLOWERS FOR LISA #14, 2016

This is a picture reversing the role of floral things. Here flowers become the vase. Maybe it's my way of breaking the sometimes rigid nature of language, so that newfound meanings and discoveries can be unearthed in the reshuffling of the names of things.

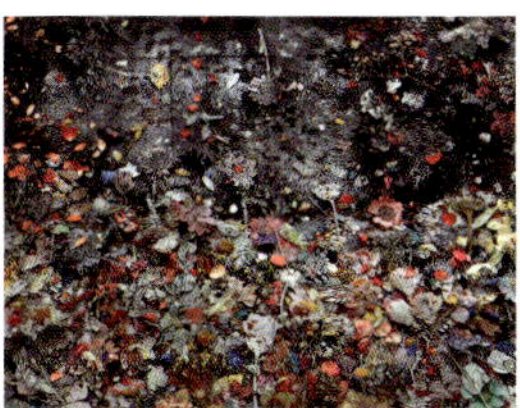

FLOWERS FOR LISA #15, 2016

This photograph suggests the edge of a flower-covered pond. The idea to picture such a scene came from my spending time walking around Claude Monet's pond in Giverny, France. The image is also a nod to Alex Katz's minimal paintings of dark ponds and brooks.

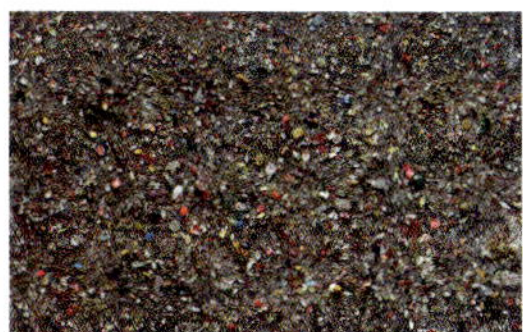

FLOWERS FOR LISA #16, 2016

I created this panorama on a small piece of wood. The surface layers are a mix of paint, flower petals, glue, and dust made by crunching dried flowers. With this image, I hoped to fashion the look of a mysterious path. Jackson Pollock's paintings loom large here. In making this work, I was thinking about the double qualities of chaos and order in his paintings. The image brings to mind a haiku by the poet Kobayashi Issa:

> In this world
> we walk on the roof of hell,
> gazing at flowers.

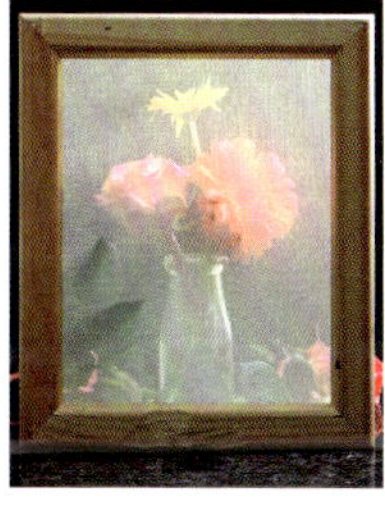

FLOWERS FOR LISA #17, 2016

Here the frame acts as a doorway into a world of softness and diffused light. In some respects this picture feels like a still from Jean Cocteau's film *Beauty and the Beast*, a wonderful work about enchantment and fantasy. It also aspires to the radiant haziness of the still-life photographs Josef Sudek made in his home in Prague.

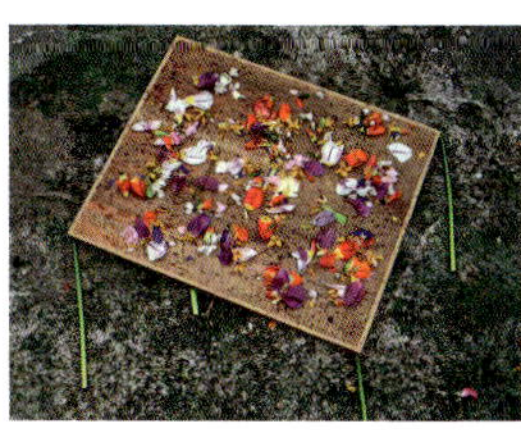

FLOWERS FOR LISA #18: MONET'S GARDENS, GIVERNY, FRANCE, 2016

I made this picture in Claude Monet's gardens in Giverny. I bought flowers like the ones growing there to crumble up, and I used stems to create the illusion of a table. If you look closely, you may notice that it had started to rain during my exposure. All the layers in this image remind me of an observation by the architect Eero Saarinen: "Always design a thing by considering it in its next larger context—a chair in a room, a room in a house, a house in an environment, an environment in a city plan."

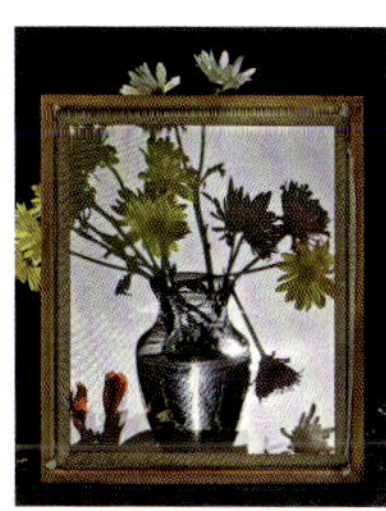

FLOWERS FOR LISA #19, 2016

For this photograph I used a silk-screen frame of the sort printmakers employ. The lovely thing about the silk is that its translucency makes nice shadows that combine with the object that produces those shadows. This frame approximates how large-format photographic cameras capture the world (upside down) on their ground glass. I like the way that, on the edges of the frame, some of the flowers in the image transform from shadow to apparently solid.

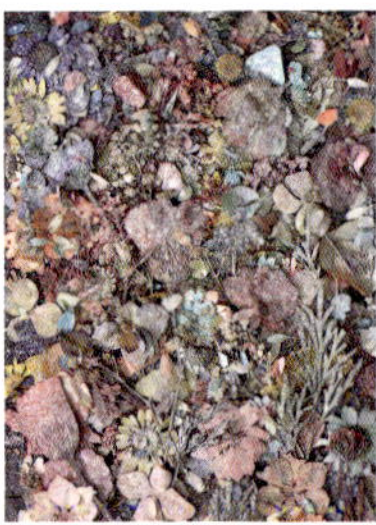

***FLOWERS FOR LISA #20*, 2016**

See numbers 15 and 16.

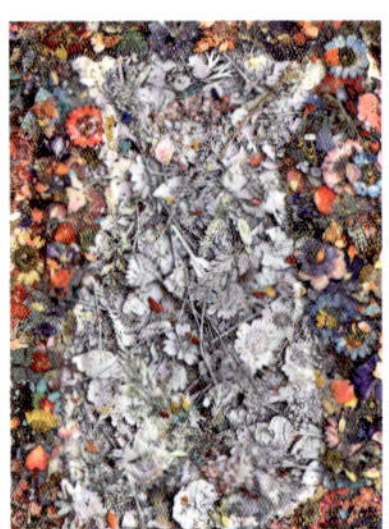

***FLOWERS FOR LISA #21*, 2016**

A variation of number 14 and inclusive of the material of number 20.

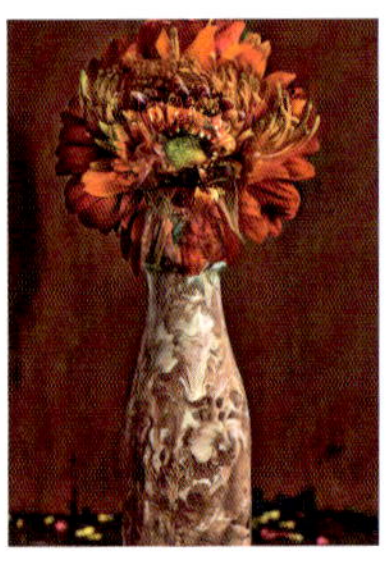

***FLOWERS FOR LISA #22*, 2016**

Here I wanted to make a portrait of a freak of nature. I'm pretty sure that I intended the palette to point to some underworld, scatological thing. The image is also an oblique reference to Chaim Soutine's paintings.

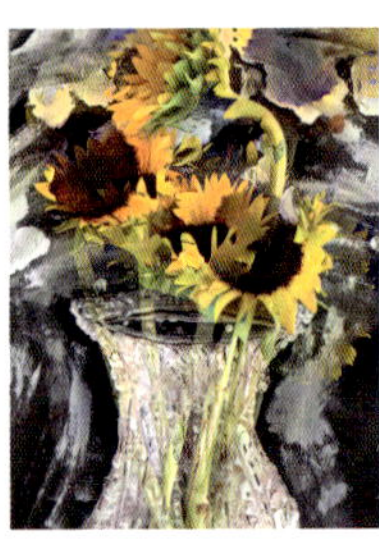

***FLOWERS FOR LISA #23: FOUR SUNFLOWERS*, 2016**

This is the first picture in the series that combines multiple exposures of real flowers, drawings, and paint. It was exciting to see these elements integrated in one picture.

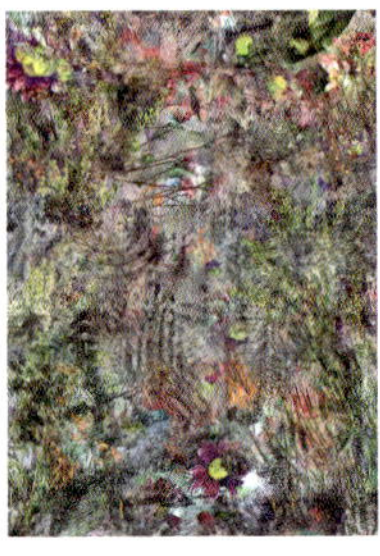

***FLOWERS FOR LISA #24*, 2016**

This image comes from multiple exposures of flower impressions and digital scans of hand painting on glass. It presents a picture of the experience of walking in a forest, seeing near and far and up and down. Odilon Redon made paintings with enchanting translucencies that approach the mystical. I aimed for something like that. My picture also reminds me of the transporting power of certain stained glass windows.

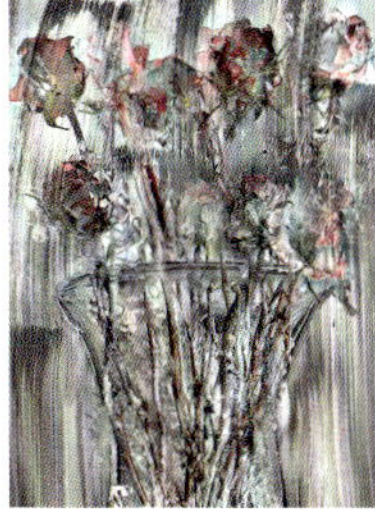

FLOWERS FOR LISA #25: SIX ROSES, 2016

This is another image for which I used multiple exposures of roses and paint, changing the flowers for each exposure. I painted the vase, too. I think it's the most painterly picture I have made so far. I used very little color, to give the picture the metallic and neutral look of a drawing and perhaps the feel of a Gerhard Richter painting.

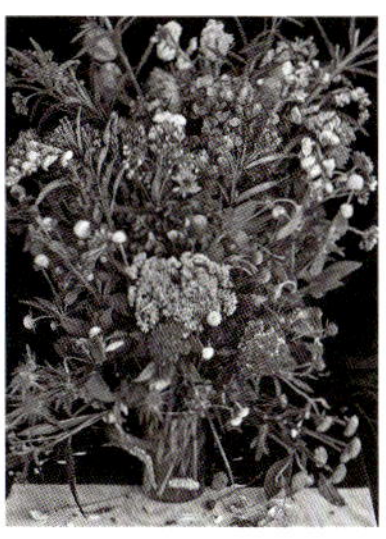

FLOWERS FOR LISA #26, 2016

Seventeenth-century Dutch floral paintings are a big influence on many of my photographs in the *Flowers for Lisa* series. In some works by Jan Brueghel the Elder and Roelandt Savery, among others, the flowers in vases are impossibly thick and high. For this still life I made the bouquets very tall and dense by positioning several layers of flowers at various depths and heights, one behind the other. Keeping the sharpness of focus the same throughout added to the illusion of a single gigantic bouquet.

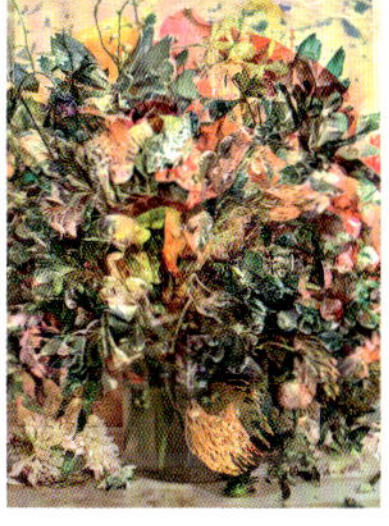

FLOWERS FOR LISA #27, 2016

Same as numbers 1 and 2 but a very fancy bouquet that a neighbor brought home from a wedding.

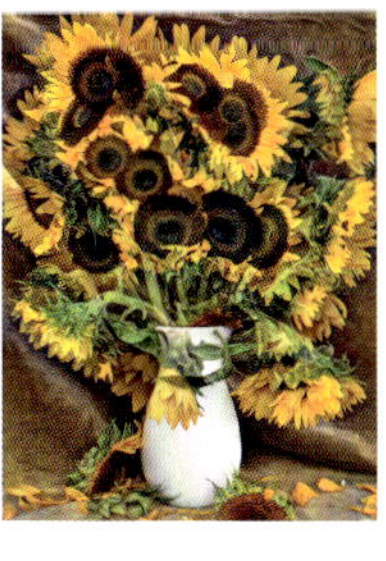

FLOWERS FOR LISA #28, 2016

There are multiple exposures in this image, but the effect is rather minimal. Van Gogh's sunflower paintings are the motivation for the picture. I like that it appears just a touch unnatural.

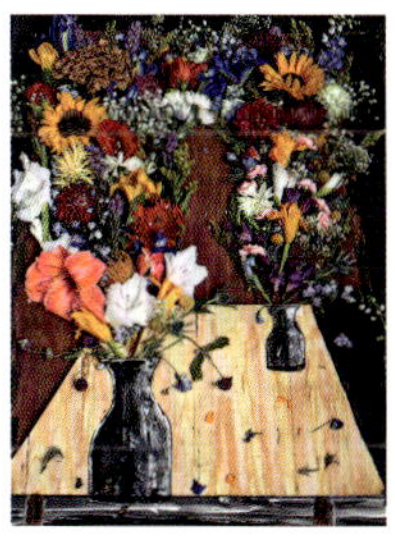

FLOWERS FOR LISA #29, 2016

See number 6.

I fabricated this space by using a forced perspective to fool the eye into believing that the bouquet on the right is farther back than the one on the left. The image has the feel of a childlike painting by a grown man. I like the statement attributed to Picasso: "Every child is an artist. The problem is how to remain an artist once he grows up."

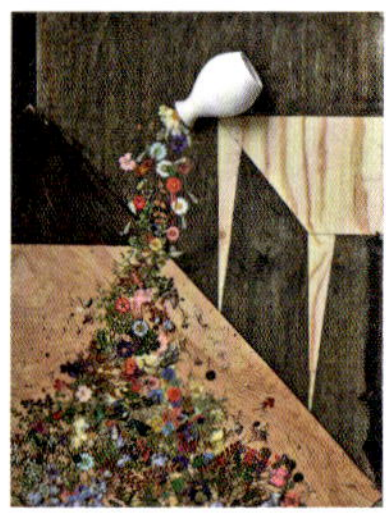

***FLOWERS FOR LISA #30*, 2016**

I'm obsessed with images and ideas about time. Some of my favorite photographs in the history of the medium have to do with studies of motion in time.

The photographs of Eadweard Muybridge, Étienne-Jules Marey, Harold Edgerton, and Berenice Abbott have all influenced my meditations on this subject. What strikes me as really weird in this photograph is that while it simulates stopped motion and the force of gravity, neither one of these things is present.

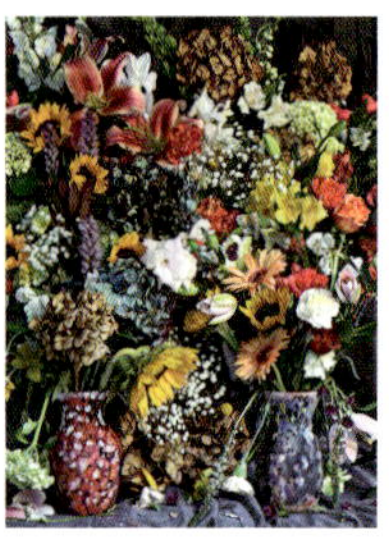

***FLOWERS FOR LISA #31*, 2016**

Photographs number 31, 32, and 33 are variations on a similar bouquet. Their construction is similar to that of number 26, with its exaggerated depth and height. All the flowers are focused sharply from near to far. I also used a telephoto lens, which flattened the feeling of depth in the picture. With these photographic techniques I was hoping to render an eerie majesty and volume in the giant bouquets.

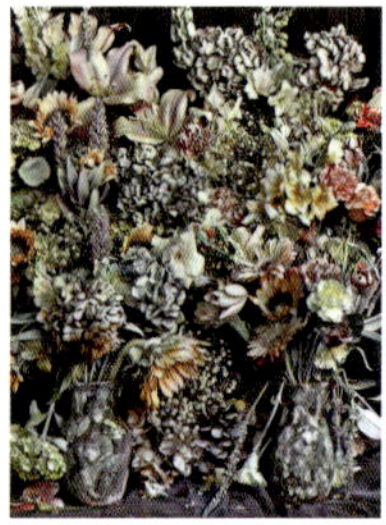

***FLOWERS FOR LISA #32*, 2016**

Same bouquet as in number 31 but painted whitish and with minor changes in arrangement because of wilting.

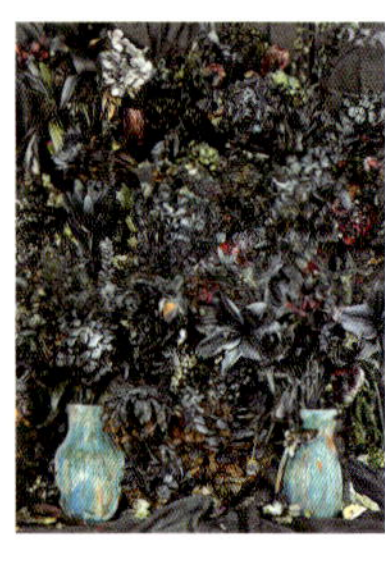

***FLOWERS FOR LISA #33*, 2016**

Same bouquet as in number 31 but painted with black.

The three bouquets in numbers 31, 32, and 33 remind me of how theme and variation are structured in music: A musical phrase is presented and then repeated in altered forms.

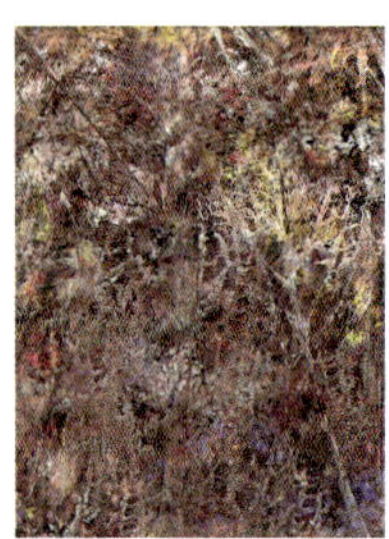

***FLOWERS FOR LISA #34: CLICHÉ VERRE*, 2016**

Cliché verre denotes a "glass negative" in French. The nineteenth-century French painters Jean-Baptiste-Camille Corot, Charles-François Daubigny, and Jean-François Millet, among others, used this method of making prints. It involves scratching drawings onto ink-coated glass. The plate is then placed on top of photographic paper and exposed to light. The result is a print born equally from printmaking and photography.

Here I pressed stems, petals, and other flower parts onto variously colored inks on glass. I then scanned the glass and printed the image.

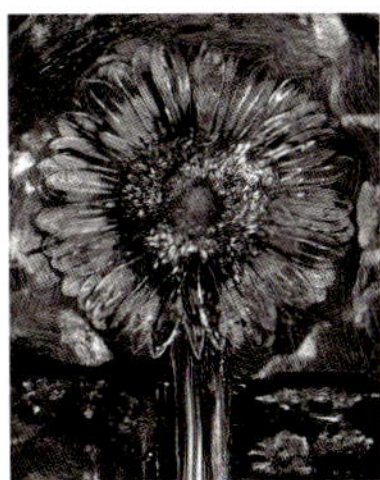

***FLOWERS FOR LISA #35: CLICHÉ VERRE*, 2017**

Another *cliché verre* picture. I applied black ink to a glass plate and then pressed a sunflower on it to leave its impression. I worked other parts of the plate to evoke weather and a territory behind the flower. In its effect, this huge flower rising out of a barren landscape reminds me of *The Colossus*, a painting by Francisco de Goya.

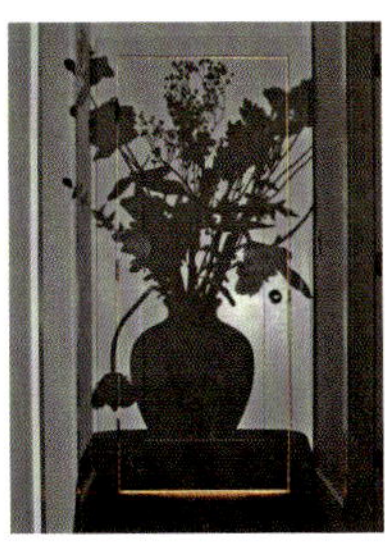

***FLOWERS FOR LISA #36*, 2017**

I set up this picture by putting a vase with flowers on a table and lighting and it from behind to throw a shadow on a doorway. The idea for this photograph came from my camera obscura experiments, in which I'm able to project the outside world into interiors.

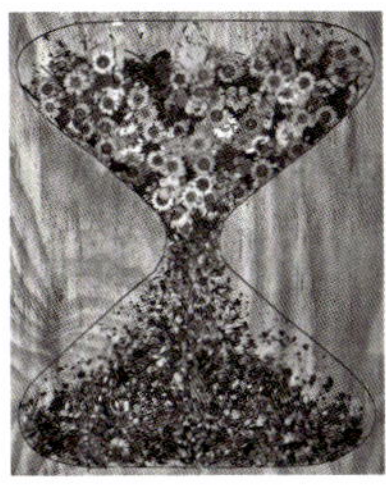

***FLOWERS FOR LISA #37*, 2017**

In earlier photographs I tried to picture time itself. All photography embodies the phenomenon of time in one form or another—it's fundamental to the medium! This version of time suggests that at every moment we are passing from whole to particle. I think that it also illustrates the formulation commonly assigned to Einstein: "Mass cannot be created or destroyed, it can only be changed from one form to another."

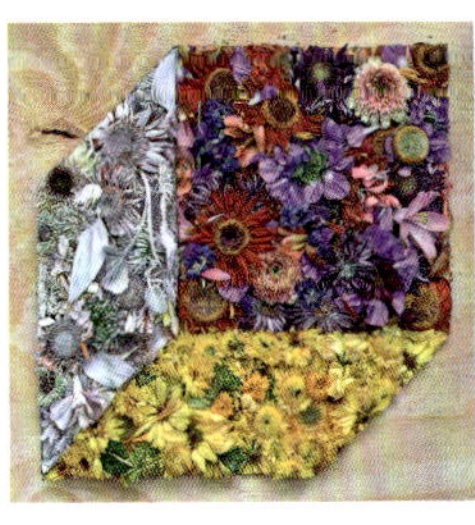

***FLOWERS FOR LISA #38*, 2017**

Here is a photograph of a common optical illusion, made with flowers. These well-known visual tricks provide access to ways of understanding how our brains can be "wrong" in perceiving the world.

Sol Lewitt made works based on platonic solid forms that transcend simple geometry to become a wordless language. This is my way of trying that.

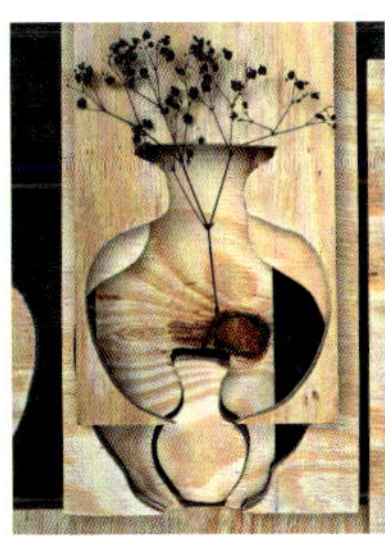

***FLOWERS FOR LISA #39: AFTER GEORGES BRAQUE*, 2017**

Cubism changed the world. This is my two cents, in gratitude. I cut plywood in various vase shapes, not knowing exactly what I would assemble. I can't tell you how much fun it was to play with these forms—for hours! I know I'm not unique in my love for plywood; Donald Judd created perfect works that make this humble material seem eternal.

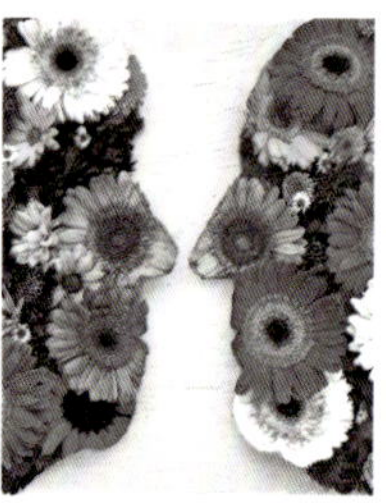

PAGE 79

FLOWERS FOR LISA #40: LISA AND ME, 2017

This image mashes (imperfectly) the optical illusion of two silhouettes turning into a vase with a vision of our marriage. It is also my adaptation of Piero della Francesca's double portrait paintings of the Duke and Duchess of Urbino.

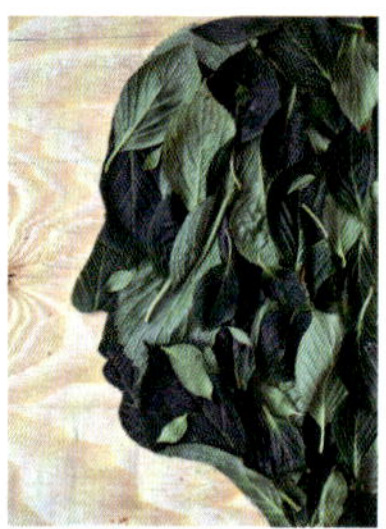

PAGE 80

FLOWERS FOR LISA #41: BRADY, 2017

Lisa and I have children, and I wanted to include them in my meditation on our marriage. This is our son, Brady.

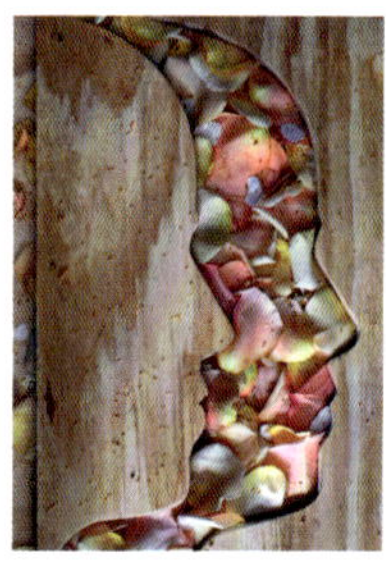

PAGE 81

FLOWERS FOR LISA #42: LAURA, 2017

Our daughter, Laura.

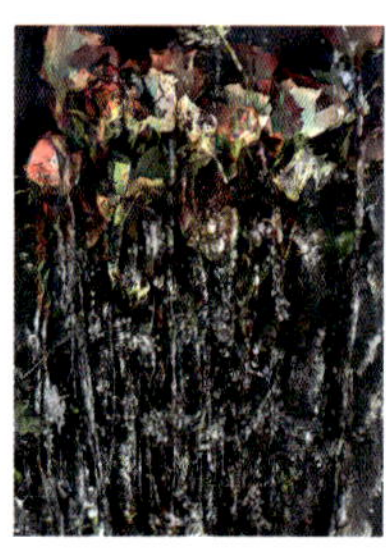

PAGE 82

FLOWERS FOR LISA #43, 2017

I think of this image as a painful walk in a gigantic burned-out forest. Maybe my mind was dwelling on the many wildfires in California at the time and their effect on perishable things like flowers. I actually burned parts of this arrangement.

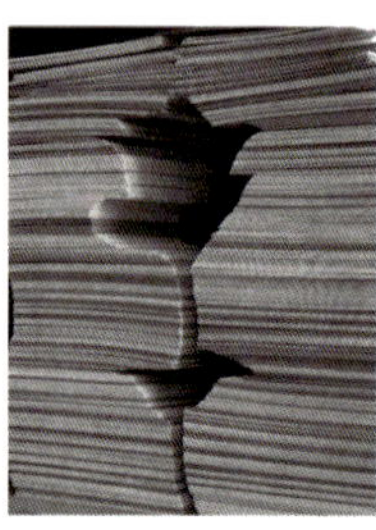

PAGE 83

FLOWERS FOR LISA #44, 2017

This image derives from earlier work I made about books and paper. I use paper the way sculptors use marble: to make solid renderings of people, things, and, in this case, a flower. I incorporate humble materials such as plywood and paper in my work because they can stand for things both common and grand at the same time. In his *Adagia*, Wallace Stevens wrote something I like a lot: "The real is only the base. But it is the base."

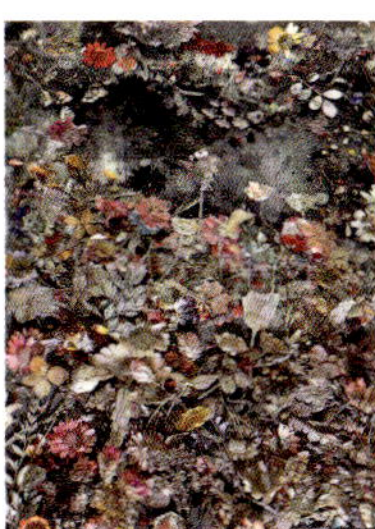

***FLOWERS FOR LISA* #45, 2017**

See numbers 15, 16, and 20.

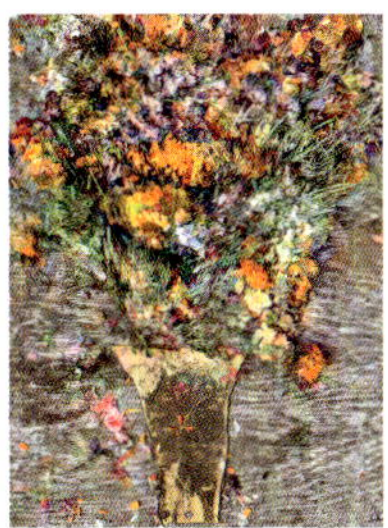

***FLOWERS FOR LISA* #46, 2017**

Same process as in numbers 1 and 2 but with a rougher result. Made on old wood with a cardboard vase.

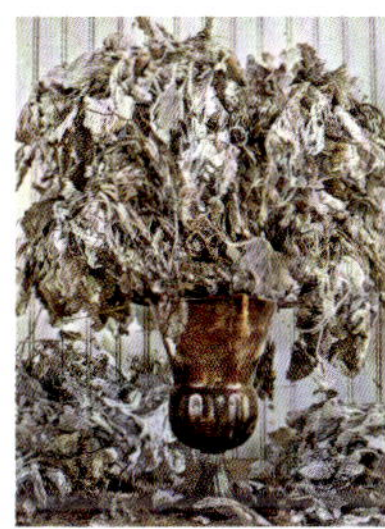

***FLOWERS FOR LISA* #47, 2017**

These are wilted flowers gathered from a garden and given a fresh composition in a makeshift bouquet. For me, this vase with dead flowers serves a function similar to that of Keats's Grecian urn. Sometimes the right object can spark meditations about life and death.

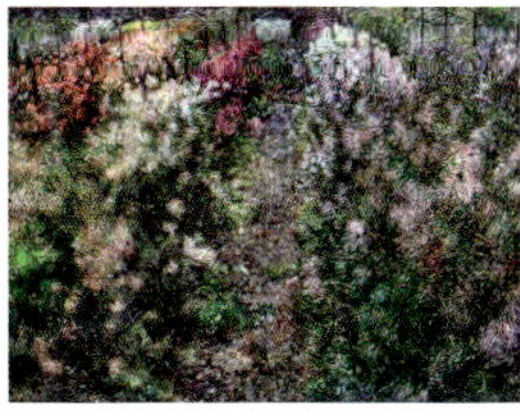

***FLOWERS FOR LISA* #48: TENT-CAMERA IMAGE, 2017**

I made this photograph at the Floret Flower Farm in Washington state. I used my tent camera, a device I invented to make landscape pictures that is part tent, part periscope. This contraption allows me to project nearby landscape views onto the ground inside the tent. A sandwich of the view and the ground makes for many interesting and painterly photographic versions of the world.

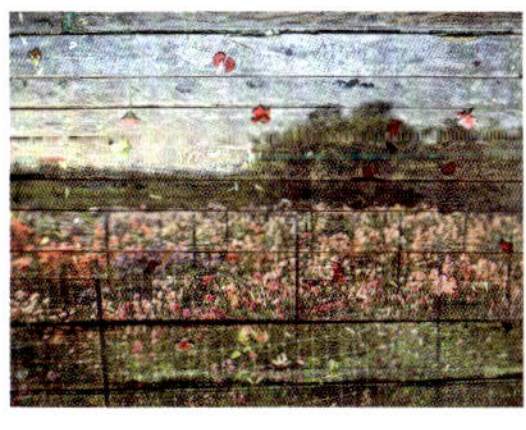

***FLOWERS FOR LISA* #49: TENT-CAMERA IMAGE, 2017**

Same as number 48.

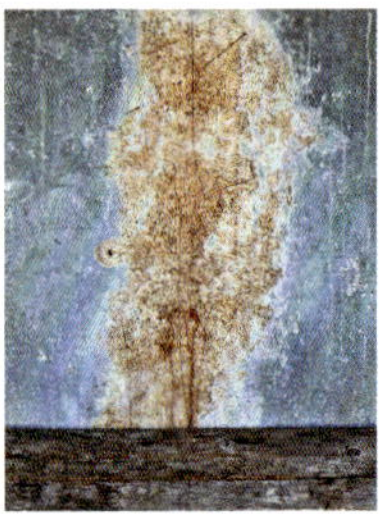

FLOWERS FOR LISA #50: RUST, 2017

Things in the world occasionally bring to mind the shapes of flowers. This is rust on a metal door that really felt like something organic growing against a beautifully speckled sky. The image is also my way of declaring: "It's a flower if I say it is."

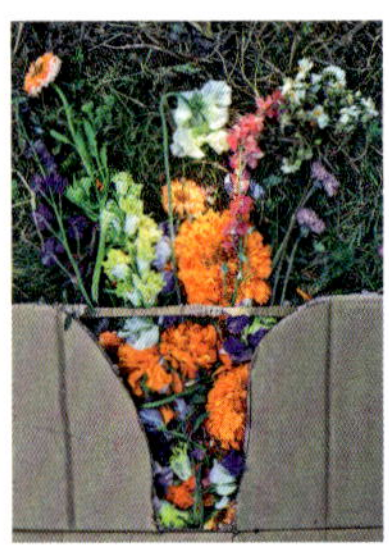

FLOWERS FOR LISA #51, 2017

A very quickly improvised still life outdoors. The late-day sunlight was going fast. These conditions placed me in the role of a painter working from life while running out of light.

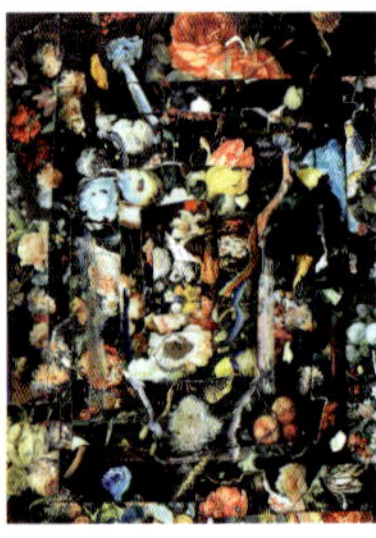

FLOWERS FOR LISA #52: AFTER HIERONYMUS BOSCH, 2017

In past work I've experimented with collage techniques, cutting and ripping all kinds of illustrations and pasting them together to be photographed. The elements here include floral illustrations from art books, parts of real flowers, and some of my own painting. To me, this composite resembles certain Hieronymus Bosch paintings. Unlike them, however, my image contains no end-of-the-world visions. Perhaps it is the cutting itself that suggests the horror in Bosch's work.

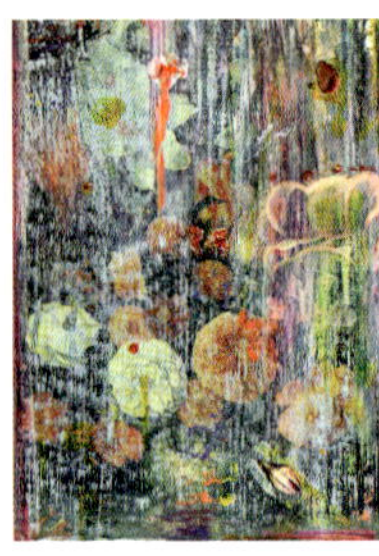

FLOWERS FOR LISA #53, 2017

This image pictures a page from an art book with floral illustrations on which I painted my own decorations. My brushstrokes inadvertently resemble rain as it appears in some well-known prints by Utagawa Hiroshige. This photograph might also be described as a palimpsest—a creation in which a new work of art is formed through its superimposition over another older piece, such that traces of the original work show through.

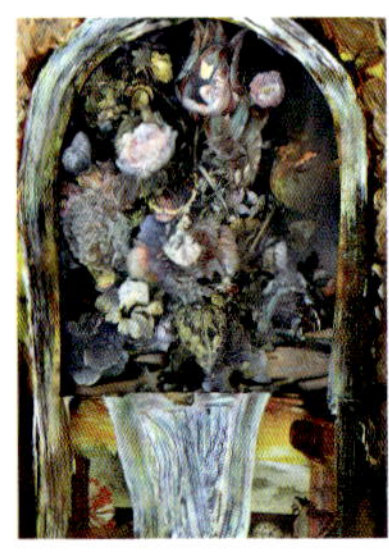

FLOWERS FOR LISA #54, 2017

I think that this may be the most complicated picture in the series. It's composed of multiple exposures of floral illustrations and my painting of the vase and corridor. I like the crudely elegant new space suggested here. I also love how wet acrylic and oil paints look when photographed. That's beautiful in itself.

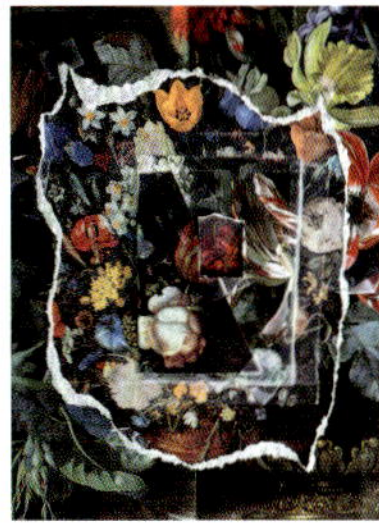

FLOWERS FOR LISA #55, 2017

See number 52.

More collage work. This one tries to show an excavation, much as archaeology reveals layers of history. I lit this picture from the side to give it a marked three-dimensional look. Everything in this image feels tactile, including the Scotch tape.

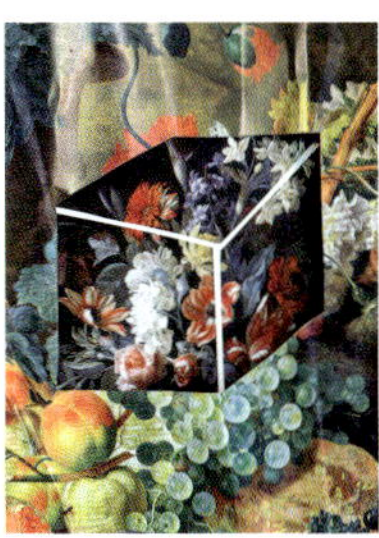

FLOWERS FOR LISA #56, 2017

Another collage idea. In this one I like the idea of two divergent things forming something new. Polyphony in music works a bit that way: A number of disparate voices are orchestrated to sound like one. Perhaps this is my visual response to that idea. It could also be a scene from my imaginary light opera about a weightless platonic shape floating above a seventeenth-century Dutch forest. The opera might be entitled *The Magic Cube.*

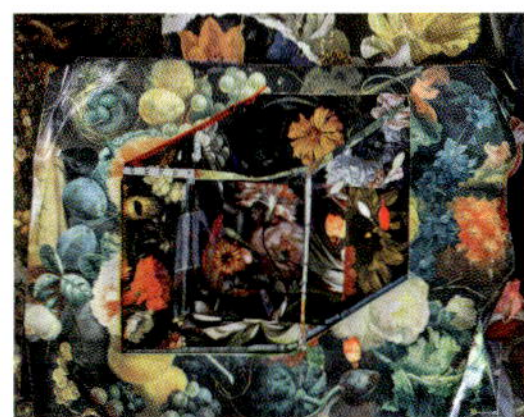

FLOWERS FOR LISA #57, 2017

Same as number 56 but more complicated.

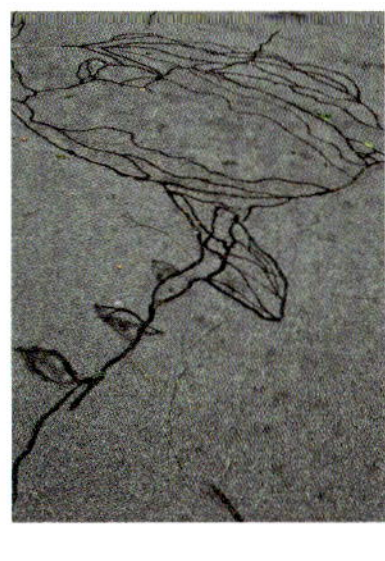

FLOWERS FOR LISA #58, 2017

Our house faces a parking lot that I see every day from our second-floor bedroom. One morning this shape in the asphalt struck me as a half-formed flower, which I finished by adding some black ink the next morning. My tripod was close to twelve feet high when I shot this.

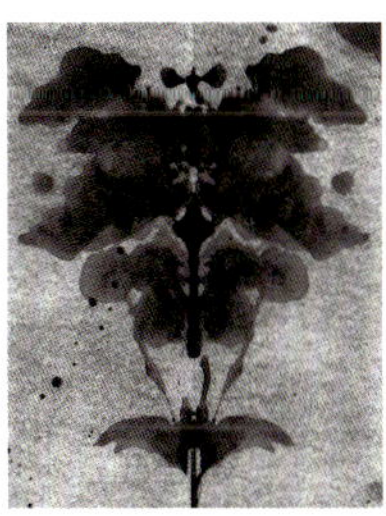

FLOWERS FOR LISA #59, 2017

This is my nod to the psychological test developed by Hermann Rorschach. I wanted to come up with symmetrical blots that gave flowers a psychological feel. I made dozens, with little success. This one came close to looking like a plant of sorts. Lisa is a therapist, and she thinks and cares a lot about the human condition. The two Rorschach pictures, numbers 59 and 60, are my acknowledgment of her profession.

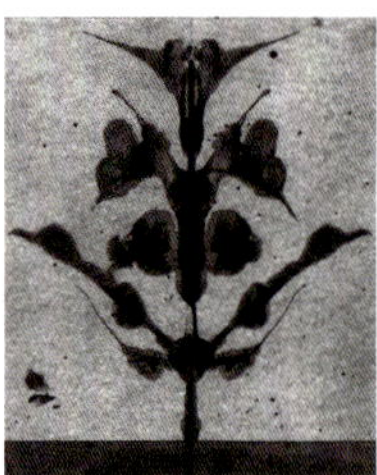

***FLOWERS FOR LISA #60*, 2017**

See number 59.

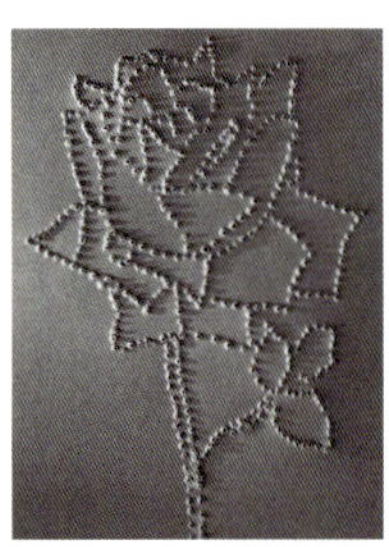

***FLOWERS FOR LISA #61: AFTER ELLSWORTH KELLY*, 2017**

I like Ellsworth Kelly's drawings of flowers and plants very much; they have such simple, effortless energy. I copied one of his drawings and then punctured it along the lines. The perforations, lit from the side, feel bold. This image made me think a lot about how all artists are influenced by artists before them—about how, in the process of feeding on the past, an artist may find his own footing. Robert Rauschenberg's famous *Erased de Kooning* drawing is a case in point.

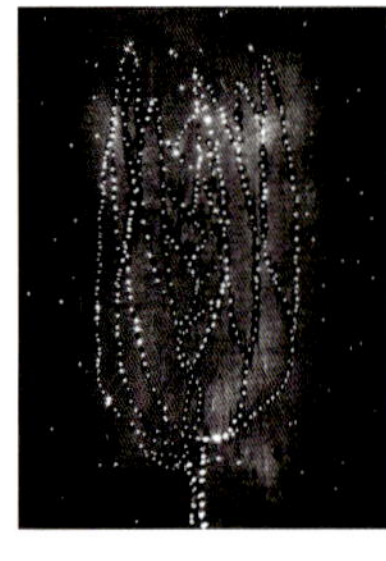

***FLOWERS FOR LISA #62: AFTER LOUISE BOURGEOIS*, 2017**

Louise Bourgeois made some curious and provocative drawings of creatures and things. My work copies a flower she drew. As in number 61, I perforated the lines of my copy, but since I wanted the image to be distinct from my Kelly-inspired picture, I lit this one from behind to achieve the appearance of the drawing mingling with a night sky.

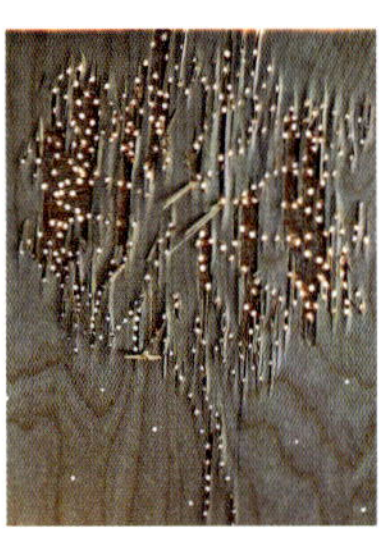

***FLOWERS FOR LISA #63*, 2017**

Same as numbers 61 and 62. Drilled plywood. More woodshop than Photoshop.

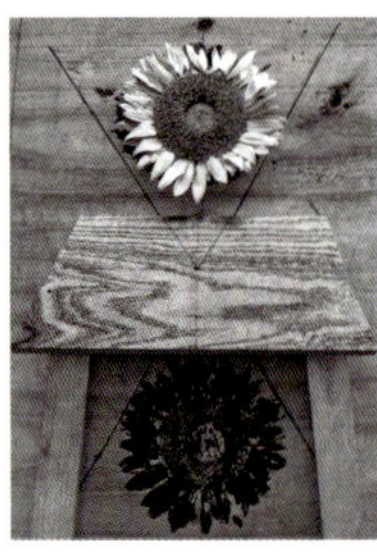

***FLOWERS FOR LISA #64: AFTER ALBRECHT DÜRER*, 2017**

In the late fifteenth and early sixteenth centuries, Albrecht Dürer made prints and drawings of machines that helped artists to draw from life. My picture pays homage to these primitive optical aids, which I consider the precursors of photographic cameras. This image also touches on the phenomenon of the camera obscura. In a totally dark chamber, make a small opening in a window facing outside and you will see the outer world projected upside down on the inside walls.

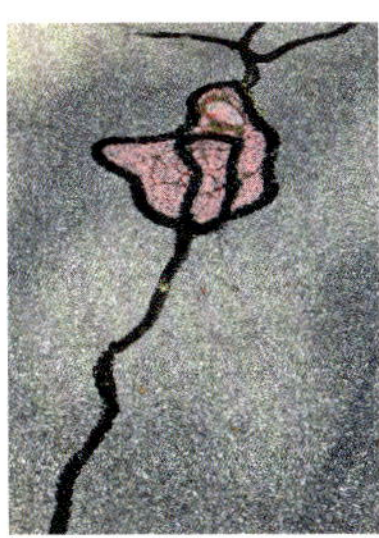

***FLOWERS FOR LISA* #65, 2017**

See number 58.

For this one I did not draw any extra black lines. Instead I colored in the tulip with pink chalk, as I might have done in my childhood.

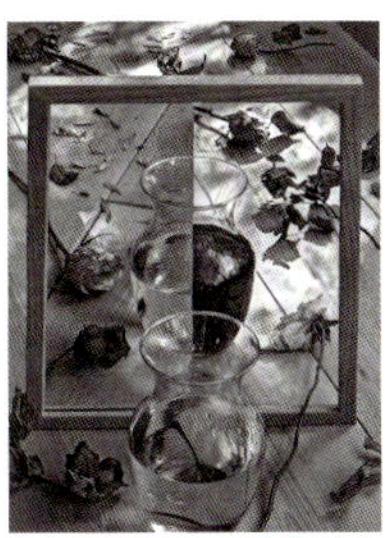

***FLOWERS FOR LISA* #66: *AFTER LEWIS CARROLL*, 2017**

In Lewis Carroll's *Through the Looking-Glass*, Alice steps into a mirror and discovers that the world on the other side is reversed. This picture is about multiple optical tricks. The left half of the frame holds a mirror. The right side is clear glass.

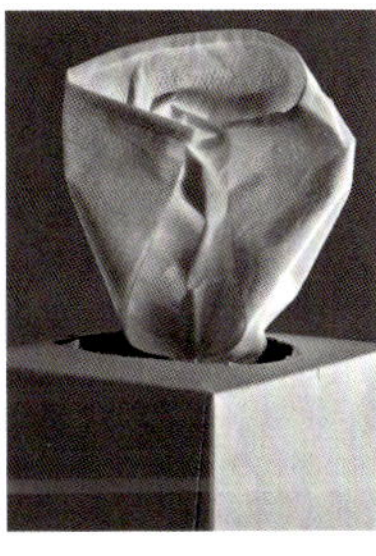

***FLOWERS FOR LISA* #67: *AFTER IMOGEN CUNNINGHAM*, 2017**

Imogen Cunningham made daring and sensual photographs of flowers. The pleasure of those pictures lies in the perfect balance of innovation and beauty that she achieved. One cannot photograph flowers without thinking about her.

This box of Kleenex is constantly producing works of art. Sometimes a Constantin Brancusi pops out. Then a Betty Woodman or an Arlene Shechet. For this tribute I was aiming for a particular flower, and I won't tell you how many boxes I ended up using to get it right.

It's also a preview of number 68.

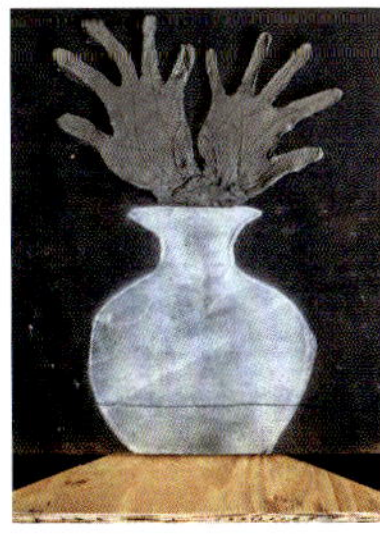

***FLOWERS FOR LISA* #68, 2017**

There is no question that *Flowers for Lisa* activated a painting gene in me. I often dream of making abstract paintings that are (in the dream) fabulously beautiful, but I am too timid to ever call myself a painter. I lack almost everything needed to make a successful painting. Whatever paint I have used in these photographs has always been in concert with photography. Here, as in other images in the series, sculpture shows up, too. I'm lucky that this photograph won't be judged by its three-dimensional subject. For me, it is the photographic rendition and not the object that carries the weight.

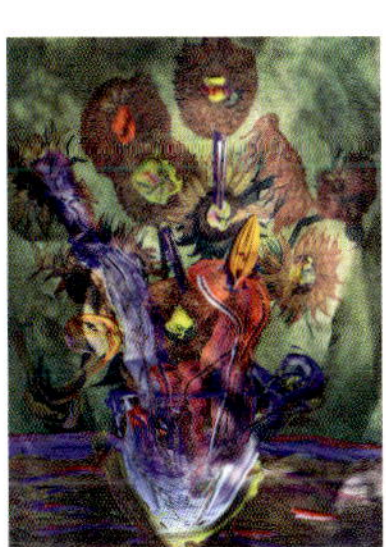

***FLOWERS FOR LISA* #69: *AFTER VINCENT VAN GOGH*, 2017**

What a sacrilege this image is! I took a book page illustrating a Van Gogh sunflower painting and added my own brushstrokes to it. I also lit segments of the page to create discrete new highlights. I hope that I made a brand-new thing out of my love for Vincent's flowers.

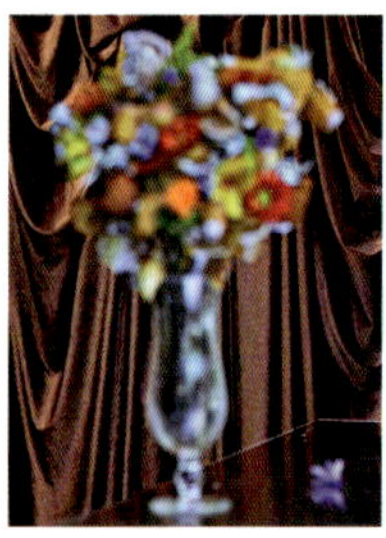

PAGE 115

***FLOWERS FOR LISA #70: AFTER DOUGLAS SIRK*, 2017**

This image is not taken directly from any scene in Douglas Sirk's *All That Heaven Allows*. I think, however, that it came from the spirit of that film, which was shot in arresting Technicolor. It has been said that Sirk liked to use certain strong colors to suggest repressed emotions and troubles in his female characters. This picture's exaggerated color may be my way of pointing to domestic unease.

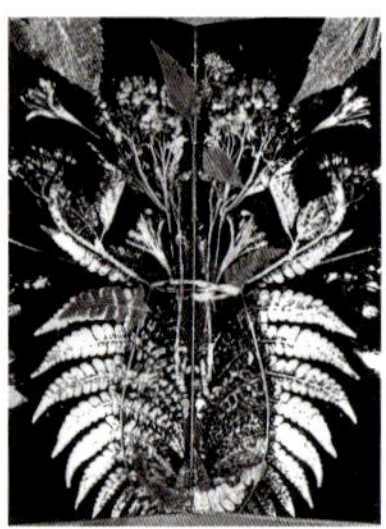

PAGE 117

***FLOWERS FOR LISA #71: AFTER ANNA ATKINS*, 2017**

Anna Atkins studied the botanical world closely and found photography, at the time of its invention, to be a perfect renderer of what she loved. Her cyanotypes look as fresh today as when they were made in the 1840s. My photograph has to do with the type of photography that's used for scientific description. I made my image by inking plants on both sides, placing halves of them on a book of blank pages, and then pressing so that a perfectly symmetrical image resulted. Like Atkins, I wanted to let nature draw itself.

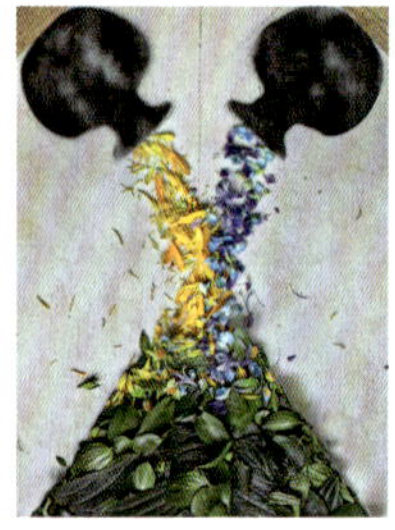

PAGE 118

***FLOWERS FOR LISA #72*, 2017**

Like number 30, this image simulates gravity. In this free fall I wanted to show a drama based on color theory—a simple lesson about the green you get when blue and yellow mix. It's also a symbolic painting about the history of Lisa and me—so far!

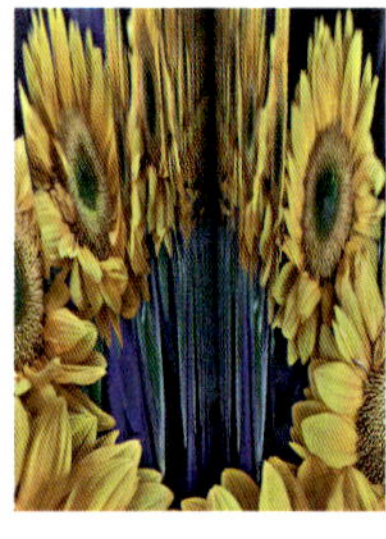

PAGE 119

***FLOWERS FOR LISA #73*, 2017**

I created this picture by placing sunflowers in front of one of those trick distorting mirrors. André Kertèsz made elegant abstract photographs with such mirrors. The image reminds me of the psychedelic posters I had hanging in my dorm room during my college days. Even back then I preferred art over the drugs. The photograph is an attempt to arrive at something hallucinogenic using straight photographic methods. Since my beginnings in photography, this has often been my approach.

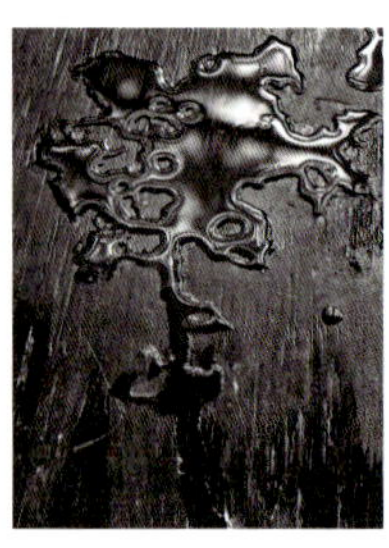

PAGE 120

***FLOWERS FOR LISA #74: AFTER MANUEL ÁLVAREZ BRAVO*, 2017**

I love how backlit water picks up and solidifies light—it looks like mercury. Manuel Álvarez Bravo made an amazing picture, entitled *El umbral*, of a woman's feet next to a puddle of water. I saw it early on in my career and it knocked me out; it's one of those images that made me want to be a photographer. Puddles, it turns out, can also create flowers.

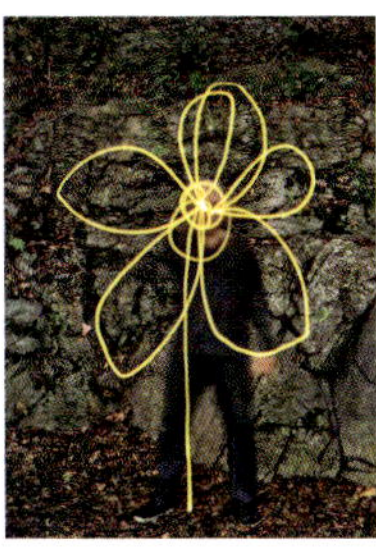

***FLOWERS FOR LISA** #75, 2017*

There is a famous long-exposure photograph, taken by Gjon Mili, of Picasso drawing flowers with a flashlight. Since I am no Picasso, it took me all evening to get it right.

I'm glad that I finally show up, somewhat hidden, near the very end of the project. The main thing is the yellow flower, not me. I really like the advice supposedly given by Konstantin Stanislavsky: "Love art in yourself, and not yourself in art."

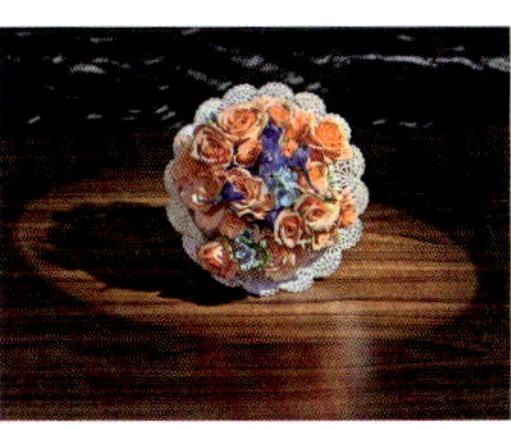

***FLOWERS FOR LISA** #76: AFTER HITCHCOCK'S VERTIGO, 2017*

In the film *Vertigo*, Kim Novak buys a nosegay and takes it with her to an art museum, where she sits contemplating a painting of a woman holding the same bouquet. The idea of creating something from that scene with flowers came to me while I was rewatching the movie. I froze a frame of the bouquet and asked a florist to make me something similar. I shot this picture with a theatrical light to shift emphasis from the actress to the flowers. This last *Flowers for Lisa* picture is a bridge to my next project, a photographic conversation inspired by Alfred Hitchcock's films.

Editors: Michael Sand and Ashley Albert
Designer: Devin Grosz
Production Manager: Anet Sirna-Bruder

Library of Congress Control Number: 2017956792

ISBN: 978-1-4197-3233-1
eISBN: 978-1-68335-321-8
Special Edition ISBN: 978-1-4197-3586-8

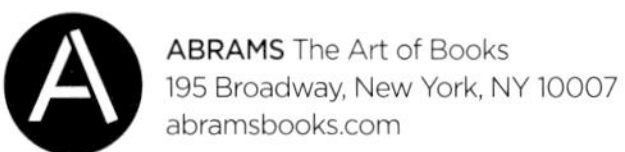